The

Essence

of

War

Other Works by Ralph D. Sawyer
Published by Westview Press

Fire and Water:
The Art of Incendiary and Aquatic Warfare in China

The Tao of War:
The Martial Tao Te Ching

Sun-tzu: Art of War

The Complete Art of War

The Seven Military Classics of Ancient China

Sun Pin:
Military Methods

One Hundred Unorthodox Strategies:
Battle and Tactics of Chinese Warfare

The Tao of Spycraft:
Intelligence Theory and Practice in Traditional China

The
Essence
of
War

Leadership and Strategy from
the Chinese Military Classics

Translated and edited by
Ralph D. Sawyer

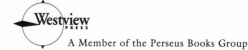

Westview
PRESS

A Member of the Perseus Books Group

Copyright © 2004 by Ralph D. Sawyer

Originally published as *The Art of the Warrior*.
Published in the United States of America by Westview Press, A Member of the Perseus Books Group, 5500 Central Avenue, Boulder, Colorado 80301-2877, and in the United Kingdom by Westview Press, 12 Hid's Copse Road, Cumnor Hill, Oxford OX2 9JJ.

Find us on the world wide web at www.westviewpress.com

Westview Press books are available at special discounts for bulk purchases in the United States by corporations, institutions, and other organizations. For more information, please contact the Special Markets Department at the Perseus Books Group, 11 Cambridge Center, Cambridge, MA 02142, or call (617) 252-5298, (800) 255-1514 or email special.markets@perseusbooks.com.

Library of Congress Cataloging-in-Publication Data
    The essence of war : leadership and strategy from the Chinese military classics / [translated, compiled, and introduced by Ralph D. Sawyer].
        p.   cm.
    Selections from the Seven military classics of ancient China. 1993; and Sun Pin's Military methods. 1995.
    Includes bibliographical references and index.
    ISBN 0-8133-9049-4 (pbk. : alk. paper)
    1. Military art and science—China.   2. War.   I. Title: Leadership and strategy from the Chinese military classics.   II. Sawyer, Ralph D.   III. Sun, Bin, 4th cent. B.C. Sun Bin bing fa. English. Selections.   IV. Wu jing qi shu. English. Selections.
    U101.E87   2004
    355.02—dc22

                                                                    2004000826

The paper used in this publication meets the requirements of the American National Standard for Permanence of Paper for Printed Library Materials Z39.48–1984.
Typeface used in this text: 11-point ITC Galliard

10   9   8   7   6   5   4   3   2   1

Contents

PART FOUR: TACTICAL ESSENTIALS

PART FIVE: TACTICAL SPECIFICS

Preface

CHINA'S GLORIOUS CULTURAL tradition, while dating back into the mists of antiquity and expressed by a nearly timeless written language, embodies many disparate intellectual threads. Never simple even at their inception, the philosophical, social, and political concepts that first evolved quickly expanded and were supplemented by religious and other abstract views derived from common life experiences compounded by perception and reflection. Over the millennia syncretic religions such as Buddhism, Zoroastrianism, and Islam were also imported from other civilizations and assimilated to greater or lesser degree, while China's tortured political history continued to haltingly unfold, often at the cost of untold suffering.

From any reasonable perspective China's continuity has been cultural rather than political, its heritage throughout one of incessant conflict as different peoples, states, and popular movements fought to control its populace and resources. These inescapable battlefield experiences eventually spawned a contemplative literature that sought to fathom the chaos of warfare and master the principles of its employment, whether offensive—in the service of Virtue—or defensive, to simply preserve the state. Like Taoism, Confucianism, and Buddhism, the three great belief systems of China, the martial culture thus produced its own body of writings and evolved a systematized, ever augmented tradition. Professional commanders and political leaders compelled to wrestle with perplexing military decisions studied and contemplated its books, but also—even if reluctantly—so did the intelligentsia because they not only encompassed tactics suitable for the battlefield, but also embodied fundamental philosophical concepts of enduring value integrated with realistic approaches to the art of living and science of management.

Largely defined by the initial conceptions and principles formulated by the great Sun-tzu around 500 BCE through his reflections on the preceding centuries of ever-escalating warfare, the Chinese military writings may be characterized as both cumulative and consistent. Moreover, despite the pronounced tendency of the literati to disparage the military profession, *The Seven Military Classics* garnered greater respect and were more widely studied than later dynastic writers have implied. Ironically, their impact not only continues undiminished but has surged phenomenally in China, Japan, Korea, and even much of Southeast Asia. In fact, the various texts are now more widely read and appreciated for tactical knowledge and essential wisdom that can be applied in many contexts, understood in many dimensions, than at any time in history.

Anyone familiar with Asian movies and television programs, especially Chinese and Japanese productions, or their American offshoots—including movies such as *The Karate Kid, The Last Dragon,* or *Big Trouble in Little China,* or serialized television offerings such as "Kung-fu," "The Master," and "Kung-fu, The Legend Continues"—will recall that teachings from the various military classics are frequently quoted by the principal characters to explain their actions or explicate plot developments. Moreover, instead of being restricted to the combat genre, in the last decade their employment has extended into popular American movies and TV programs, including *Wall Street, The Art of War,* the prime-time cartoon hit, "The Simpsons," and especially "The Sopranos." In many cases the original source has been obscured, and a number of famous lines, including Sun-tzu's "one who knows the enemy and knows himself will not be endangered in a hundred engagements" and "subjugating the enemy without fighting is the greatest achievement," have virtually entered idiomatic language.

As a result of this extensive media exposure coupled with their previous historical importance, the Chinese military classics have come to furnish a common conceptual vocabulary for China and the civilizations conversant with its culture, particularly Japan. The influence originates not merely in the subtle, unconscious assimilation of their subject matter on a daily basis, but also as the consequence of assiduous study, imaginative contemplation, and deliberate application to many spheres of life and activity. Such contemporary vigor no doubt stems from the remarkable scope of the texts, a corpus of writings whose authors pondered and incorporated defining beliefs from Confucianism, Legalism, and Taoism to proffer strategic measures and tactical remedies for a wide variety of problems and situations. They provide a psychology of human behavior, motivation, and evaluation; formulate theories and procedures for command and control; and discuss principles for grand strategy and political action. Rather than being idle theory, they are founded and continually focus upon human nature, for it is people who create civilization and culture, men who fight and die.

Fully cognizant of the tragic consequences of any conflict, the writings consistently emphasize that war should be avoided whenever possible and consequently stress that victory should be secured with minimal bloodshed, at the lowest possible cost for both combatants. Yet the authors equally condemn any failure to decisively extirpate evil and perversity, to vanquish tyrannical demagogues such as Hitler or King Chou, as heinous and inimical to any professed concern for humanity. However, the highest ideal in any conflict—whether actual combat or on a more abstract battlefield—remains conquering without ever engaging the enemy or inflicting any bloodshed at all. This outcome can be realized by creatively shaping the total circumstances to bring overwhelming strategic power to bear—as in the 1991 and 2003 Iraq conflicts—and thereby subjugate the awestruck enemy with little or no vicious fighting.

The continued popularity of the eight military writings excerpted to compose *The Essence of War* is attested by the wide range of concrete expressions presently seen throughout Asia, but especially China and Japan. At this writing in early 2004, the vast populace of an economically burgeoning China (where people now focus upon profits rather than diatribe) consistently exhaust full print runs of contemporarily formatted classic military writings within days, even hours, of their ssue, immediately vaulting them into the best-seller category together with books on computers and entrepreneurial schemes. The range of these surprisingly popular works subsumes not just the theoretical writings, but also historically derived material focusing upon the methods and strategies of famous, often romanticized, generals and political leaders such as Liu Pang and Ts'ao Ts'ao. No doubt resurgent national pride coupled with the sudden acceptability of lessons from China's earlier feudal period, previously condemned under strict Maoist doctrine, sustains this interest as China, in common with other Asian states, flexes its economic muscles and demands greater international recognition.

These modern versions have not been confined solely to the printed word—or rather, Chinese characters in either their ancient or simplified forms—but have frequently ventured into the wildly successful media form of cartooning. Even then several variations have appeared, with serialized novels about Sun-tzu's life and other famous commanders competing vigorously with simplified retellings of classic writings arranged into a series of discrete lessons. A phenomenon that began in the early 1980s, cartoon editions have already brought most of the definitive writings of China's cultural heritage to a generation that previously had neither time nor interest to pursue them. Due to their enormous success—millions of copies having been sold in Taiwan alone—some of the more famous classics by Sun-tzu and Confucius have been published in two or three competing editions drawn by different artists, and a few have been translated into English, primarily for distribution throughout Southeast Asia and among second- and third-generation Chinese and Japanese in foreign lands who no longer retain or never acquired reading fluency in their native languages.

While many of the current publications simply represent vernacular language translations of ancient classics whose archaic language has become incomprehensible to modern speakers, others have selectively reorganized and reformatted the material to focus upon critical problems and lessons in life. The most popular selectively apply principles and concepts from Chinese military thought to the world of business,

including general strategy, competition for market sha
perception of openings. Several have also transcend
universal tendency to conceive of business activities sim
terms of warfare to envision their applicability in the ind
ual's quest to survive and flourish within corporate cultu
(They are especially prevalent in Japan despite—or perha
because of—the culture's vaunted emphasis upon teamwork
and faceless cooperation, but may also be found in China and
Taiwan as well.) Other variants focus upon the lessons to be
learned for interpersonal relations; offer tactics for romance
and sexual offense and defense; suggest strategies for resolving life crises; and adapt principles to competitive sports.
Measures derived from the classics have even been suggested
for conquering the stock market, accompanied by extensive
charts and detailed graphs purporting to show the effectiveness of various strategies. In short, their influence is universal,
their presence ubiquitous. They not only affect those who actually read them, but also mold the perspective from which
matters are framed and factors evaluated. In fact, the classic
Chinese military writings excerpted here—*The Seven Military
Classics* and *Military Methods*—have been reintroduced into
China's military curricula and are being actively studied by
officers at every level—not necessarily for tactical specifics,
but for general principles and guidance. Thus they significantly shape conceptualization, perceptual parameters, and
the very categories of possibility themselves.

Although sayings from the military classics also appear in
the fortune cookies distributed as part of the after-meal ritual
in many American Chinese restaurants, the lessons and
thoughts should neither be underestimated nor trivialized.
Inherently profound, they have significantly affected the
views and understanding of many Asian political and military
leaders over the past century, including the present generation in China and earlier ones in Japan. Moreover, ever since
Sun-tzu's *Art of War* was first translated some two centuries
ago, they have furnished and continue to underlie many of
the fundamental concepts and essential tactics of modern
warfighting throughout the world, including the United
States where recent army doctrine has heavily stressed ma-

...ire. Many of the actual tactics found in contem-
ne...ical manuals, even embodied in several Marine
p...ts, often read like quotations from the Chinese mil-
...tings themselves.

...mpiling the present work our intent has been to pro-
...eaders with an accessible, conveniently arranged com-
...dium of the astounding material preserved by *The Seven*
...litary Classics and the recently rediscovered *Military Meth-*
...ds. Apart from Sun-tzu's *Art of War*, which has received extensive exposure in the West through several important
translations, the others have not previously been translated
except in our own publications. Although a number of repet-
itive and uninteresting passages have been eliminated, the
most germane and stimulating have all been retained. However, rather than being a mere abridgment, *The Essence of War*
arranges the thoughts of each of the classical military theorists under forty-one topics, grouped into five general categories that progress from broad orientations to specific
concepts and tactical lessons, much as in the famous *Six Secret*
Teachings, one of *The Seven Military Classics.*

The selections have been chosen in accord with three criteria: theoretical importance, especially critical passages that set
forth or explicate a strategist's basic concepts and tactics; historical significance, particularly materials that reflect critical
historical developments in either culture or military science;
and contemporary relevance, perhaps providing a useful mir-
ror for burning modern issues or application in life's wider
domains. Every effort has been made to incorporate the major variations found in the eight individual books on focal
topics such as the Tao of warfare, command and control, the
unorthodox, and requisite characteristics of commanders.
Sometimes the differences are subtle, at others glaring, often
expressive of time's unremitting progression and the con-
comitant escalation of the scope of battle and the problems
thereby entailed.

The individual selections are provided in full, except where
extraneous or possibly confusing historical names and detailed
events might obfuscate an otherwise clear passage. However,
throughout we have sought to retain self-explanatory, focal

material that can be read and pondered irrespective ⟨
milieu, experience, and intent. Insofar as the introd
has been kept reasonably brief in order to include as ⟨
textual material as possible, the selections are largely
contained. The introductory sketches for the individ
books merely orient them within the vastness of Chinese h.
tory in order to reprise the fascinating biographies for th
traditionally ascribed authors, while a few pages provide the
essentials of military capability to aid in conceptualizing the
concrete possibilities for tactical realization and envisioning
the circumstances that stimulated their formulation. Further
information, including extensive endnotes, may readily be
found in our translations of the original historical works, *The
Seven Military Classics of Ancient China* and Sun Pin's *Military Methods*.

Ralph D. Sawyer
RalphSawyer.com

Chronology of Approximate Dynastic Periods

Dynastic Period	Years
Legendary Sage Emperors	2852–2255 BCE
Hsia	2205–1766
Shang	1766–1045
Chou	
Western Chou	1045–770
Eastern Chou	770–256
Spring and Autumn	722–481
Warring States	403–221
Ch'in	221–207
Former Han (Western Han)	208 BC–8 CE
Later Han (Eastern Han)	23–220
Six Dynasties Period:	222–589
Three Kingdoms	222–280
Wei-Chin	220–316
Northern and Southern Dynasties	265–589

Sui	589–618
T'ang	618–907
Five Dynasties (Northern China)	907–959
Ten Kingdoms (Southern China)	907–979
Sung	960–1126
Southern Sung	1127–1279
Yüan (Mongol)	1279–1368
Ming	1368–1644
Ch'ing (Manchu)	1644–1911

Introduction

THE CIVIL AND MARTIAL TRADITIONS IN CHINA

Until the advent of hot weapons and their gradual, often blundering adoption by the world's armies, China's military science was, as in many other areas, whether for better or worse, virtually light-years ahead of Western practices. When the Greeks were struggling to escape the confining nature of the phalanx and its single tactic of the mass collision, China had already perfected numerous formations and methods of deployment, as well as an underlying hierarchical organization based upon the "squad of five" that, when coupled with precise training methods, allowed articulation, segmentation, and the execution of both orthodox and unorthodox tactics. Only centuries of Confucian domination as the orthodox state philosophy perhaps prevented the development and acceptance of the advanced firepower that characterized the West subsequent to the longbow at Agincourt and the powerful but slow-firing crossbow that itself did not appear in an effective role until a great many centuries after its first use in China during the Warring States period. However, China's comparative stagnation or decline in the military sphere remains a question much debated, certainly one deeply related to its approach to science and technology in general and the prevailing doctrine of cultural superiority that entailed the ideal of subjugating external enemies solely by Virtue, even when the latter was vividly absent.

Virtually from the earliest dynasties, and certainly from the Chou, China's intellectual tradition consciously distinguished *wen* and *wu*, respectively the "civil" (or "cultural") and the "martial." Apart from the entrenched, often hypocritical literati serving in the bureaucracy, more realistic thinkers esteemed them both equally, seeing in them, just as in the dynamically complementary *yin* and *yang*, the necessary counterparts for the development and preservation of the state, the means to civilization and a civilized life for the entire populace under the ruler's benevolent and sagacious leadership. The military thinkers naturally focused upon the martial, perhaps in response to its dire neglect as dynasties became more effete and corrupt, but—if the military classics can be taken as evidence for their actual views—they rarely overemphasized it. Confucianism eventually became the recognized embodiment of the *wen Tao*, the Tao of culture, whereas the various martial arts, including the science of military tactics, organization, and command, were synonymous with *wu Tao*, the Tao of the martial, also known in Japanese as *budo*. King Wen, the first king of the Chou dynasty, is traditionally portrayed as the cultural king who fathered Chou civilization and nurtured its power, but it was his successor, King Wu, the martial king, who conquered the perverse and oppressive Shang state and thus established the Chou dynasty. Thereafter, the martial frequently engendered a renewal of the civil, while the civil, becoming extreme, fostered a return of the martial.

The Tao (or Way) of the martial delimited its own inner realm and made equal, if not more rigorous, demands upon its students because they had to perfect themselves not only in the theories of their art, frequently from texts and other writings, but also in physical training and combat skills. Even the early Confucians—progenitors of what might be termed the pristine form of Confucianism—adopted a realistic attitude while loudly espousing the new virtues of righteousness and benevolence for all cultivated men. Confucius himself, generally considered the first teacher, would have all men practice the six arts—propriety, music, archery, charioteering, composition, and mathematics—and stated that when the perfected man was compelled to extirpate evil and restore order, once having donned his armor his visage would be terrible and his stature awesome. Moreover, he repeatedly emphasized the courage and demeanor of the perfect man, the highest ideal of Confucianism, in selflessly pursuing the true path, in sustaining others and disciplining himself to the Good. Even the pedantic Mencius, who followed a century later and significantly spread the doctrine of Confucianism, also accepted the need for campaigns of rectification to eliminate evil and nurture the people, just as advocated in the section entitled "History of Warfare."

Despite incessant barbarian incursions and major military threats throughout their history, except during the ill-fated expansionistic policies of the Former Han dynasty, or under dynamic young rulers such as T'ang T'ai-tsung during a dynasty's founding reign, Imperial China was little inclined to pursue military solutions to external aggression. Ethnocentric rulers and ministers instead preferred to believe in the myth of cultural attraction, whereby their vastly superior Chinese civilization, founded upon virtue and reinforced by opulent material achievements, would simply overwhelm the hostile tendencies of the uncultured. Frequent gifts of the embellishments of civilized life, coupled with music and women, would distract and enervate even the most warlike peoples. If they were unable to either overawe them into submission or bribe them into compliance, other mounted nomadic tribes could be employed against the troublemakers, following the time-honored tradition of "using barbarian against barbarian."

According to Confucian thought, which became the orthodox philosophy and prescribed state view in the Former Han, the ruler need only cultivate his Virtue, accord with the seasons, and implement benevolent policies to successfully attract universal support and foster stability. Although there were dissenting views, except under rulers such as Sui Yang-ti (reigned 605–617 CE) who sought to impose Chinese suzerainty on external regions (and thereby impoverished the nation), military affairs were pressed unwillingly, with most of the bureaucracy inclined to disdain anything associated with them and the profession of arms.

At the same time there was a vibrant tradition of self-cultivation in the martial arts that developed from the Han onward, frequently being amalgamated with other intellectual edifices, such as Taoism, Buddhism, and various minor religious and sectarian views, and often integrated into peasant revolution-

ary movements, being assiduously practiced as part of the prescribed self-discipline. Moreover, bravos and stalwarts often
swaggered across the historical stage, being much admired by
the people at large, although officially condemned as sources
of discordant values and unruly examples of personal courage
that frequently resulted in brigandage at the expense of state
order and security. This tradition, long romanticized in popular literature, has in recent decades been graphically exploited
by the innumerable martial-arts films produced in China, Taiwan, and Japan that portray both heroes and villains vigorously, even painfully, pursuing the highest combat skills as an
end in itself, as well as to extirpate brutal oppressors on behalf
of the weak and downtrodden. As such, they no doubt symbolize the "fist in the face of authority" that many wish to display but lack the courage and power to attempt.

THE HERITAGE OF CHINESE MILITARY THOUGHT

Although Imperial China suffered from almost constant
warfare throughout its long history, particularly from the
Warring States through the T'ang, military thought, the
complex product of experience and analysis, was disparaged
and actively shunned for the last thousand years. Self-styled
Confucians—whether sincerely or hypocritically—ignored
the Master's original teachings and eschewed not only the
profession of arms, but all aspects of military activity from the
Han dynasty onward, even growing more vociferous in their
condemnation with the passage of centuries. However, irrespective of their civilized and cultured self-perception, the nation could not be without armies or generals, particularly in
the face of constant "barbarian" threats and ongoing conflicts
with volatile nomadic peoples. Accordingly, a number of early
military treatises continued to be valued and studied, thereby
managing to survive, while the turmoil of frequent crises
grudgingly fostered generations of professional military figures and additional strategic studies. Yet in comparison with
the Confucian classics and various other orthodox writings
the military corpus remained minuscule, numbering at most
a few hundred books of every length and description.

Individual chapters of several writings by influential Warring States period philosophers also focused upon military matters, often with radical impact, while their orientations and perspectives affected the fundamental assumptions of tactical thought. Many famous thinkers pondered the major questions of government administration and military organization; motivation and training; the nature of courage; and the establishment of policies to stimulate the state's material prosperity. The *Tso Chuan* and other historical writings similarly record the thoughts of many key administrators and preserve the outlines of famous strategies, although battlefield tactics are minimally presented.

A number of the ancient strategic monographs became relatively famous, and scholars in the Sung period (circa 1078 CE) collected, edited, and assembled six important survivors, augmenting them with a T'ang dynasty book, to comprise *The Seven Military Classics*. Thus codified, the seven works thereafter furnished the official textual foundation for government examinations in military affairs, concurrently providing a common ground for tactical and strategic conceptualization. To them may now be added an eighth military classic dating from the middle Warring States period, Sun Pin's recently recovered *Military Methods*.

BASIC CONTENTS AND HUMANISTIC THRUST OF THE MILITARY WRITINGS

The terrible realities of the Warring States period persuaded many observers that—in the words of Sun-tzu—"warfare is the greatest affair of state, the basis of life or death, the Tao to survival or extinction." While there were dissenting voices, primarily among those who would seek refuge amidst the remote woods or mountains, most inhabitants of the era agreed. In fact, the famous general Wu Ch'i even criticized one powerful ruler for cowardice in consigning his people to death by failing to adequately prepare against their enemies. Moreover, there were those who advocated warfare as a state policy, who wanted to employ military means to expand the country by violently subjugating and brutally annexing other states rather than developing defensive forces simply to ensure their own survival. Battlefield success, except for the wounded and dead, was seductive, often bringing apparently easy gains. People quickly became flushed with the rewards and emotional surge of victory, stimulating a more realistic counterview that emphasized that frequent battles can only debilitate a country. However, the early *Ssu-ma Fa* advocates a balanced perspective: "Even though a state may be vast, those who love warfare will inevitably perish. Even though calm may prevail under Heaven, those who forget warfare will certainly be endangered."

In contrast to the Confucians and Taoists who envisioned warfare as having evolved from a period of sagely government in some lost antiquity through human actions and misdeeds, many thinkers in the Warring States period concluded that violence and conflict are inherent in the human condition, whether simply innate or brought about by unconstrained desire resulting in fierce competition for limited material goods. Accordingly, to alleviate suffering and ensure a semblance of order so that "All under Heaven" might pursue their lives in security and tranquility, the Virtuous had to create and then employ the principles of warfare in the service of humanity. Unfortunately, despite cherished ideals, rulers in the Warring States period were consumed by the ever more tortured quest to survive and major conflicts were waged to avenge insults, expand territory, or greedily acquire riches. Had they succeeded in their humanitarian approach to the challenges of conflict resolution, the unrealized ideal of the military strategists might have fashioned a far different world.

Within the purview of what might be termed grand strategy, virtually all the military theorists believed that for states to survive and conquer their enemies, they must develop a substantial material base, undermine the enemy's strength, and create administrative organizations that can function effectively in both peace and war. Accordingly, most of them strongly advocated the need for benevolent rulers and emphasized the people's welfare because a well-ordered, prosperous, and satisfied people might both physically and emotionally support their government. Moreover, only materially sufficient societies can generate the resources required to train and instruct the people; have the capability to stimulate a positive, committed spirit among the populace; raise the supplies essential to military campaigns; and nurture the values that would truly motivate its soldiers. Naturally, benevolent governments immediately become attractive beacons to the dispirited and oppressed and also create confidence among enemy populaces that, should military intercession establish a new regime in their state, its new rulers would not mimic the errors of the just deposed monarchs.

While governments must be founded upon moral standards and should assiduously practice virtue, they can only govern effectively by creating and strictly implementing a system of rewards and punishments. The rewards and punishments must be clear, immediate, and universally imposed so that they will become part of the national consciousness. Although laws and punishments should be restrained, never multiplied, those necessary to the state's survival should be rigorously enforced. Punishments should extend to the very highest ranks, rewards to the lowest, for then they will prove effective and people will be motivated to observe them irrespective of their positions, whether their transgressions might be detectable or not. Values inimical to the state, such as private standards of courage, should be severely discouraged, but tolerance must be extended to allies, and efforts made to avoid violating their local customs.

The ruler, and by implication all ranking members of government and military, should intensively cultivate the universally acknowledged virtues: benevolence, righteousness, loyalty, credibility, sincerity, courage, and wisdom. Relevant policies must invariably be implemented by a strong bureaucracy composed of talented men carefully selected after insightful evaluation. Since people love profits, pleasure, and virtue, and detest death, suffering, and evil, the ruler should develop and foster these in common with them. Ideally he must perceive their needs and desires, and avail himself of every source of information to understand their condition.

Personal emotions should never be allowed to interfere with the impartial administration of government, nor should the ruler's pleasures, or those of the bureaucracy, become excessive, thereby impoverishing the people and depriving them of their livelihood. The ruler should strive to eliminate every vestige of evil in order to forge a persona which dramatically contrasts with the enemy's perversity, vividly presenting the people with a diametrically opposed alternative. Righteousness must always dominate personal emotions and desires, and the ruler should not only actively share both hardship and pleasure with his people, but also project an image of doing so. This will personally bind them to him, and guarantee their allegiance to the state.

Commanding generals must be carefully selected and properly invested in their role with a formal ceremony conducted at the state altars, being thereafter entrusted with absolute authority over all military matters. Once they have assumed command, the ruler cannot interfere with their actions or decisions, primarily because valuable opportunities might be lost or actions forced that endanger the army, but also to prevent any of the officers from questioning the general's authority by presuming on their familiarity with the king. Generals and commanders should embody critical characteristics in balanced combinations to qualify them for leadership, while always being free from traits that might either lead to judgmental errors or be exploitable, and thereby doom their forces.

Within the just-described policies and orientations, much of the eight classic military books are devoted to elaborating fundamental strategic concepts, such as the orthodox and unorthodox, outlining principles for military organization and command, and advising both general rules and detailed tactics for typical combat situations. As they are all well represented in the categorized selections, it need only be noted that Sun-tzu's views, while the most famous and influential, do not represent the entire corpus of Chinese military thought. Rather, there are many explications, variations, and even contrary developments, as well as much material addressed to numerous fundamental topics he never considered. Naturally the strategists' ability to conceptualize basic military principles was shaped and constrained by the nature and capability of the forces in their era, but they largely transcended concrete limitations imposed by time and terrain to discern far more visionary patterns. While the context is distinctly military, their applicability and understanding remain unconstricted.

CONFLICT AND WEAPONS IN WARRING STATES CHINA

Insofar as all intellectual pronouncements, even those of a military nature, inevitably derive from concrete milieus, a brief explication of the nature of conflict in the Warring States period beyond the tangential depictions incorporated in the biographical sketches below may aid in fathoming some of the more enigmatic statements. Over the centuries, Chinese military thought mirrored the ongoing evolution in weapons, economic conditions, and political power while creating the framework for strategic conceptualization and stimulating the development of battlefield methods. Tactics appropriate to the dawn of the historical Shang period in which limited numbers of nobility manning chariots would engage similar forces in fairly brief, circumscribed conflicts changed in response to increased manpower, greater speed and mobility, the rise of the infantry as the critical combat arm, and the invention of more powerful shock and missile weapons. However, a critical kernel of thought that focused upon basic questions, including organization, discipline, evaluation, objectives, and fundamental principles, retained its validity and continued to be applied until the Ch'in eventually conquered and unified the empire, thereby signifying the end of the Warring States period.

By the commencement (in 403 BCE) of the Warring States period, the setting for six of the eight books incorporated in *The Essence of War*, the pace of political and military events had become virtually incomprehensible. The heritage of the immediately preceding Spring and Autumn period had itself been frequent warfare in which any state, even the most powerful, could be vanquished if it failed to prepare its defenses and train its soldiers. Its conflicts had segmented China into seven powerful survivors, each contending for control of the realm, and another fifteen ill-fated minor states for them to prey upon. Their feudal lords had by then evolved into despotic monarchs who were compelled to nurture extensive economic and political bureaucracies just to survive. In order to effectively suppress external threats, virtually every ruler had to consider radical new ideas and seek powerful methods to expand their agricultural bases. The immigration of disaffected people from other states was also encouraged by policies providing them with land, and tenancy and land ownership concurrently developed. Moreover, after 500 BCE durable iron implements came into general use that, when coupled with drainage and irrigation projects, vastly increased the food reserves and therefore strength of some regions. Trade and commerce began to flourish and a class of influential merchants arose who, although officially despised, proved important to the development of logistics.

During the Warring States period the scale of conflict surged phenomenally, sustained by an ever expanding population and increasing material prosperity. Whereas in the Shang dynasty a few thousand men had constituted an army, even the weaker states easily fielded 100,000; the strongest, in the third century BCE, reportedly maintained a standing army of nearly a million, and mobilized 600,000 for a single campaign. In one battle between Ch'in and Ch'u, the total number of combatants apparently exceeded one million, an astounding figure even after discounting for inaccuracy and exaggeration. Numerical strength became critical, for in the immediately previous campaign against Ch'u, Ch'in had suffered a severe defeat with an army of some 200,000 soldiers. Naturally casualties also escalated rapidly, with at least 100,000 from Wei dying at the battle of Ma-ling in 341 BCE; as many as 240,000 in the combined forces of Wei and Han perishing at I-ch'ueh in 295 BCE; and 450,000 men of Ch'u being slaughtered at Ch'ang-p'ing in 260 BCE. Campaigns of such magnitude required lengthy periods for logistical preparation, mobilization, and engagement. Instead of a few days or weeks on the march with perhaps a couple of days in battle as in the Shang, months and even years were necessary while battles raged for tens of days and stalemates persisted for a year or more.

Managing the employment of such vast resources and manpower demanded great expertise, and the profession of arms quickly developed. While the newly free masses were generally registered and subjected to military training on a seasonal basis, being conscripted for combat when necessary, the army's core had to be composed of practiced, disciplined officers and soldiers. Consequently the recognition and retention of individuals proficient in the military arts became essential, and rewards, including position, honors, and rank, for valor, strength, and military achievements, proliferated. Basic physical qualifications for members of the standing army, as well as for elite units, arose and were stringently maintained. Moreover, as talent had grown in importance in the Spring and Autumn period, resulting in social mobility, bureaucracies staffed by capable individuals had begun to expand, and had now largely displaced administrations staffed by members of the ruler's clan and the formerly entrenched nobility. The establishment of districts permitted central governments to wield greater power over their states and quickly mobilize army resources as required.

These massive armies suddenly made drill manuals and deployment methods, as well as the tactics they would be designed to execute, indispensable. Consequently, an extensive body of military theory appeared, stimulated not only by battlefield and training requirements, but also by new political theories and individual philosophies. Numerous military books were thus composed during the Warring States, their theories finding rigorous employment thereafter.

The commander's qualifications and responsibilities similarly changed during the period. The formulation and execution of strategy became so complex, a general's replacement could result in an army's defeat and the endangerment of an entire state. Even though rulers continued to meddle in army matters with catastrophic results, often at the instigation of jealous ministers or traitorous officials, professional officers who specialized solely in military affairs became dominant. While the ideal early Warring States commander was normally an effective, even exemplary civilian administrator such as the famous Wu Ch'i, toward the end of the period the civilian realm had become estranged from the realities of warfare.

During the Shang and early Chou periods, battles had been fought on agricultural and otherwise open, undefended terrain with campaign armies encountering only scattered cities during their advance. Some fortifications always seem to have existed, such as the thick neolithic and Shang dynasty stamped earth walls still being discovered, but basically forces could roam about unhampered until encountering them. In the Warring States period the feudal lords undertook the expanded defense of borders, constructing "great walls," ramparts, forts, and guard towers throughout the countryside to defend their entire territory against incursion. States protected their land more than their people, and the objectives of warfare changed as each state sought not to capture prisoners and plunder for riches, but to thoroughly vanquish their enemies by seizing their lands, exterminating their armies, gaining political control of their populace, and administratively annexing their territory.

Throughout the Warring States period fortified cities, previously just military and administrative centers, grew enormously in significance as industry, trade, and population all flourished and naturally evolved as focal points in the road network. Accordingly, whereas in the Western Chou and Spring and Autumn periods it was advisable to circumvent these isolated cities rather than wasting men and resources besieging and assaulting them, their capture or destruction advanced simultaneously, with siege engines, giant shields, battering rams, catapults, overlook towers, and other mobile equipment appearing in large numbers. Specialists in the technologies of assault and defense were necessary, and the Mohists, who both mastered defensive techniques and created countersiege measures, became famous for their dedication to assisting the targets of aggression. Sun-tzu's well-known condemnation of urban assaults thus became outdated by the time of Sun Pin's analysis of vulnerable and impregnable targets in his *Military Methods* just 150 years later.

Prior to the official start of the Warring States period the technology for mass producing bronze weapons had long been fully realized. Despite the increasing perfection of iron and steel technology that began in the Spring and Autumn period, elegant, functional bronze weapons continued to be carried by the remnants of the nobility and much of the army's masses as well. In fact, the manufacture and extensive employment of iron weapons seems to have been more identified with the peripheral but highly aggressive state of Ch'in, possibly playing a role in its ability to field and equip the massive armies that eventually overwhelmed its enemies.

In the Warring States period the preferred Shang and Chou weapon—the massive halberd or dagger-ax—which had been a charioteer's implement *par excellence*, had been supplanted in the ever-expanding infantry forces by smaller, single hand versions with a spear point affixed to the top. This new weapon, carried by infantrymen for use in close combat, combined the lethal hooking capability of the old halberd blade—essentially a dagger with a curved lower edge affixed at ninety degrees to the shaft—with the stabbing and thrusting potential of a spear or a modern bayonet. However, spears themselves were still employed in a supplementary role and, in accord with prevailing theory that weapons should be mixed in type in order to provide the means for both aggressive and defensive action at close and long ranges, daggers and hatchets continued to be available for close fighting. Leather armor more suited to the increasingly active role played by infantrymen had developed and continued to benefit from ongoing improvements in tanning and leather working capabilities. Both large and small shields—the former often employed in coordinated fighting tactics—offered considerable protection against shock action and projectiles. Bronze helmets had long been fabricated to deflect missiles and glancing blows, and thin bronze plates were affixed as outer protection on both armor and shields, although most shields were constructed from wood and staves or upon wooden frames. None of them were significantly supplanted by iron versions until the end of the Warring States period.

The sword, romanticized in Japan and the West as the warrior's soul and imaged as a real man's only true weapon, was far less significant in China than in early Europe. It evolved slowly from the late Shang onward, apparently from daggers or spear-tips, coincident with the consistent advances in metallurgical skills that saw all weapons becoming longer, stronger, and more complex. Short versions had appeared in limited quantities by the end of the Western Chou, but true swords, particularly those capable of slashing rather than stabbing, did not become common until the middle of the Warring States period. Thereafter, they rapidly proliferated until comprising an essential component of every unit's arms.

Long before the Warring States period, the early compound bow had evolved to become a reflex weapon whose pull may have reached 160 pounds. Bronze arrowheads continued to be employed, particularly in unusual shapes for specialized purposes, but inexpensive iron arrowheads were rapidly introduced, lowering ammunition costs considerably as the technology for multiple cavity casting became widespread—an important consideration since massed volley fire had become an important tactic. The traditional bow was also supplemented from the middle Warring States by large numbers of crossbows, probably being exploited as described in Sun Pin's *Military Methods*. These highly powerful weapons had a far slower rate of fire than the traditional bow and required, even with various ingenious methods for cocking, considerable strength. However, improvements made during the late Warring States period led to the development of large, automatically cocking versions mounted on chariots, as well as hand-held bows capable of firing multiple bolts and repeating or essentially automatic models with top mounted magazine-style feeds.

The chariot, which had comprised the basic fighting unit during the late Shang, Western Chou, and Spring and Autumn periods, remained important until well into the Warring States when it was gradually superseded by large infantry masses and eventually, during the third century BCE, minimally supplemented by the cavalry. Chariots from the late Shang onward had normally carried three men: the driver in the center, an archer on the left, and a warrior with the halberd to the right. Five chariots had initially comprised a squad, the basic functional unit, with five squads composing a brigade. Each chariot included a complement of between ten and twenty-five close supporting infantry, with an additional vanguard of perhaps 125 men in later times. Training for chariot warfare in the early Warring States period included large-scale mobilizations that replaced Shang and Chou royal hunts, although given the difficulty of developing driving skills and the fighting expertise appropriate to a racing chariot, extensive practice must have been necessary. An expensive weapon, requiring numerous specialized craftsmen to build and maintain, its use had at first been confined to the nobility, minimally supported by conscripted commoners, but by the Warring States period, with some states even fielding 10,000 chariots, physical qualifications came to take precedence.

In early times chariot battles had largely resolved into a number of individual clashes, with personal combat supposedly being governed by appropriate ceremonial constraints, although this is probably a later romanticization. The horse had only been employed in conjunction with the chariot, with the cavalry never becoming noticeable until late in the Warring States period. Even in the Spring and Autumn period when the scope of warfare had dramatically increased due to the predatory campaigns of the stronger states and necessarily involved greater numbers of peasants as integral infantry elements, combat had remained centered on the chariot, at least on open terrain. Concepts of chivalry had initially prevailed, with the ethics of battle dictating adherence to the proper forms, although conscripted infantry were little bound by them. Within a century, however, only the foolish and soon to be defeated were burdened by the old code of ethics, and the ancient style of individual combat—despite personal challenges offered to instigate battle—outmoded.

The growth of mass infantry armies was also accompanied by developments in articulation, deployment, and maneuvering capabilities; the abandonment of the chariot as a fighting platform and core of the initial onslaught; and the reluctant adoption of barbarian practices to create the cavalry. Under constant pressure from mounted steppe horsemen, various perceptive commanders and rulers realized the need to develop their own cavalry. While the history of the horse in China is still emerging, it appears that King Wu-ling of Northern Chao deliberately forced the assumption of the "barbarian style of dress"—short jacket and trousers instead of the much revered indigenous long coat of the Chinese—over vehement objections in 307 BCE to facilitate adoption of the cavalry. Mounted horsemen had apparently been challenging the Chinese states since the fifth century, probably evolving from Iran and the steppe region, and foreign horses had long been famous in China for their speed and endurance. The King created the first known cavalry, immediately providing the state with a vastly increased offensive potential. Of course the saddle, if any, was extremely primitive, being only a rolled blanket, while stirrups did not appear until the end of the Han. Consequently the rider was burdened with the difficult task of simultaneously controlling his horse and either shooting his bow or striking with his shock weapon. Acting from such an unstable platform their effectiveness was somewhat limited, and stemmed more from their great speed and mobility than inherent fighting power. However, the development of the cavalry, mentioned only briefly in the military books prior to *Questions and Replies*, freed armies from being confined to open, chariot accessible terrain, allowing fuller exploitation of ravines, valleys, forests, hilly fields, and mountains through diffuse deployment. Supported by vast hordes of armored infantrymen wielding spears, crossbows, and eventually iron swords, warfare on an unprecedented scale suddenly became both possible and inevitable. In the final century of conflict, the third century BCE, which witnessed the growth and decisive triumph of Ch'in, massive campaigns requiring hundreds of thousands of men, executing both explosive and persisting strategies, decimated the populace and countryside. In those days the strategies and methods of the famous tacticians were repeatedly tested and applied, and proven to have a timeless validity.

In order to better understand the inherent importance of the indigenous military classics within the Chinese tradition, several brief historical and political points might be noted. First, military works were frequently not permitted in private hands, and their possession could be construed by state authorities as evidence of a conspiracy. (The T'ai Kung's *Six Secret Teachings* would be particularly fatal, being a book advocating and instructing revolution.) Second, many of these teachings were at first transmitted through generations, often orally and usually secretly. Eventually they were recorded, committed to written form on bamboo slips, sometimes becoming public knowledge, whether deliberately or inadvertently. Designated government officials periodically gathered them for state use, depositing them in imperial libraries where they were so highly valued as to have been exempted from the infamous book burnings of the Ch'in dynasty. Once stored away in government archives they would be accessible only to some few officially appointed professors of the classics, a restricted number of high officials and military commanders, and the emperor himself. Even these privileged individuals might still be denied perusal of the critical writings, especially if they were related to the imperial family and might pose a threat to his royal power.

Even after they were committed to manuscript form, whether on bamboo, silk, or eventually paper after the Han dynasty, patriots sometimes felt compelled to remove them from public domain. For example, the famous general Chang Liang, who played a major role in overthrowing the tyrannical Ch'in dynasty and establishing the Han, apparently had the sole copy of *Three Strategies of Huang Shih-kung*, from which he had personally profited, buried in his casket. However, his efforts were not entirely successful, for the text seems to have resurfaced when his tomb was vandalized in the fourth century. This attitude is further illustrated by the well-known, although perhaps apocryphal, refusal of Li Ching, the famous T'ang strategist and general to whom *Questions and Replies* is attributed, to provide his emperor with more than defensive knowledge and tactics. In Li's view, strategies for aggressive action should not be disseminated because the empire was already at peace, and they could only interest and aid disaffected individuals who might want to incite revolution and precipitate warfare.

The seven books preserved in the *Seven Military Classics*, as traditionally arranged since the Sung dynasty, are: Sun-tzu's *Art of War*, *Wu-tzu*, *Methods of the Ssu-ma (Ssu-ma Fa)*, *Questions and Replies between T'ang T'ai-tsung and Li Wei-kung*, *Wei Liao-tzu*, *Three Strategies of Huang Shih-kung*, and *T'ai Kung's Six Secret Teachings*. In addition, the recently rediscovered *Military Methods*, another Warring States text, essentially constitutes an eighth military classic.

Although uncertainty abounds regarding the authorship and dating of most of these books, as well as to what extent they are composite books drawing upon common ground and lost writings, the traditional order found in the *Seven Military Classics* unquestionably is not chronological. Sun-tzu's *Art of War* has generally been considered the oldest and greatest extant Chinese military work, even though the purported author of *Six Secret Teachings*, the T'ai Kung, was active hundreds of years earlier than the historical Sun-tzu. Materials preserved in *Ssu-ma-Fa* reputedly extend back into the early Chou; the *Wu-tzu* may have been recorded by Wu Ch'i's disciples, while suffering from later accretions; and *Three Strategies* probably follows the *Wei Liao-tzu*, yet traditionalists still associate it with the T'ai Kung. Accordingly, the likely chronological order (with many caveats and unstated qualifications) might well be: initial period, *Ssu-ma Fa* and *The Art of War*; second period, *Wu-tzu*; third period, *Military Methods*, *Wei Liao-tzu*, *Six Secret Teachings*, and then *Three Strategies*; and finally the T'ang or Sung dynasty *Questions and Replies*. With the exception of the latter, all the works may therefore be considered products of the Warring States period, obviating any further need for detailed discussions of their provenance and evolution. However, the traditional biographies of the purported authors will be found in the introductory sketches below.

Six Secret Teachings purportedly records the T'ai Kung's political advice and tactical instructions to Kings Wen and Wu of the Chou dynasty in the eleventh century BCE. Although the present book certainly dates from the Warring States period, some scholars believe it reflects the tradition of Ch'i military studies, and therefore preserves at least vestiges of the oldest strata of Chinese military thought. The historic T'ai Kung, to whom *Six Secret Teachings* is attributed, has been honored throughout Chinese history as the first famous general and the progenitor of strategic studies. Furthermore, in the T'ang dynasty he was even accorded his own state temple as the martial patron, thereby attaining officially sanctioned status approaching that of Confucius, the revered civil patron.

A complete work that not only discusses strategy and tactics, but also proposes the government measures necessary for forging effective state control and attaining national prosperity, *Six Secret Teachings* is grounded upon, or perhaps projected back into, monumental historical events. The Chou kings presumably implemented many of these policies, enabling them to develop their agricultural and population base, gradually expand their small border domain, and secure the allegiance of the populace, until they could finally launch the decisive military campaign that defeated the powerful Shang dynasty and overturned its six-hundred-year rule.

Six Secret Teachings is the only military classic written from the perspective of revolutionary activity, for nothing less than a dynastic revolution was their aim. Attaining this objective required perfecting themselves in the measures and technologies of the time and systematically developing policies, strategies, and battlefield tactics not previously witnessed in Chinese history. The Chou kings were compelled to ponder employing limited resources and restricted forces to attack a vastly superior, well-entrenched foe whose campaign armies alone probably outnumbered their entire population. In contrast, the other strategic writings focus upon managing military confrontations in which both sides start from relatively common military and government infrastructures. Furthermore, while nearly all the military texts adhere to the basic concept of "enriching the state through agriculture and strengthening the army," many tend to emphasize strategic analysis and battlefield tactics rather than the fundamental measures necessary to even create the possibility of confrontation.

The epoch-making clash between the Chou and Shang, as envisioned by the Chou themselves and idealistically portrayed in later historical writings, set the moral tone and established the parameters for the dynastic cycle concept. The archetypal battle of virtue and evil, the benevolent and righteous acting on behalf of all the people against a tyrant and his coterie of parasitic supporters, truly commenced with their conflict. The Shang's earlier conquest of the Hsia, while portrayed as similarly conceived, occurred before the advent of written language, and was only a legend even in antiquity. However, the Chou's determined effort to free the realm from the yoke of suffering and establish a rule of Virtue and benevolence became the inspirational essence for China's moral self-perception. As dynasties decayed and rulers became morally corrupt and increasingly ineffectual, new champions of righteousness would appear to confront the oppressive forces of government, rescue the people from imminent doom, and return the state to benevolent policies. Moreover, in the view of some historians, the Shang-Chou conflict marked the last battle between peoples, for commencing with the Chou dynasty military engagements within China proper were essentially internal political clashes. However, ongoing confrontations between the agrarian central states and the nomadic steppe peoples continued throughout Chinese history, reflecting in part the self-conscious identity that the people of the central states emphasized in contrast with their "barbarian" neighbors.

As portrayed in such historical writings as the *Shih Chi*, in accord with good moral tradition and the plight of the people the Shang had ascended to power by overthrowing the last evil ruler of the previous dynasty, the Hsia. After generations of rule the Shang emperors, perhaps due to their splendid isolation and constant indulgence in myriad pleasures, are recorded as having become less virtuous and capable. Their moral decline inexorably continued until the final ruler appeared, whom history has depicted as evil incarnate. Among the many perversities attributed to him were imposing heavy taxes; forcing the people to perform onerous labor services, mainly to provide him with lavish palaces and pleasure centers; interfering with agricultural practices, thereby causing widespread hunger and deprivation; personal debauchery, including drunkenness, orgies, and violence; the brutal murder of innumerable people, especially famous men of virtue and loyal court officials; and the development and infliction of inhuman punishments. Unfortunately, the king was also talented, powerful, and fearsome, and therefore able to exert tyrannical control over his frightened subjects.

Into this state of Chou—insignificant when compared with the strength and expanse of the mighty Shang that continued to assert at least nominal control over some three thousand small states and fiefs—came the eccentric T'ai Kung, whose personal name was Chiang Shang. An elderly, somewhat mysterious figure whose early life was virtually unknown even then, he had perhaps found the Shang ruler insufferable and feigned madness to escape court life and his power. He disappeared only to resurface in the Chou countryside at the apocryphal age of seventy-two and become instrumental in Chou affairs. After faithfully serving their court for approximately twenty years subsequent to his first encounter with King Wen, he was enfeoffed as King of Ch'i following the great conquest, perhaps as much to stabilize the eastern area and remove him as a military threat as to reward him for his efforts.

According to traditional sources, the state of Chou was dramatically established when Tan Fu, their leader, personally emigrated over the mountains south into the Wei River valley to avoid endangering his people, and subsequently abandoned so-called barbarian customs to embrace the agricultural destiny of his ancestors. These actions immediately characterized him as a paragon of Virtue, and endowed the Chou, and subsequently China, with a sedentary, agrarian character. However, Chi Li, Tan Fu's third son, successfully waged aggressive campaigns against neighboring peoples and rapidly expanded their power base. Initially the Shang court recognized his achievements and sanctioned his actions, granting him the title of earl, but eventually imprisoned him despite his marriage to one of their royal princesses.

While a detailed history of Shang-Chou relations awaits further archaeological discoveries, it appears that several other members of the Chou royal family, including King Wen, were connected by marriage with the Shang. However, generations before the Chou migrated into the Wei River valley, the famous Shang king Wu Ting conducted several military expeditions to subjugate them. Shang kings also frequently hunted in Chou domain, but apparently grew apprehensive and abandoned the practice as Chou's might increased.

In his old age King Wen of the Chou was similarly imprisoned by the tyrannical Shang ruler for his loyal remonstrance, but finally gained his freedom through lavish bribes gathered by his family and other virtuous men. The gifts presented were in fact so generous and impressive that King Wen, who continued to profess his submission to the Shang, was even designated as the "Western Duke" or "Lord of the West." When the title was conferred, he was presented with a bow, arrows, and axes, symbolic of the attendant military responsibilities that ironically required he actively protect the empire from external challenges. He immediately returned to his small state on the western fringe of the Shang empire, where the remoteness of the Wei River valley proved immensely advantageous. Dwelling in essentially barbarian territory, they enjoyed the stimulus of vigorous military activity, the harvests of a fertile area, and the secrecy that relative isolation would permit. Because King Wen could implement effective policies to foster the state's material and social strength without attracting undue attention, the Chou had the luxury of seventeen years to prepare for the ultimate confrontation.

Apart from his storied longevity, the initial interview is also marked by the mythic aura that frequently characterizes predestined meetings between great historical figures. As recorded in *Six Secret Teachings*, the diviner had noted signs portending the appearance of a great Worthy and accordingly informed King Wen. The king therefore observed a vegetarian fast for three days to morally prepare for the meeting and ensure attaining the proper spiritual state of mind. When he finally encountered him, the T'ai Kung quickly broached the ultimate subject of revolution, of overthrowing the Shang, by responding to the king's inquiry about fishing in allegorical terms. Immediately thereafter he abandoned metaphors to openly advise the king that the realm, the entire world, could be taken with the proper humanitarian measures and an effective government. Startled by his directness, although probably assuming it was the working of Heaven, the king immediately acknowledged the T'ai Kung as the true Sage critical to realizing their dreams, and resolved to overthrow the Shang dynasty. Thereafter the T'ai Kung served as advisor, teacher, confidant, Sage, military strategist, and possibly commander-in-chief of the armed forces to Kings Wen and Wu over the many years necessary before final victory could be realized.

The *Shih Chi* chapter that recounts the history of the state of Ch'i contains a brief biography of its founder, the T'ai Kung, which provides additional information and records the developments that led to the famous interview which purportedly is preserved in chapter one of *Six Secret Teachings*: "T'ai Kung Wang, Lü Shang, was a native of the Eastern Sea area. One of his ancestors had once served as a labor director and been successful in assisting Yü in pacifying the waters. In the interval between Emperor Shun and the Hsia dynasty he was enfeoffed at Lü, or perhaps at Shen, and surnamed Chiang. During the Hsia and Shang dynasties some of the sons and grandsons of the collateral lines were enfeoffed at Lü and Shen, some were commoners, and Shang was their descendant. His original surname was Chiang, but he was subsequently surnamed from his fief, so was called Lü Shang.

"Lü Shang, impoverished and in straits, was already old when, through fishing, he sought out King Wen, the Lord of the West. When the Lord of the West was about to go hunting, he divined about the prospects. The diviner prognosticated: 'What you will obtain will be neither dragon nor serpent, neither tiger nor bear. What you will obtain is an assistant for a hegemon or king.' Thereupon the Lord of the

West went hunting, and indeed met the T'ai Kung on the sunny side of the Wei River. After speaking with him he was greatly pleased and said, 'My former lord, the T'ai Kung, said "There should be a Sage who will come to Chou, and Chou will thereby flourish." Are you truly this one or not? My T'ai Kung looked out [*wang*] for you for a long time.' Thus he called him T'ai Kung Wang, returned with him in his carriage, and established him as strategist.

"Someone has said: 'The T'ai Kung had extensive learning, and once served King Chou of the Shang. Since King Chou lacked the Tao, he left him. He traveled about exercising his persuasion on the various feudal lords but did not encounter anyone suitable, and in the end returned west with the Lord of the West.'

"Someone else has said: 'Lü Shang was a retired scholar who had hidden himself on the seacoast. When the Lord of the West was confined at Yu-li, San-i Sheng and Hung Yao, having long known him, summoned Lü Shang. Lü Shang also said, "I have heard that the Lord of the West is a Worthy, and moreover excels at nurturing the old, so I guess I'll go there." The three men sought out beautiful women and unusual objects on behalf of the Lord of the West, and presented them to King Chou in order to ransom him. The Lord of the West thus managed to return to his state.'

"Although the ways they say Lü Shang came to serve the Lord of the West differ, still the essential point is that he became strategist to Kings Wen and Wu. After the Lord of the West was extricated from Yu-li and returned to Chou, he secretly planned with Lü Shang and cultivated his Virtue in order to overturn Shang's government. The T'ai Kung's affairs were mostly concerned with military authority and unorthodox stratagems, so when later generations speak about armies and the Chou's secret balance of power, they all honor the T'ai Kung for making the fundamental plans.

"The Lord of the West's government was equitable, even extending to settling the conflict between the Yu and Jui. The *Book of Odes* refers to the Lord of the West as King Wen after he received the Mandate of Heaven. He attacked Ch'ung, Mi-hsü, and Chüan-i, and constructed a great city at

Feng. If All under Heaven were divided into thirds, two thirds had already given their allegiance to the Chou. The T'ai Kung's plans and schemes occupied the major part.

"When King Wen died, King Wu ascended the throne. In the ninth year, wanting to continue King Wen's task, he mounted an attack in the east to observe whether the feudal lords would assemble or not. When the army set out, the T'ai Kung wielded the yellow battle ax in his left hand, and grasped the white pennon in his right, in order to swear the oath:

> *Ts'ang-ssu! Ts'ang-ssu!*
> *Unite your masses of common people*
> *with your boats and oars.*
> *Those who arrive after will be beheaded.*

Thereafter he went to Meng-chin. The number of feudal lords who assembled of their own accord was eight hundred. The feudal lords all said, 'King Chou can be attacked.' King Wu said, 'They cannot yet.' He returned the army and made the Great Oath with the T'ai Kung.

"After they had remained in Chou for two years, King Chou of the Shang killed prince Pi-kan and imprisoned Chi-tzu. King Wu, wanting to attack King Chou, performed divination with the tortoise shell to observe the signs. They were not auspicious, and violent wind and rain arose. The assembled Dukes were all afraid, but the T'ai Kung stiffened them to support King Wu. King Wu then went forth.

"In the eleventh year, the first month, on the day *chia-tzu* he swore the oath at Mu-yeh and attacked King Chou of the Shang. King Chou's army was completely defeated. King Chou turned and ran off, mounting the Deer Tower. They then pursued and beheaded him. On the morrow King Wu was established at the altars: The Dukes presented clear water; K'ang Shu-feng of Wei spread out a variegated mat; the T'ai Kung led the sacrificial animals; and the Scribe Yi chanted the prayers, in order to announce the punishment of King Chou's offenses to the spirits. They distributed the money from the Deer Tower, and gave out the grain in the Chü-ch'iao granary, in order to relieve the impoverished people. They enfeoffed Pi-kan's grave, and released Chi-tzu from imprisonment. They moved the nine cauldrons of authority, rectified the government of Chou, and began anew with All under Heaven. The T'ai Kung's plans occupied the major part.

"Thereupon King Wu, having already pacified the Shang and become King of All under Heaven, enfeoffed the T'ai Kung at Ying-ch'iu in Ch'i. The T'ai Kung went east to go to his state, traveling slowly, staying overnight en route. The innkeeper said, 'I have heard it said that time is hard to get but easy to lose. Our guest sleeps extremely peacefully. Probably he isn't going to return to his state.' The T'ai Kung, overhearing it, got dressed and set out that night, reaching his state just before first light. The Marquis of Lai came out to attack, and fought with him for Ying-ch'iu. Ying-ch'iu bordered Lai whose populace were members of the Yi tribe. They took advantage of the chaos under King Chou, and assumed that the newly settled Chou would not be able to assemble the distant quarters to battle with the T'ai Kung for his state.

"When the T'ai Kung reached Ch'i he rectified the government in accord with their customs; simplified the Chou's forms of propriety; opened up the occupations of the merchants and artisans; and facilitated the realization of profits from fishing and salt. The people turned their allegiance to Ch'i in large numbers, and Ch'i became a great state.

"Then when King Ch'eng of the Chou was young, Kuan Shu and Ts'ai Shu revolted, and the Yi people of the Huai River valley turned against the Chou. So King Ch'eng had Duke Chao K'ang issue a mandate to the T'ai Kung: 'To the east as far as the sea, the west to the Yellow River, south to Mu-ling, and north to Wu-ti, completely rectify and put in order the five marquis and nine earls.' Thus Ch'i was able to conduct a campaign of rectification against the rebellious and became a great state. Its capital was Ying-ch'iu. Probably when the T'ai Kung died he was more than a hundred years old.

"The Grand Historian comments: 'I traveled the expanse of Ch'i from Lang-yah, which belongs to Mt. T'ai, north to where it fronts the sea, two thousand kilometers of fertile land. Its people are expansive, and many conceal their knowledge. It's their Heaven-given nature. Taking the T'ai Kung's Sageness in establishing his state, isn't it appropriate that Duke Huan of Ch'i later flourished and cultivated good government, and was thereby able to assemble the feudal lords in a covenant. Vast, vast, truly the style of a great state!"

Despite this detailed biography in Ssu-ma Ch'ien's generally reliable *Shih Chi*, over the millennia Confucian skeptics even denied the T'ai Kung's very existence. Others, perturbed by the confusing traditions regarding his origin, consigned him to a minor role. (While the details of his initial encounter with King Wen seem likely to remain unknown, the T'ai Kung was probably a representative of the Chiang clan with whom the Chou was militarily allied and had intermarried for generations.) Both justified their views by citing the absence of references in the traditionally accepted archaic texts that supposedly provide an authentic record of these epoch-making events, and they generally appear to be following the second great Confucian, the pedantic Mencius, in refusing to accept the brutal nature of military campaigns and the inevitable bloodshed. In fact, King Wu's herculean efforts over the many years prior to the conquest, and his achievements in imposing rudimentary Chou control over the vast Shang domain, also tend to be slighted. Consequently, the two figures historically associated with sagacity, virtue, and the civil—King Wen and the Duke of Chou—are revered, while the strategist and final commander, the representatives of the martial, are ignored and dismissed. However, other scholars and historians, after examining the numerous stories and references to him in disparate texts, winnowing away the legendary and mythic material, have concluded that the T'ai Kung not only existed, but also played a prominent role, much as described in the *Shih Chi* biography. No doubt, as with the Hsia dynasty, whose formerly mythic existence assumes concrete dimensions with the ongoing discovery of ancient artifacts, the T'ai Kung will eventually be vindicated by historical evidence.

Ssu-ma Fa is a terse, enigmatic text dating from about the fourth century BCE when it was probably compiled from materials dating far back into antiquity. Virtually every account of its inception identifies it with the state of Ch'i, historically the fount of military studies that possibly received their initial impetus from the T'ai Kung himself, the first king of Ch'i. Thereafter, throughout the Spring and Autumn and the Warring States periods, military studies flourished in Ch'i, being represented by Sun-tzu, Sun Pin, and Wei Liao-tzu, with certain families such as Sun, T'ien, and Ch'en being particularly noteworthy. The renowned strategist Sun Pin may have been active at the time of *Ssu-ma Fa*'s compilation, possibly even been a contributor, and in fact was a distant relative of Ssu-ma Jang-chü, to whom the work is traditionally attributed. Furthermore, the style and character of the writing reportedly identifies it as a product of the middle Warring States, the era of the fourth century BCE, and apart from the two books by Sun-tzu and Sun Pin, it has traditionally been accorded far more authenticity than any of the other military writings.

The title, *Ssu-ma Fa*, might be best translated as *The Methods of the Minister of War*, for the character *fa*, whose basic meaning is law, encompasses the concept of methods, standards, and techniques or art, as in Sun-tzu's famous *Art of War*. However, no single term adequately covers the scope of the content, because *Ssu-ma Fa* discusses laws, regulations, government policies, military organization, military administration, discipline, basic values, grand strategy, and strategy.

One often-disputed story associated with the book suggests that the famous general T'ien Jang-chü was instrumental in the great victories achieved under King Ching of Ch'i. Because he had held the post of *Ssu-ma* in this campaign, in accord with common practice he was granted the privilege of assuming the title as a family surname. Thereafter, when *Ssu-ma Fa* was originally compiled under King Wei, it apparently included General T'ien Jang-chü's strategic concepts and thus acquired the title *Ssu-ma Jang-chü Ping-fa, The Military*

Methods of Ssu-ma Jang-chü. His well-known biography in the *Shih Chi* not only records these events, but also illustrates the measures he felt were necessary to wrest immediate psychological control of the troops and create the awesomeness that would command obedience: "Ssu-ma Jang-chü was a descendant of T'ien Wan. During the time of Duke Ching of Ch'i, Chin attacked the major cities of A and P'in, and Yen invaded the river district of Ho-shang. Ch'i's army suffered complete defeat, and Duke Ching was sorely troubled. Yen Ying then recommended Jang-chü, saying: 'Even though Jang-chü is descended from one of T'ien's concubines, still in civil affairs this man is able to attach the masses, and in martial affairs is able to overawe the enemy. I would like my Lord to test him.' Duke Ching summoned Jang-chü and spoke with him about military affairs. He was greatly pleased with him, and appointed him as General of the Army to lead the soldiers in resisting the armies of Yen and Chin.

"Jang-chü said, 'I was formerly lowly and menial. If my Lord pulls me out from amidst my village, and places me above the high officials, the officers and troops will not be submissive, and the hundred surnames will not believe in me. Since I am insignificant and my authority light, I would like to have one of my Lord's favored ministers, someone whom the state respects, as Supervisor of the Army. Then it will be possible.' Thereupon Duke Ching assented and deputed Chuang Ku.

"Jang-chü, who had already taken his leave, made an agreement with Chuang Ku, saying: 'Tomorrow, at midday, we shall meet at the army's gate.' Jang-chü raced ahead to the army, set up the gnomon and let the water drip in the water clock, awaiting Ku. Ku, who had always been arrogant and aristocratic, assumed that since the commanding general had already reached the army while he was only the Supervisor, it was not extremely urgent. His relatives from all around, who were sending him off, detained him to drink. Midday came and Ku had not arrived. Jang-chü then lay down the standard, stopped the dripping water, and went into the encampment. He advanced the army, took control of the soldiers, clearly publicizing the constraints and bonds. When the constraints had been imposed it was already evening, and then Chuang Ku arrived.

"Jang-chü said: 'How is it that you have arrived after the appointed time?' Ku acknowledged his fault, saying, 'High officials and relatives saw this simpleton off, thus he was detained.' Jang-chü said: 'On the day a general receives the mandate of command he forgets his home; when he enters the army and takes control of the soldiers he forgets his loved ones; when he takes hold of the drumsticks and urgently beats the drum he forgets himself. At present, enemy states have already invaded our land and there is unrest and movement within the state. Officers and soldiers lie brutally cut down and exposed on the borders. Our ruler does not sleep soundly, nor enjoy the sweet taste of his food. The fate of the hundred surnames hangs upon you, so what do you mean that you were being seen off?'

"He summoned the provost marshal and inquired: 'What is the army's law regarding those who arrive after the appointed time?' He replied: 'Offenders should be decapitated!' Chuang Ku was terrified and ordered a man to race back and report it to Duke Ching, asking to be saved. The messenger had already left but not yet returned when Jang-chü beheaded Ku in order to publicize the enforcement of discipline within the Three Armies. All the officers within the Three Armies then shook with fear.

"Somewhat later an emissary dispatched by Duke Ching bearing a tally to pardon Ku raced into the army. Jang-chü said: 'When the general is with the army, there are orders of the ruler that are not accepted.' He queried the provost marshal: 'What is the law regarding racing into the army?' The provost marshal said: 'He should be beheaded.' The emissary was terrified. Jang-chü said, 'We cannot slay the ruler's emissary.' Then he beheaded the emissary's attendant, severed the carriage's left stanchion, and beheaded the horse on the left in order to instruct the Three Armies. He dispatched the Duke's emissary to return and report, and then moved the army out.

"The officers and soldiers next encamped, dug wells, lit the cookfires, and prepared their drink and food. He asked about those with illnesses, had physicians prescribe medicine, and personally looked after them. Whenever he received his salary and rations, he personally divided them up equally with his officers and troops. He compared the strong and weak among them, and only after three days took control of the soldiers. The sick all sought to go on the march, fervently struggling to join him in battle. When Chin's army heard about it, they abandoned their position, and departed. When Yen's army heard about it, they forded the river and dispersed. Thereupon he pursued and attacked them, subsequently retaking all the territory within the borders of the old fiefs, returning with the soldiers. Before he reached the state capital he disbanded the units, released them from the military constraints, swore a covenant, and thereafter entered the city. Duke Ching and his high officials greeted him in the suburbs, rewarded the troops, and completed the rites before returning to rest. After that he interviewed T'ien Jang-chü and honored him as Great Master of the Horse [*Ta Ssu-ma*]. The T'ien clan daily grew more honored in Ch'i.

"After this, subordinates of the high officials Pao, Kao, and Kuo harmed him, slandering him to Duke Ching so the duke forced Jang-chü to retire. Shortly thereafter he fell extremely ill and died. Consequently the followers of T'ien Ch'i and T'ien Pao bore a grudge against Kao, Kuo, and the others. Later with T'ien Ch'ang they killed Duke Chien, and completely exterminated the Kao and Kuo clans. Subsequently Ch'ang's great grandson T'ien Ho was able to establish himself as King Wei of Ch'i. In employing the army to effect Ch'i's awesomeness he greatly imitated Jang-chü's methods, and the feudal lords all paid court to Ch'i. King Wei also had the high officials seek out and discuss the strategy of the ancient *Ssu-mas*, appending Jang-chü's methods within them. Thus the book is called the *Military Methods of Ssu-ma Jang-chü*.

"The Grand Historian comments: 'I have read the *Ssu-ma Ping-fa*. It is vast, expansive, deep, and far reaching. Even the Three Dynasties, in their campaigns of rectification, still could not exhaust its meaning. Its language as well deserves some praise. However, how could one such as Jang-chü, commanding the army in a minor way on behalf of a small country, have the leisure to realize the *Military Methods of the Ssu-ma*? As the world already has numerous copies of the *Ssu-ma Ping-fa* I have not discussed it, but have written Jang-chü's biography.' '

The Grand Historian's comments eventually stimulated historical doubts about Jang-chü's possible role, even though the biography clearly indicates that his thoughts were merely appended among those of the early Masters of the Horse. Yet another account found in the histories suggests that Jang-chü was actually evil and dissolute, hardly a figure of any merit, and that any work he might have penned has been lost. Irrespective of its evolution, the present book apparently assumed essentially final form about the middle of the fourth century, the approximate time of Mencius's youth, more than a hundred years after the death of Confucius (551–479 BCE), probably contemporary with the composition of Sun-tzu's *Art of War* or perhaps Sun Pin's *Military Methods*. Unfortunately, all the editions presently available appear to be merely remnants of a once-extensive work, amounting to only five chapters out of the one hundred and fifty-five reportedly extant in the Han dynasty. However, these five seem to have been faithfully transmitted ever since the T'ang dynasty and probably represent original material whose kernel records early Chou practices, supplemented by paragraphs dating from the Warring States period.

SUN-TZU'S *ART OF WAR*

Of the *Seven Military Classics* only Sun-tzu's *Ping-fa*, traditionally known as *The Art of War*, has previously received much exposure in the West. First translated by a French missionary roughly two hundred years ago, it was reportedly studied and effectively employed by Napoleon and possibly by certain members of the Nazi High Command. For two thousand years it remained the most important military treatise in Asia, known at least by name even to the common people. Chinese, Japanese, and Korean military theorists and professional soldiers have all studied it, and many of the strategies played a significant role in Japan's storied military history, commencing about the eighth century CE. Over the millennia the book's concepts have stimulated intense debate and vehement philosophical discussion, commanding the attention of significant figures in all realms. Although rendered into English numerous times, further translations continue to appear.

The Art of War has long been recognized as China's oldest and most profound military treatise, all other works being relegated to secondary status at best. Traditionalists attribute the book to the historical Sun Wu, who is portrayed in *Shih Chi* and *Spring and Autumn Annals of Wu and Yüeh* as active in the last years of the sixth century, beginning about 512 BCE. In their view the book preserves his strategic and tactical concepts and principles and should therefore be dated to this period. Over the ages more skeptical scholars have questioned the work's authenticity, citing certain historical discrepancies and anachronisms to justify their positions. Although all the arguments have varying degrees of merit and credibility, the most extreme not only deny Sun Wu's military role, but even his very existence. However, a balanced view— taking into account the evolving nature of warfare, the rising need for military and bureaucratic specialization, the personalities involved, the complexity of the politics, and the fragility of recorded material—might well conclude that the historical Sun Wu existed, and not only served as a strategist and possibly general, but also composed the core of the book that bears his name. Thereafter the essential teachings were perhaps transmitted within the family or a close-knit school of disciples, being improved and revised with the passing decades, while gradually gaining wider dissemination. The early text may even have been edited by his famous descendant Sun Pin, who also extensively employed its teachings in his own *Military Methods*, and simultaneously made the Sun name even more glorious.

Shih Chi, famous throughout Asia as China's first true history and a literary masterpiece, includes several biographies devoted to distinguished military strategists and generals, including Sun-tzu. However, a somewhat later work, *Spring and Autumn Annals of Wu and Yüeh* recounts a very similar but rather more interesting version of Sun Wu's career and experiences: "In the third year of King Ho-lü's reign, Wu's generals wanted to attack Ch'u, but no action was taken. Wu Tzu-hsü and P'i spoke with each other: 'We nurture officers and make plans on behalf of the king. These strategies will be advantageous to the state, and for this reason the king should attack Ch'u. But he has put off issuing the orders, and does not have any intention to mobilize the army. What should we do?'

"After a while the King of Wu queried Wu Tzu-hsü and Po P'i: 'I want to send forth the army. What do you think?' Wu Tzu-hsü and Po P'i replied: 'We would like to receive the order.' The King of Wu secretly thought that the two of them harbored great enmity for Ch'u and was deeply afraid that they would take the army out only to be exterminated. He mounted his tower, faced into the southern wind and groaned. After a while he sighed. None of his ministers understood the king's thoughts. Wu Tzu-hsü secretly realized the king would not decide, so he recommended Sun-tzu to him.

"Sun-tzu, whose name was Wu, was a native of Wu. He excelled at military strategy, but dwelled in secrecy far away from civilization, so ordinary people did not know of his ability. Wu Tzu-hsü, himself enlightened, wise, and skilled in discrimination, knew Sun-tzu could penetrate and destroy the enemy. One morning when he was discussing military affairs he recommended Sun-tzu seven times. The king of Wu said: 'Since you have found an excuse to advance this officer, I want to have him brought in.' He questioned Sun-tzu about military strategy, and each time that he laid out a section of his book the king couldn't praise him enough.

"Greatly pleased, he inquired: 'If possible, I would like a minor test of your military strategy.' Sun-tzu said: "It's possible. We can conduct a minor test with women from the inner palace.' The king said, 'I agree.' Sun-tzu said: 'I would like to have two of your Majesty's beloved concubines act as company commanders, each to direct a company.' He ordered all three hundred women to wear helmets and armor, to carry swords and shields, and stand. He instructed them in military methods, that in accord with the drum they should advance, withdraw, go left or right, or turn around. He had them know the prohibitions and then ordered, 'At the first beating of the drum you should all assemble, at the second drumming you should advance with your weapons, and at the third deploy into military formation.' At this the palace women all covered their mouths and laughed.

"Sun-tzu then personally took up the sticks and beat the drum, giving the orders three times, and explaining them five times. They laughed as before. Sun-tzu saw that the women laughed continuously, and wouldn't stop. Sun-tzu was enraged, his eyes suddenly opened wide, his sound was like a terrifying tiger, his hair stood on end under his cap, and his neck broke the tassels at the side. He said to the Master of Laws, 'Get the executioner's axes.'

"Sun-tzu then said: 'If the instructions are not clear, if the explanations and orders are not trusted, it is the general's offense. When they have already been instructed three times, and the orders explained five times, if the troops still do not perform, it is the fault of the officers. According to the rescripts for military discipline, what is the procedure?' The Master of Laws said: 'Decapitation!' Sun-tzu then ordered the beheading of the two company commanders, the king's favorite concubines.

"The King of Wu ascended his platform to observe just when they were about to behead his beloved concubines. He had an official hasten down to them with orders to say, 'I already know the general is able to command forces. Without these two concubines my food will not be sweet. It would be appropriate not to behead them.'

"Sun-tzu said: 'I have already received my commission as commanding general. According to the rules for generals, when I, as a general, am in command of the army even though you issue orders to me, I do not have to accept them.' He then had them beheaded.

"He again beat the drum, and the women went left and right, advanced and withdrew, and turned around in accord with the prescribed standards without daring to blink an eye. The two companies were silent, not daring to look around.

Thereupon Sun-tzu reported to the King of Wu: 'The army is already well ordered. I would like your Majesty to observe them. However you might want to employ them, even sending them forth into fire and water will not present any difficulty. They can be used to settle All under Heaven.'

"The King of Wu was suddenly displeased. He said: 'I know that you excel at employing the army. Even though I can thereby become a hegemon, there is no place to exercise them. General, please dismiss the army and return to your dwelling. I am unwilling to act further.'

"Sun-tzu said: 'Your Majesty only likes the words, he isn't able to realize their substance.' Wu Tzu-hsü remonstrated: 'I have heard that the army is an inauspicious affair and cannot be wantonly tested. Thus if one forms an army but does not go forth to launch a punitive attack, then the military Tao will be unclear. Now if Your Majesty sincerely seeks talented officers and wants to mobilize the army to execute the brutal state of Ch'u, become hegemon of All under Heaven, and overawe the feudal lords, if you do not employ Sun-tzu as your general, who can ford the Huai, cross the Ssu, and traverse a thousand kilometers to engage in battle?'

"Thereupon the King of Wu was elated. He had the drum beaten to convene the army's staff, assembled the troops, and attacked Ch'u. Sun-tzu took Shu, killing the two renegade Wu generals, Princes Ka-iyu and Chu-yung."

The *Shih Chi* biography differs from the above version in two fundamental respects: first, it identifies Sun-tzu as a native of Ch'i rather than Wu. This would place his background in the state that enjoyed the heritage of the T'ai Kung's military thought. Accordingly, many traditional scholars have asserted that he was well versed in *Six Secret Teachings* and similar writings, although it should be noted that much, if not all, of *Six Secret Teachings* was probably composed well after Sun-tzu's *Art of War*. Moreover, the state of Ch'i, originally on the periphery of the ancient Chou political world, was well known for nurturing a diversity of views and imaginative theories. Since the *Art of War* clearly embodies many Taoist conceptions and is philosophically sophisticated, he may well have been a man of Ch'i.

Second, the *Shih Chi* biography adds a brief description of Sun-tzu's achievements: "To the west the king defeated the powerful state of Ch'u, and advanced into Ying. To the north he overawed Ch'i and Chin, and manifested his name among the feudal lords. This was due to Sun-tzu imparting power to him." Some military historians have identified Sun Wu with the campaigns against Ch'u that commenced in 511 BCE, the year after his initial interview with King Ho-lü. Although he is never mentioned in any recorded source as having sole command of the troops, following Wu's conquest of Ying, the capital of Ch'u, his name completely disappears. Perhaps he realized the difficulty of surviving under the unstable political conditions of his time, or possibly feared he would be executed by the new king, Fu-chai, after becoming entangled in Po P'i's machinations, and set an example for later ages by retiring to obscurity, leaving his work behind.

Sun Wu remains an enigma not only because of the absence of historical data in the so-called authentic texts of the period, but also because his life never generated the anecdotes and illustrative stories frequently found about famous figures in the works of succeeding periods. Not only is his background and early history completely unknown, it remains unclear whether he was born in Wu or Ch'i, and whether he had studied military strategy and served in a command capacity before venturing to instruct the King of Wu or simply was a peripatetic thinker capitalizing upon an employment opportunity. (The dramatic way in which he illustrated his theories about military organization and discipline with three hundred of the king's concubines, and thereby received his appointment, may well be apocryphal.) Many theories have been vociferously advanced to explain Sun Wu's invisibility, chief among them that most of the credit that was rightly his was attributed to his mentor, Wu Tzu-hsü, because the latter was more prominent and his life, a living melodrama writ large, provided a natural focal point for tales of intrigue and portraits of achievement. Remarkably, among those who deny Sun-tzu's very existence, some have advanced the theory that he and Wu Tzu-hsü were identical, one and the same individual.

WU CH'I'S *WU-TZU*

Unlike the semilegendary Sun-tzu, Wu Ch'i, also termed Wu-tzu by later generations, was a famous historical figure. His exploits and achievements, both military and administrative, were truly outstanding, and shortly after his death his name became inextricably linked with Sun-tzu's. According to the *Shih Chi,* whenever people discussed military theory Sun and Wu were invariably mentioned together, and Ssu-ma Ch'ien's famous biographical chapter permanently canonized that bond.

Wu Ch'i was a complex man of contradictions, and even his *Shih Chi* biography does not depict him favorably. Extremely talented, he advocated the fundamental Confucian beliefs, although his behavior visibly contradicted them. He embraced the concept of benevolence as the essential foundation for government, yet reputedly killed his own wife. He ignored his mother's mourning rites, a heinous offense in Confucian eyes, in order to keep a vow, clearly emphasizing trustworthiness over filial emotion and its respectful expression. While he attained great power and encouraged the development and preservation of distinctions, he personally eschewed the visible comforts available to a commanding general, sharing every misery and hardship with his troops.

Born about 440 BCE into the tumultuous era that witnessed the initial conflicts of the incessant warfare that would eventually reduce the number of powerful states from seven to one, he immediately realized that states could survive only if they fostered both military strength and sound government. As a young man he reputedly studied with two of the founding disciples of Confucianism, perhaps for as long as three years. Subsequently he journeyed to find a receptive ear, yet lost favor even after great accomplishments. Eventually he was murdered about 351 BCE in Ch'u, a victim of the enmity incurred by his draconian measures to strengthen the military and the state.

According to subsequent historical writings Wu Ch'i not only was never defeated in battle, but rarely suffered the ignominy of a stalemate, while compiling a remarkable record of decisive victories against the superior forces of entrenched states. He too has been widely regarded as China's first great general and credited with such notable achievements as governing and holding the West Ho region; pacifying Yüeh (the south China region); commanding the forces of Lu to gain an overwhelming victory against Ch'i; leading Wei to thrash Ch'in's growing power numerous times; and stabilizing the government of Ch'u. Thus his views and methods, to the extent they may be preserved in the *Wu-tzu*, are not merely theoretical, but were founded and thoroughly tested in reality.

Wu Ch'i's reputation for impressive administrative contributions, especially the institution of innovative measures and controls to organize the state and instill order, first as Protector of the West River Commandery, and later as prime minister of Ch'u, has frequently caused him to be ranked with the famous Legalist Lord Shang. Numerous anecdotes portray his emphasis upon certitude, one of the few virtues he both espoused and personally embodied. Stories about him abound in works originating in the centuries after his death.

The *Wu-tzu* not only comprises one of *The Seven Military Classics*, but it has also long been valued as one of the basic foundations of Chinese military thought. Although less strident than *The Art of War*, it seriously considers all aspects of war and battle preparation, as well as suggesting generally applicable strategies for resolving certain tactical situations. Over the centuries traditional Confucian scholars, with their classical prejudices toward style and artifice, denigrated the *Wu-tzu* because of the language's comparative simplicity, condemning as well its realistic policies and perceived brutality, but the text remains lucid and commanding.

The core of the *Wu-tzu* was probably composed by Wu Ch'i himself, then expanded and revised by his disciples, perhaps from their own memories or court recordings. Much of the original appears to have been lost, but what remains has been edited into a succinct, fairly systematic, and remarkably comprehensive work. Although earlier versions of the text apparently date back to at least the fourth century BCE, it probably assumed its present form in the Han dynasty. Fortunately, unlike some of the military classics, few textual problems exist, with only small differences among editions. Naturally some passages are common to other, presumably later works, but the focus, concepts, and stage of development are distinctly different.

Wu Ch'i's life and values being closely intertwined, his dramatic biography from *Shih Chi* merits translation in full: "Wu Ch'i, a native of Wey, loved military operations. He once studied with Tseng-tzu, then went on to serve the ruler of Lu. When the state of Ch'i attacked Lu, the ruler wanted to commission Wu Ch'i as a general, but since he had taken a woman of Ch'i as his wife the ruler doubted him. Thereupon Wu Ch'i, who wanted to become famous, killed his wife to show he had no connection with Ch'i. Lu finally appointed him as a general, and in this capacity he attacked Ch'i, destroying their forces.

"Someone in Lu who hated Wu Ch'i said to the ruler: 'Wu Ch'i is cruel and suspicious. When he was young his family had accumulated a thousand ounces of gold. He traveled about seeking official appointment but was never successful, and eventually exhausted the family's resources. When members of his district laughed at him he killed more than thirty of his detractors and then went east, through the gate of Wey's outer wall. On parting from his mother he bit his arm and swore a blood oath: "Until I become a ranking minister I will not reenter Wey." Then he went to serve Tseng-tzu. He had only been there a short while when his mother died but he did not return home. Tseng-tzu despised him for this and severed all relationship with him. Wu Ch'i then went to Lu and studied military arts in order to serve you. You doubted his intentions so he killed his wife to obtain the post of general. Now Lu is a small state, and if it should attain a reputation for being victorious in battle the other feudal lords will plot against it. Moreover, Lu and Wey are brothers, so if you employ Wu Ch'i you will be casting aside Wey.' The ruler grew suspicious of Wu Ch'i and dismissed him.

"At that time Wu Ch'i happened to hear that Marquis Wen of Wei was a Worthy and wanted to serve in his court. Marquis Wen questioned Li K'o about him: 'What sort of a man is Wu Ch'i?' Li K'o replied, 'Ch'i is greedy and licentious, but in the employment of troops even the famous general Ssu-ma Jang-chü could not surpass him.' Upon hearing this Marquis Wen appointed him as a general. Wu Ch'i commanded an attack on Ch'in that seized five enemy cities.

"In his position as general Wu Ch'i's custom was to wear the same clothes and eat the same food as the men in the lowest ranks. When sleeping he did not set out a mat, while on the march he did not ride a horse or in a chariot. He personally packed up his leftover rations, and shared all labors and misery with the troops.

"Once when one of his soldiers had a blister he personally sucked out the pus for him. The soldier's mother heard about it and wept. Someone said to her, 'Your son is only an ordinary soldier, while the general himself sucked out the pus. What is there to weep about?' The mother retorted, 'That isn't it. In years past Duke Wu sucked his father's blister. His father went to war without hesitating and subsequently died at the hands of the enemy. Now Duke Wu again sucks my son's blister so I don't know where he will die. For this reason I weep.'

"Because Marquis Wen felt that Wu Ch'i excelled in employing the army, was scrupulous and fair-handed, and able to obtain the complete allegiance of his troops, he appointed him as Protector of the West River Commandery to fend off the states of Ch'in and Han.

"When Marquis Wen died, Wu Ch'i continued to serve Marquis Wu, his son. Marquis Wu voyaged by boat down the West River. In midstream he looked back and exclaimed to Wu Ch'i, 'Is it not magnificent! The substantiality of these mountains and rivers, this is the jewel of Wei.' Wu Ch'i replied: 'The real jewel lies in Virtue, not in precipitous defiles. Formerly the Three Miao had Tung-t'ing Lake on the left and P'eng-li Lake on the right, but they didn't cultivate Virtue and righteousness and Yü obliterated them. The place where Chieh of the Hsia dynasty resided had the Yellow and Chi Rivers on the left, Mt. T'ai and Mt. Hua on the right, the cliffs of I-ch'üeh in the south, and the slopes of Yang-ch'ang to the north. But in his practice of government he didn't cultivate benevolence and T'ang displaced him. The state of the tyrant Chou of the Yin dynasty had Mt. Meng-men on the left, Mt. T'ai-hang on the right, Mt. Ch'ang to the north, and the great Yellow River flowing to the south, but in his practice of government he didn't cultivate Virtue and King Wu killed him. From this perspective the state's jewel is Virtue, not the precipitousness of its defiles. If you do not cultivate Virtue, all the men in this boat will become your enemies.'

'Excellent,' said Marquis Wu. Thereupon he enfeoffed Wu Ch'i as Protector of the West River Commandery, and his reputation grew enormously.

"Wei then established the post of Minister, naming T'ien Wen to the office. Wu Ch'i was unhappy so he accosted T'ien Wen. 'Could we please discuss merit and attainments?' T'ien Wen agreed. Wu Ch'i asked, 'Who is better at commanding the Three Armies, causing the officers and soldiers to take pleasure in dying in battle, and ensuring that enemy states do not dare plot against us—you or me?' 'I am not as capable as you,' T'ien Wen replied. Wu Ch'i then asked him, 'Who is better, you or I, in administering the bureaucracy, gaining the support of the people, and filling the storehouses and arsenals?' T'ien Wen again replied, 'I am not as good as you.' 'In serving as Protector of the West River Commandery so that Ch'in's troops dare not establish villages in their eastern regions, while Han and Chao act submissively as honored guests, who is better?' T'ien Wen acknowledged, 'You are.'

"Wu Ch'i then proceeded, 'In all three of these you are inferior to me, yet your position has been placed above me. Why?' T'ien Wen said, 'The ruler is young, the state doubtful, the major ministers not yet supportive, while the common people do not trust the government. At this time should the role fall to you, or to me?' After Ch'i was silent for a very long time he said, 'It should belong to you.' 'This is why I am placed over you.' Wu Ch'i then knew he was not as good as T'ien Wen.

"After T'ien Wen died Kung Shu became Minister. He had married a princess of Wei and wanted to damage Wu Ch'i. Kung Shu's servant said to him, 'It would be easy to eliminate Wu Ch'i.' Kung Shu asked how, and his servant replied:

'Wu Ch'i is constrained, incorruptible, and likes fame. Accordingly, you should first say to Marquis Wu, "Wu Ch'i is a Worthy while your state is small. Moreover you have a border area of fertile land abutting the strong state of Ch'in. Therefore I fear Wu Ch'i will not remain loyal." The Marquis will then ask what should be done and you should say: "Test him by extending an offer of marriage with a princess. If Ch'i intends to stay he will certainly accept her; if not he will invariably decline. With this divine his intent." Then you should summon Wu Ch'i and return with him, while also making the princess angry so that she treats you contemptuously. When Wu Ch'i sees that the princess holds you in contempt he'll certainly decline.'

"Thereafter, when Wu Ch'i saw the princess treat the Minister of Wei contemptuously, he did in fact decline Marquis Wu's offer. Marquis Wu grew suspicious and did not trust him any longer. Wu Ch'i, fearing he might be charged with some offense, subsequently departed for the state of Ch'u.

"King Tao of Ch'u, who had previously heard that Wu Ch'i was a Worthy, appointed him as Minister upon his arrival. Wu Ch'i made the laws clear, examined the ordinances, eliminated unimportant offices, and dispersed distant royal relatives in order to nourish and support fighting men. He emphasized strengthening the army and destroying the vociferous proponents of the horizontal and vertical alliances. To the south he pacified the Pai Yüeh. In the north he seized Ch'en and Ts'ai, and forced the Three Chin to withdraw. To the west he successfully attacked Ch'in. The other feudal lords were troubled by Ch'u's growing strength, while all the royal family members wanted to harm him. When King Tao died the imperial relatives and chief ministers revolted and attacked Wu Ch'i. He ran to the king's body and hid beneath it. When his assailants shot their arrows, striking him, they thereby struck King Tao as well.

"After King Tao had been buried and the prince enthroned, he had the Minister of Justice execute all those who had shot at Wu Ch'i and struck the king's corpse. Those who were judged guilty and executed, and also had their families exterminated, numbered more than seventy.

"The Grand Historian comments: 'When referring to armies and regiments, the habit of the contemporary age is to always speak of Sun-tzu's thirteen chapters and Wu Ch'i's strategy. Since many people have them now I have not discussed them, but instead written about what their actions accomplished. There is a common saying: "One able to perform an action cannot invariably speak about it; one able to speak about something is not invariably able to perform it." Wu Ch'i tried to persuade Marquis Wen that the strategic advantages of power conferred by the substantiality of the terrain's configuration are not as good as Virtue. However his actions in Ch'u, on account of his harsh oppressiveness and the paucity of his beneficence, caused him to lose his life. Was it not tragic!'" Even in death Wu Ch'i managed to conceive and successfully execute a strategy to gain revenge, for he knew that in trying to kill him his enemies would desecrate the king's body and eventually be executed!

Modern scholars, troubled by the inclusion of such detrimental material as Wu Ch'i killing his wife, have studied the biography in considerable detail and concluded it is an amalgamation of the disparate, even condemnatory materials probably available to the Grand Historian. Opinion divides over Wu Ch'i's historical accomplishments, with much of the *Shih Chi* record being rejected as romantic embellishment, anachronistic, or simply dubious. However, given the numerous references to Wu Ch'i in the extant literature from the two centuries following his death, it can probably be concluded that he served in the capacities enumerated, and was a highly effective strategist and commander. Moreover, the more significant anecdotes among these other writings not only provide interesting information about the man and his character, but also indicate the important principles generally associated with his name and prominently illustrated by his lifelong behavior.

Wu Ch'i reputedly valued credibility—which can only be established through the sincere, ongoing preservation of one's word—above all else. An anecdote commented upon by Han Fei-tzu portrays this paramount commitment: "Wu Ch'i went out and happened to encounter an old friend. He stopped him and invited him to eat dinner with him. The friend replied, 'I will. In a short time I'll go back and eat with you.' Wu Ch'i said, 'I will wait for you to dine.' By nightfall the friend had not come, but Wu Ch'i waited for him without eating. Early the next morning he had someone seek out his friend, and only when the friend had come back did he eat with him. Han Fei-tzu commented: 'When small acts of faith are achieved, great faith is established. Therefore the wise ruler accumulates good faith. When rewards and punishments are not trusted, prohibitions and ordinances will not be effected. For this reason Wu Ch'i waited for his friend to eat.' "

Another incident from *Han Fei-tzu* portrays Wu Ch'i as divorcing his wife for a minor transgression—rather than killing her, as in his *Shih Chi* biography—in order to preserve his credibility. His brother-in-law even rationalized this action in terms of his zealous commitment to the law: "Wu Ch'i, who was a native of Tso-shih in Wey, had his wife weave a silk band. When he measured it and found it to be narrower than desired, he had her change it. She assented but when it was complete he measured it again and the result was still inaccurate. Wu Ch'i was enraged but his wife replied: 'When I began I set the warp, and it could not be changed.' Wu Ch'i sent her away. She then asked her older brother to seek her readmission, but her brother said: 'Wu Ch'i is a man of law. He works with the laws so that he may attain great achievements in a large state. Therefore he must first put the laws into practice with his wife, and thereafter implement them in government. You have no hope of seeking to return.' His wife's younger brother was well favored by Wey's ruler, so he sought the ruler's intercession on her behalf with Wu Ch'i. Wu Ch'i did not listen, but instead left Wey and went to Ching."

Still a third version of the story perceives her dismissal as resulting from working too assiduously, thereby surpassing—rather than falling short of—what he had required: "Wu Ch'i, showing his wife a silk band, said: 'Weave a silk band for me, making it like this.' When it was finished he compared them, and the one she had made was especially good. Wu Ch'i said, 'I had you weave a silk band, making it like this one, but now this one is especially good. How is that?' His wife replied, 'The materials employed are alike, but I concentrated upon making it better.' Wu Ch'i said: 'It is not what I said to do.' He had her change her clothes and return to her family. Her father went to request that he take her back, but Wu Ch'i said, 'In the Ch'i family there are no empty words!'" This explanation fully accords with the Legalist emphasis upon not exceeding the prescribed role, generally proclaimed a canonical virtue by the military thinkers within the context of battlefield situations.

Another cardinal doctrine of the strategists was the inviolate nature of rewards and punishments because they embody and symbolize the administrative system's credibility. Successfully motivating men not only requires both rewards and punishments, but also the absolute certainty that they will invariably be implemented in every single instance. Wu Ch'i unflinchingly believed in the power of the twin handles, as Lord Shang termed them, and especially in the ability of rewards to motivate men so strongly that they will risk their lives and chance everything. While instruction, organization, training, and the development of a sense of shame must precede any manipulation of the human spirit, the underlying effect of credibility in attaining a desired objective is well illustrated by the following incident: "When Wu Ch'i was serving as Protector of the West River Commandery, the state of Ch'in maintained a small fortified watchtower near the border. Wu Ch'i wanted to attack it, for if he did not eliminate it, it would be extremely harmful to the farmers. However, it was not worth summoning armored troops to eliminate it. Therefore he leaned a carriage shaft against the North Gate and issued an ordinance that stated: 'Anyone who can move this outside the South Gate will be rewarded with superior lands and an excellent house.' For a while no one moved it, then someone did succeed in moving it. Upon his return from the South Gate Wu Ch'i rewarded him in accord with the ordinance. Shortly thereafter he set a picul of red beans outside the East Gate, and issued an ordinance that stated: 'Anyone able to move this outside the West Gate will be rewarded as in the first case.' The people competed to move it. Then Wu Ch'i sent down an order. 'Tomorrow when we attack the tower, whoever can ascend it first will be appointed as a high official and rewarded with superior lands and a house.' The people fought to race to the tower, attacking and seizing it in a single morning."

The *Shih Chi* biography indicates that Wu Ch'i once studied with Tseng-tzu; however, as this is chronologically impossible, it was probably Tseng Shen, Tseng-tzu's son, perhaps for as long as three years. If he incurred Tseng Shen's condemnation for blatantly violating the precepts of filial behavior—one of the cornerstones of Tseng-tzu's recension of Confucianism—he may have rejected formal studies in favor of military pursuits, presumably his first inclination. However, throughout the *Wu-tzu* he advocates policies based upon four fundamental Confucian virtues: benevolence, righteousness, the forms of propriety, and the Tao of Heaven. This fully accords with the new reality of the Warring States period because state governments were becoming significantly dependent upon the willing consent and participation of the populace in military enterprises. The famous, although probably fabricated, discussion with Marquis Wu while floating down the West River clearly expresses his belief in Virtue rather than simple, strategic advantage. Another interview with the Marquis, at the start of his reign, reflects the same concern, but coupled with an advocacy of practicing accessible government while retaining political power and preventing the nobles from encroaching upon the people: "Marquis Wu asked Wu Ch'i about the initial reign year. Wu Ch'i replied: 'It is said that the ruler of a state must be cautious about the beginning.' 'How does one go about being cautious about the beginning?' 'Make it upright.' 'How does one make it upright?' 'Make wisdom enlightened. If wisdom is not enlightened how can you perceive the upright? Listen widely and select from what you hear, so as to make wisdom enlightened. For this reason, in antiquity when the ruler first held court, the high officials were each allotted one speech, the officers allowed one audience, and if the common people requested admittance they would be heard. If the nobles made any inquiries they would certainly be answered, and they would not refuse any who came from the four quarters. This can be termed not plugged up or obscured. In apportioning salaries they made certain to extend them to everyone, while in the employment of punishments they were invariably accurate. The ruler's mind had to be benevolent. He thought of the ruler's profit and the elimination of the people's harm. This can be termed not losing the people. The ruler personally had to be upright, the intimate ministers carefully selected. The high officials could not hold more than one office concurrently, while the handles for controlling the people did not lie with one clan. This can be referred to as not losing the balance of authority and strategic power. This is the meaning of the *Spring and Autumn Annals*, and the basis of the initial reign year.' "

A dramatic passage in the *Lü-shih Ch'un-ch'iu* describes Wu Ch'i's prophetic words upon departing from Wei, providing another version of the slander story incorporated in the *Shih Chi* biography: "When Wu Ch'i governed the area outside the West River, Wang Ts'o slandered him to Marquis Wu of Wei. Marquis Wu had an emissary summon him. When Wu Ch'i reached the gate on the far shore he stopped his carriage and rested. Looking toward the West River several tears fell from his eyes. His servant addressed him: 'I have observed your intentions. You have cast aside the world as if throwing away a pair of straw sandals, yet now you weep as you leave the West River region. Why?'

"Wu Ch'i wiped the tears away and replied: 'You do not understand. If the ruler truly knew me and had me exhaust my abilities, Ch'in could certainly be destroyed, and with the West River region he could become a true king. But now the ruler listens to the ideas of slanderers and does not know me. It will not be long before the West River region belongs to Ch'in. Henceforth the state of Wei will diminish.' Wu Ch'i subsequently left Wei and entered Ch'u. Wei diminished day by day, while Ch'in grew correspondingly greater. This is what Wu Ch'i saw first and wept about." Wu Ch'i's radical, emotional commitment to his political beliefs, as well as his desire to exert himself on behalf of the state, clearly manifest themselves in such passages.

Several incidents provide glimpses of Wu Ch'i's activities in Ch'u, apparently confirming that King Tao quickly entrusted him with power and influence. Seeking to strengthen the central government, and thereby the state and army, Wu Ch'i proposed policies that invariably antagonized entrenched interests: "Formerly Wu Ch'i instructed King Tao of Ch'u about Ch'u's customs. 'The chief ministers are too powerful, the hereditary lords too numerous. In this sort of situation, above they press upon the ruler, while below they oppress the people. This is the Tao for impoverishing the state and weakening the army. It would be better to take back all ranks and emoluments from the hereditary lords after three generations; diminish the salaries and allowances of the hundred officials; and reduce all unnecessary offices in order to support selected, well-trained officers.' King Tao had implemented his suggestion for a year when he died. Wu Ch'i was then torn apart in Ch'u."

Another version in the same third-century BCE book further explicates his policies for populating the countryside and emasculating the stagnant nobility: "Wu Ch'i addressed the King of Ch'u: 'What Ch'u has in surplus is land, but what is insufficient is people. Now if your lordship takes what is insufficient to increase what is in surplus, then I cannot do anything.' Thereupon the king ordered the nobles to go out and fill the vast, empty lands. They all found it extremely bitter. When the King of Ch'u died the nobles all came to the capital where the king's corpse was lying in the upper hall. The nobles acting together shot arrows at Wu Ch'i. Wu Ch'i yelled, 'I'll show you how I use weapons.' He pulled out an arrow and ran. Prostrating himself over the corpse he stuck the arrow in and yelled out, 'The ministers are revolting against the king!' Then Wu Ch'i died. However, according to Ch'in law anyone who exposed a weapon before the king's body should be subject to the severest penalty—capital punishment and the extirpation of their families to three degrees. Wu Ch'i's wisdom can certainly be said to have been acute."

Chinese tradition has long viewed the military arts as being a "contrary virtue," a concept perhaps originally espoused by the mythical Lao-tzu in the *Tao Te Ching* and eventually embraced even by many of the military writings, including the

Wu-tzu. Consequently, prolonged involvement and extensive experience were thought to doom its practitioners to misfortune and disaster as indicated by these two fictional interviews in the *Shuo Yüan*: "When Wu Ch'i was serving as Protector of Yüan, during a tour of inspection he reached Hsi where he asked Ch'u I-chiu: 'The king, not knowing that I am a petty man, has made me Protector of Yüan. Sir, how would you instruct me?' Duke Ch'u did not reply.

"After a year the king made Wu Ch'i Director of Ordinances. During his tour of inspection he reached Hsi and again asked Ch'u I-chiu, 'I inquired of you, but you didn't instruct me. Now the king, not knowing that I am a petty man, has made me Director of Ordinances. Sir, would you examine how I am acting?' Duke Ch'u said, 'What are you going to do?' Wu Ch'i said, 'I am going to level the ranks of nobility in Ch'u and even their emoluments; reduce what is in excess and continue what is insufficient; and polish the armor and weapons in order to contend for All under Heaven at the appropriate time.'

"Duke Ch'u said: 'I have heard that in the past those that excelled at governing states did not change the old, nor alter the usual. Now you are about to level the ranks of Ch'u's nobility and even their emoluments, reduce what is surplus and continue what is insufficient. This is changing the old and altering the usual. Moreover, I have heard that weapons are inauspicious implements, and that conflict is a contrary Virtue. Now you secretly plot contrary Virtue, and love to employ inauspicious implements. Reaching out for what men abandon is the extreme of contrariness; implementing licentious and dissolute affairs is not advantageous. Moreover, when you employed the troops of Lu, although you should not have gained your intentions in Ch'i, you realized them. When you employed the troops of Wei you should not have been able to realize your intentions against Ch'in, but you gained them. I have heard it said, "If one is not the man for disaster he cannot complete disaster." I formerly found it strange that my ruler had frequently acted contrary to the Tao of Heaven, but up to now had not met with any misfortune. Alas, it was probably waiting for you.'

"Wu Ch'i fearfully said, 'Can it still be altered?' Duke Ch'u said, 'It cannot.' Wu Ch'i said, 'I plan on behalf of others.' Duke Ch'u said, 'A prisoner whose punishment has been determined cannot change it himself. You would best be honest and sincerely implement the affairs of government, for the state of Ch'u has nothing more valued than raising up the worthy.'"

From a historical perspective that had witnessed Ch'in's slow evolution to power and subsequent meteoric collapse, the milieu that saw the rise of state Confucianism and also the pervasive expression of Taoism in such syncretic texts as the *Huai-nan tzu*, gave voice to a condemnatory view: "On behalf of Ch'in, Lord Shang instituted the mutual guarantee laws, and the hundred surnames were resentful. On behalf of Ch'u, Wu Ch'i issued orders to reduce the nobility and their emoluments, and the meritorious ministers revolted. Lord Shang, in establishing laws, and Wu Ch'i, in employing the army, were the best in the world. But Lord Shang's laws eventually caused the loss of Ch'in, for he was perspicacious about the traces of the brush and knife, but did not know the foundation of order and disorder. Wu Ch'i, on account of the military, weakened Ch'u. He was well practiced in such military affairs as deploying formations, but didn't know the balance of authority involved in court warfare."

From such passages it would appear that Wu Ch'i actually wielded significant political power and tried to implement typically Legalist reforms. Whether he enjoyed such influence in Wei's central government is more problematic, for although Li K'o and other ministers apparently embarked on such programs, Wu Ch'i's administrative impact and power were probably confined to the West River region where he may have been virtual dictator.

SUN PIN'S *MILITARY METHODS*

In the centuries just before the founding of the first imperial dynasty in 221 BCE, four great military figures were commonly recognized as having been instrumental in strengthening their states and wresting power over the realm: Sun-tzu in Wu, Sun Pin in Ch'i, Wu Ch'i in Wei, and Shang

Yang in Ch'in. Until recently only Sun Pin lacked his own work because one that had been identified with him in the Han imperial library, entitled *Military Methods*, had been lost, causing many scholars in later centuries to insist it had never existed. However, some two thousand years after its last recorded existence, remnants of his book were dramatically recovered in 1972 when a Han dynasty military official's tomb revealed hoard of bamboo strips that preserved numerous ancient writings on military, legal, and other subjects. Amazingly, the various writings had fortuitously been placed in the tomb either to aid the departed in the other world or, more likely, deliberately preserve them for posterity even though the tomb should never again be opened.

Unfortunately, although many of the strips are perfectly preserved, over the centuries portions of others have suffered varying degrees of damage, ranging from complete physical disintegration to the partial obliteration of the ancient characters. Moreover, because the rolled-up strips simply collapsed into structureless piles when the cords binding them together decayed, the original organization has been significantly obscured. However, after painstaking reconstruction much of the contents have tentatively emerged, revealing incisive conceptions and integrated tactics. While some of the chapters remain hopelessly fragmented and opaque, incredibly several are almost perfectly preserved. Even in this imperfect condition the *Military Methods* remains a remarkable middle Warring States text, one that presumably embodies the views of the great strategist who was active in Ch'i at least from 356 until 341 BCE and perhaps lived until near the end of the century.

As to the date of the original *Military Methods* and to what degree the recovered copy represents an embellished or otherwise altered version, it appears that the book is based upon Sun Pin's thought and teachings, but was compiled and edited by his disciples. Sun Pin himself, perhaps wishing to emulate his famous predecessor, may have composed a prototext or developed a kernel of fixed teachings, and then his disciples or family members reworked it into the present form. The first fifteen chapters are cast in the dialogue form common to other early writings (such as the *Mencius*) and almost always indicate the speaker. The second part of the book may have originally comprised extended discussions on concrete topics (such as is found in the critical chapter on the unorthodox and orthodox) that Sun Pin had not put into dialogue form or simply had not been formatted in the same way by his students. Sun Pin obviously acquired disciples during his lifetime, for they are mentioned in the text questioning him about his discussions with King Wei and T'ien Chi. Coupled with other internal evidence, this suggests they may have finished *Military Methods* about the end of his life or compiled it shortly thereafter from memory to preserve the master's teaching.

Virtually every traditional source identifies Sun Pin as Suntzu's lineal descendant, although the actual relationship may well have been somewhat less direct. Several family trees have been suggested, but they are all dubious reconstructions that naturally ignore the possibility that Sun-tzu himself may not have existed. The common view identifies Sun Pin as Suntzu's grandson, but since more than a century separates their active years, "great-grandson" or even "great-great-grandson" is more likely. Assuming that Sun Pin would have been at least twenty-five during the unfolding of the Kuei-ling campaign in 354 to 353 BCE yields a projected birth year of approximately 380 BCE, consistent with a statement in his *Shih Chi* biography placing him more than a century after Sun-tzu.

Even though he enjoys a joint biography with Sun-tzu in Ssu-ma Ch'ien's famous *Shih Chi*, virtually nothing is known about Sun Pin's life and background. Recently numerous popular editions and even several scholars have supplied surprisingly embellished biographies for Sun Pin in their modern editions, but essentially they all derive from inferences based upon the *Shih Chi* biography and a few brief references in other writings associated with the period. Sun Pin's life and accomplishments, as reprised by Ssu-ma Ch'ien some two centuries after his death, are preserved as follows: "About a hundred years after Sun-tzu died there was Sun Pin. Sun Pin was born between Ah and Chüan in Ch'i, and was also a direct descendant of Sun-tzu. Sun Pin had once studied military strategy together with P'ang Chüan. P'ang Chüan was already serving in the state of Wei, having obtained appointment as one of King Hui's generals. Realizing that his abilities did not come up to Sun Pin, he secretly had an emissary summon Sun Pin. When Pin arrived P'ang Chüan feared that he was a greater Worthy than himself, and envied him. By manipulating the laws he managed to have him sentenced to the punishment of having his feet amputated and his face branded, wanting to thereby keep him hidden so that he would not be seen by the king.

"An emissary from the state of Ch'i arrived at Liang in Wei. Sun Pin, who was banished from the court because of his punishment, secretly had an audience with him, and exercised his persuasion. Ch'i's emissary found him to be remarkable and clandestinely brought him back to Ch'i in his carriage. T'ien Chi, Ch'i's commanding general, regarded him well and treated him as an honored guest.

"T'ien Chi frequently gambled heavily on linked horse races with the princes. Sun Pin observed that the fleetness of his horses did not differ much from theirs. The horses had three grades—upper, middle, and lower. Thereupon Sun Pin said to T'ien Chi, 'My lord should bet again for I am able to make you win.' T'ien Chi trusted him and wagered a thousand gold coins with the king and princes. When they approached the time for the contest Sun Pin then said: 'Put your lowest team of horses against their best; your best team against their middle one; and your middle team against their lowest one.' When the three teams raced, T'ien Chi lost one race but won two, so that in the end he gained the king's thousand gold coins. T'ien Chi then introduced Sun Pin to King Wei. King Wei questioned him about military affairs, and appointed him as a strategist.

"Thereafter the state of Wei attacked Chao. Chao was sorely pressed, and requested aid from Ch'i. King Wei of Ch'i wanted to appoint Sun Pin as commanding general, but Pin respectfully declined saying, 'It is not possible for a man who has been mutilated by punishment.' Thereupon the king appointed T'ien Chi as commanding general, and Sun Pin as strategist. Pin traveled in a screened carriage, making plans while seated.

"T'ien Chi wanted to lead the army into Chao, but Sun Pin said, 'Now one who would untie confused and tangled cords does not strike at them with clenched fists. One who would disengage two combatants does not strike them with a halberd. While they stand opposed to each other you should hit their vacuities. Then as their dispositions counter each other and their strategic power is blocked, the difficulty will be resolved by itself. Now Wei and Chao are attacking each other, so Wei's light troops and elite soldiers must certainly all be deployed outside their state, with only the old and weak remaining within it. Wouldn't it be better to lead the troops on a forced march to Ta-liang, occupying their roads and striking their newly vacuous points? They will certainly release Chao in order to rescue themselves. Thus with one move we will extricate Chao from its encirclement and reap the benefits of Wei's exhaustion.' T'ien Chi followed his plan, and Wei did indeed abandon Han-tan, engaging Ch'i in battle at Kuei-ling. Ch'i extensively destroyed Wei's army.

"Thirteen years later Wei and Chao attacked the state of Han. Han reported the extremity of its situation to Ch'i. Ch'i ordered T'ien Chi to take command and go forth, proceeding straight to Ta-liang. When general P'ang Chüan of Wei heard about it, he abandoned his attack on Han and embarked on his return. Ch'i's army had already passed by and was proceeding to the west. Sun Pin said to T'ien Chi, 'The soldiers of the Three Chin (Han, Wei, and Chao) are coarse, fearless, and courageous, and regard Ch'i lightly. Ch'i has been termed cowardly. One who excels in warfare relies upon his strategic power and realizes advantages from leading the enemy where he wants. As *The Art of War* notes, "One who races a hundred kilometers in pursuit of profit will suffer the destruction of his foremost general; one who races fifty kilometers in pursuit of profit will arrive with only half his army." Have our army of Ch'i, upon entering Wei's borders, light one hundred thousand cooking fires. Tomorrow make fifty thousand, and again the day after tomorrow start thirty thousand cooking fires.'

"P'ang Chüan, after advancing three days, greatly elated said: 'Now I truly know that Ch'i's army is terrified. They have been within our borders only three days, but more than half the officers and soldiers have deserted.' Thereupon he abandoned his infantry, and covered double the normal day's distance with only light, elite units in pursuit of them. Sun Pin, estimating his speed, determined that he would arrive at Ma-ling at dusk.

"The road through Ma-ling was narrow, and to the sides there were numerous gullies and ravines where troops could be set in ambush. There he chopped away the bark on a large tree until it showed white and wrote on it: 'P'ang Chüan will die beneath this tree.'

"Then he ordered ten thousand skilled crossbowmen to wait in ambush on both sides, instructing them, 'At dusk, when you see a fire, arise and shoot together.' In the evening P'ang Chüan indeed arrived beneath the debarked tree. He saw the white trunk with the writing, struck a flint, and lit a torch. He had not finished reading the message when ten thousand crossbowmen fired en masse. Wei's army fell into chaos and mutual disorder. P'ang Chüan knew his wisdom was exhausted and his army defeated, so he cut his own throat, saying, 'I have established this clod's fame!' Ch'i then took advantage of the victory to completely destroy their army, and returned home with Imperial Prince Shen of Wei as prisoner. Because of this, Sun Pin's name became known throughout the realm, and generations have transmitted his *Military Methods.*" This dramatic biography no doubt found strong echoes in Ssu-ma Ch'ien, for both had endured the humiliation of corporeal punishment yet achieved historical greatness.

WEI LIAO-TZU

The *Wei Liao-tzu* was named after a shadowy historical figure whose surname was Wei and personal name was Liao. (The character "tzu," meaning master and indicating respect, was added by the compilers of his book.) One view holds that Wei Liao probably lived in the last half of the fourth century BCE, an era when mendicant persuaders indiscriminately sought receptive ears among the various feudal lords, irrespective of their moral qualifications. The opening chapter's format implies that the *Wei Liao-tzu* records his response to King Hui of Wei's obsessive search for the military and political knowledge that would not only strengthen the state's sagging defenses, but also furnish the means to vanquish its enemies and avenge its losses. When he failed to secure employment with King Hui, apparently because the king lacked confidence in policies that would require the cultivation of virtue in addition to the simple implementation of military measures, Wei Liao departed.

A laconic historical note in the *Shih Chi* also suggests that an otherwise unknown Wei Liao offered advice to the youthful king of Ch'in, who eventually unified all of China and became known as the first emperor, Ch'in Shih Huang-ti. However, in 237 BCE the king seized power from his ministers and immediately began to expel all foreign advisers and favored retainers. No further mention of Wei Liao's activities or role in Ch'in survives, although the policies he apparently suggested were implemented with considerable success.

Whatever his personal history, Wei Liao was an insightful strategist and perceptive observer who realized that only by integrating the civil and martial could a state be assured of surviving in the tumultuous Warring States environment. Since he never illustrated his discussions with examples from personal military experience and is not historically noted as a commander, and since the book is almost devoid of actual tactics, it appears he was strictly a theoretician. However, his extensive military knowledge is evident from the frequent inclusion of passages found in the present *Six Secret Teachings, The Art of War*, and other military books, and from his detailed description of army organization and discipline.

The extant text, while essentially consistent, appears to combine two distinct works because the first twelve chapters are more philosophical and general in scope, frequently concerned with grand strategy, while the last twelve focus upon the nature and problems of organization, discipline, command, and structure. This has prompted various theories about the possible authors and their relationship with these texts. Scholarly interest in the *Wei Liao-tzu* has recently increased because several chapters, still fairly well preserved on bamboo slips, were discovered stored away in a Han dynasty tomb. While there are numerous minor differences in wording and the bamboo slip edition is characterized by a somewhat more philosophical orientation than the current *Wei Liao-tzu*, only a few significantly affect the traditional understanding of the orthodox received passages.

The style and historical content of the book suggest a composition date around the end of the fourth century BCE and, based upon the bamboo slip edition, it clearly assumed its present form before the inauguration of the Han in 206 BCE, contrary to skeptical claims denigrating it as a much later fabrication. Therefore, it might tentatively be concluded that the *Wei Liao-tzu* may actually be based upon Wei Liao's court conversations with King Hui in the fourth century BCE, perhaps with additional, detailed material about military organization appended by someone from his family or school within the century after his death.

THREE STRATEGIES OF HUANG SHIH-KUNG

In addition to *Six Secret Teachings*, two other military writings have traditionally been attributed to the T'ai Kung: *Three Strategies of Huang Shih-kung*, and the esoteric *Yin Fu [Hidden Symbols]*. As with most ancient Chinese works there are numerous problems with the text of the *Three Strategies* and the usual questions about its authenticity. However, even if the book were a "valueless forgery" as claimed by a number of biased Confucians who vehemently denounced its purported brutality, the work would still demand serious study because of its antiquity, complex content, and manifest influence on subsequent military thinkers in China and eventually Japan. In its present form the language, subject matter, presentation, and visible Taoist influence suggest it dates toward the end of the first century BCE, but incorporates Warring States views throughout.

Three Strategies apparently first attained historical prominence through Chang Liang's critical accomplishments in establishing the power and consolidating the authority of the

Han dynasty during the turmoil and violent insurrections which overthrew the repressive, short-lived imperial Ch'in dynasty. The story of its sudden appearance typifies semi-legendary Chinese historical accounts, although circumstances can be construed to suggest a possible line of transmission extending back through the obscurity of time to the T'ai Kung himself. According to this tradition, *Three Strategies* preserves the aging sage's pronouncements after being enfeoffed as King of Ch'i, a state initially on the periphery of Chou culture, following the conquest of the Shang dynasty. Subsequently the individual spontaneous statements, recorded in disjointed fashion, underwent collection, editing, and systematizing. The task would probably have been performed by Ch'i's official court historian, with the work thereafter being secretly preserved by successive generations because of its great military value. It is assumed that since the T'ai Kung had already composed *Six Secret Teachings*, his comments when peace had been attained throughout the realm would mainly expand and supplement the earlier treatise. This would account for the more extemporaneous character of the material, and for the absence of many focal military topics, such as battlefield command and tactics.

According to the provenance suggested by these traditionalists, *Three Strategies* then surfaced when transmitted by a nondescript old fellow to Chang Liang a decade before he became famous and powerful. The *Shih Chi* vividly records the incident: "Once when Chang Liang was leisurely strolling across the Hsia-p'ei bridge he encountered an old man wearing the poor garb of a retired gentleman. When the old fellow reached the place where Chang was standing he deliberately lost his shoe over the side of the bridge. Looking at Chang he commanded, 'Young fellow, go down and fetch my shoe.' Chang Liang was startled by this, and wanted to beat him soundly, but because of the man's age he repressed his impulse.

"Chang went down below the bridge and got the shoe. Upon returning the old man ordered, 'Put it on my foot.' As Chang had already gone and retrieved the shoe, he formally knelt down and put it on. Once he was wearing the shoe the old man smiled and departed. Chang Liang was quite surprised, and continued staring at him. After the old man had gone about a few hundred yards he returned and said, 'Son, you can be taught. Five days from now, at dawn, meet me here.' Chang Liang felt this was strange, but he knelt and assented.

"Five days later, at dawn, Chang went to the bridge. However, the old fellow was already there and upbraided him: 'When you make an appointment with an old man, how can you arrive after him?' He then departed, saying: 'In five days we will meet even earlier.' Five days later, when the cock first crowed, Chang Liang went there. However, the old fellow was first again, and once more he was angry. 'How can you come after me?' As he departed he yelled, 'In five days come again, even earlier!'

"In another five days, before the night was half over, Chang Liang went there. In a little while the old man also arrived and was happy. 'This is the way it should be,' he said. Then, taking out a book, he continued: 'If you read this you can become a teacher of kings. Ten years from now you will flourish. In thirteen years you will see me on the northern bank of the Chi River. The yellow rock at the foot of Ku-ch'eng mountain will be me.' Then he departed without another word, never to be seen again. In the morning Chang Liang looked at the book and discovered it to be the T'ai Kung's military strategy. He thereafter regarded it as something exceptional, and constantly studied and worked over the book."

The old man may have been a proud descendant of Ch'i's official state historian, a worthy whose family had preserved the secret teachings for generations as suggested by his detailed knowledge of the area. In fact, he identified himself with a large "yellow rock" [*huang shih*], a reference that would eventually give the book its name, *Three Strategies of the Duke of Yellow Rock*. Since Ch'i was one of the last states vanquished by the infamous Ch'in, the Duke of Yellow Rock would have been amply motivated to assist in overthrowing the now tortured dynasty. Providing this essential work of strategy to a young fugitive already being hunted for attempting to assassinate the emperor would be a highly appropriate gesture.

QUESTIONS AND REPLIES BETWEEN T'ANG T'AI-TSUNG AND LI WEI-KUNG

Li Yüan, the powerful Sui official who eventually founded the T'ang dynasty (reigning under the title T'ang Kao-tsu), has traditionally been portrayed as being forced into revolting by the combined influences of popular prophecies and the machinations of his son, Li Shih-min (T'ang T'ai-tsung). Li Yüan not only commanded the strongest provincial army, but was directly related to the previous dynasty's imperial family, as well as powerful semibarbarian aristocratic families in the Northwest region. Entrusted with suppressing several of the sporadic revolts that had begun to appear in 613 CE, his success augmented his authority and solidified his control over the strategic province of Shansi. Initiated in the fifth month of 617 CE, the revolt quickly gathered major support from a number of other rebels and strong generals, and by the eleventh month Li Yüan had captured the capital. In the fifth month of 618 CE, the year of Sui Yang-ti's murder, he formally ascended the throne to establish the T'ang dynasty.

The T'ang established itself through the talents of its skilled generals; the adoption of Sui institutions; the populist appeal of its positions; and a benevolent pacification policy, especially in the south. Three generals particularly distinguished themselves, including Li Ching, the strategist to whom the seventh *Military Classic* is attributed, and Li Shih-min, second son of Li Yüan who became T'ang T'ai-tsung upon his usurpation of the throne in 617 CE. Both were active in the founding and integration of the empire, with the future emperor being depicted as heroically leading his elite troops in many pitched conflicts.

T'ang T'ai-tsung, who asks the questions and offers short observations in the classic, apparently received a Confucian education; therefore he was thoroughly versed in the classics and histories, as well as being extremely skilled in the martial arts. He reportedly commanded troops by the age of fifteen, and after contributing to the establishment of the T'ang as both a strategist and commander, was instrumental in subduing numerous challenges to the new state, including segments of the Western Turks. He finally became emperor by displacing his father, although only after murdering his older brother, the designated heir. Stories of his prowess and famous horses abound in popular Chinese history.

As emperor he consciously cultivated the image of a proper ruler, one responsive to the needs of the people, willing to accept criticism and advice. The country was truly unified, both politically and culturally. Measures were enacted to reduce the plight of the people and stimulate the economy. Government expenditures were reduced, and effective administration imposed throughout the nation. With the passage of time, and perhaps distance from the uncertainties of the initial period, he eventually became more independent, intolerant, and extravagant. However, the formative years of the T'ang saw the rebirth of thought and culture, the resurgence of a civilization that would dazzle Asia for three centuries.

Li Ching, who lived from 571 to 649 CE, began his career under the Sui, serving in the northwest in a military capacity. He eventually joined the T'ang forces just after the fall of the capital, Ch'ang-an, to become one of T'ang T'ai-tsung's earliest associates and supporters. Thereafter he commanded T'ang troops in the suppression of both internal and external challenges, the great conquest of the Western Turks (for which he became famous), and the pacification of the south. Thus if *Questions and Replies* actually preserves his conversations with T'ang T'ai-tsung, or even a large part of them, the strategies they discuss were not only theoretical concepts, but had been personally tested and employed by them in critical battles.

Li Ching's biography in the *Hsin T'ang-shu* not only illuminates the turbulent career of a successful T'ang dynasty commander and politician, but also portrays the man and his strategies in action: "Li Ching, whose personal name was Yao-shih, was a native of San-yüan in the Metropolitan prefecture. In appearance tall and elegant, he was thoroughly versed in the classics and histories. He once said to those close to him, 'In this life a man wants to attain wealth and rank through accomplishments. Why must one compose passages like the Confucians?' Whenever his uncle Han Ch'in-hu discussed military affairs with him, he would sigh in amazement and say, 'If one can't discuss Sun-tzu and Wu-tzu with this man, who can one discuss them with?' When Li Ching served the Sui dynasty as Chief of the Palace Attendants, Niu Hung, Minister for the Ministry of Personnel, saw him and remarked, 'This is a talent to assist a king!' The Left Vice Director for State Affairs, Yang Su, placing his hand upon his great seat, said to him, 'My lord, in the end you should sit here!'

"At the end of the Ta-yeh period he served as Vice Magistrate of Ma-i District. When T'ang Kao-tsu attacked the Turks, Li Ching observed that Kao-tsu was marked by extraordinary ambition. He had himself arrested for being disloyal to Kao-tsu and sent to Chiang-tu in order to urgently report Kao-tsu's revolutionary intentions. When he reached Ch'ang-an the road was blocked. Kao-tsu then conquered the capital and captured Li Ching. He was about to have him beheaded when Ching cried out: 'My Lord raised troops to eliminate perversity and chaos on behalf of All under Heaven. If you want to achieve the great affair of becoming emperor, how can you slay a righteous man because of personal enmity?' Li Shih-min also interceded on his behalf, and he was released, being brought into the government as a member of the Three Capital Guards. He accompanied Li Shih-min on the campaign to pacify Wang Shih-ch'ung, and for his achievements was appointed a commander.

"Hsiao Hsien occupied Chiang-ling, so Kao-tsu issued an imperial edict to Li Ching to pacify the area. Accompanied by a few light cavalrymen he crossed to Chin-chou to confront several tens of thousands of barbarian Teng-shih-luo bandits encamped in the mountain valleys of the region. King Yüan of Lu-chiang had not been victorious, so Ching planned the attack for him, forcing the enemy to withdraw. They proceeded to Hsia-chou, where they were blocked by Hsien's army and could not advance. The emperor assumed he was procrastinating and issued an imperial edict to the Supervisor-in-Chief, Hsü Shao, to behead Ching. Shao entered a plea on Ching's behalf and he was spared.

"The Man (barbarian) peoples in K'ai-chou under Jan Chao-tse then invaded K'uei-chou. Hsiao-kung, King of Chao Commandery, engaged them in battle but without gaining any advantage. Ching led eight hundred men to destroy their encampment and strategic defiles, establishing an ambush which resulted in slaying Chao-tse and capturing five thousand prisoners. The emperor exclaimed to his attendants, 'Employing men of achievement is not as good as using those who have erred. This is certainly true in Li Ching's case.' Thereupon he personally drafted his citation, saying, 'You are blameless for what is already past. I have long forgotten previous events.' Li Ching subsequently planned the strategy for ten campaigns against Hsien.

"By imperial edict Ching was appointed as Commander-in-Chief of the Campaign Army, concurrently serving as Aide to Hsiao-kung's Campaign Army, with both armies' administrative matters all being entrusted to him. In August of the fourth year of the Martial Virtue reign period [621 CE], he reviewed the troops in K'uei-chou. It was the time of the autumn floods, with heavy waves on the vile, overflowing waters of the Yangtze River. Hsien believed Ching would not be able to descend so he did not establish any defenses. Ching's generals also requested they await the calming of the river before advancing. Ching said: 'For the army the most critical affair is for its speed to be spiritual. Now the men have just assembled and Hsien does not yet know it, so if we take advantage of the water to attack his fortifications, it will be like being unable to cover one's ears at a thunderclap. Even if he is able to suddenly summon his troops, he will lack the means to oppose us, and we will certainly capture him.' Hsiao-kung followed his plan, and in the ninth month the navy attacked I-ling.

"Hsien's general Wen Shih-hung encamped at Ch'ing-chiang with several tens of thousands of troops. Hsiao-kung wanted to attack him, but Ching said: 'You cannot! Shih-hung is a stalwart general, while those below him are all courageous men. Now when they have newly lost Ching-men they will all be full of ardor to oppose us. This is an army that can rescue the defeated and cannot be opposed. It would be better to go to the southern riverbank and wait for their spirit to abate, and then take them.' Hsiao-kung didn't listen, but instead left Ching behind to guard the encampment, and personally went forth to engage them in battle. After being soundly defeated, he returned. The bandits then employed boats to disperse and plunder the countryside. Ching saw their disarray, and let his army loose to destroy them. They seized more than four hundred while ten thousand of the enemy drowned.

"Thereupon, leading a vanguard of five thousand light cavalry, he raced to Chiang-ling. They besieged the city and encamped, subsequently destroying generals Yang Chün-mao and Cheng Wen-hsiu, and taking four thousand armored soldiers prisoner. Hsiao-kung continued the advance, and Hsien was terrified. He summoned the troops of the Chiang-nan region, but when they didn't arrive, surrendered the next day. Ching entered their capital. His orders were quiet but strict, and the army did not loot the city.

"Some of his generals requested that Ching confiscate the family wealth of Hsien's generals who had opposed them in order to reward the army. Ching said: 'The army of a True King has sympathy for the people and seizes the guilty. They were coerced into coming, so if we confiscate their wealth because the army opposed us, which they fundamentally did not wish to do, we make no allowance for the real rebels. Now that we have just settled Ching and Ying, we should display generosity and magnanimity in order to pacify their hearts. If they surrender and we confiscate their wealth, I am afraid that from Ching south they will strengthen their walls and increase their emplacements. Forcing them into a desperate defense is not excellence in planning.' He stopped their actions and did not confiscate their wealth. Because of this the line of cities between the Chiang and Han Rivers competed with each other to submit.

"For his achievements he was appointed Duke of Yung-k'ang District, and acting Prefect for Ching-chou Prefecture.

Thereupon he crossed the mountains to K'uei-chou, and dispatched emissaries along different routes to proclaim the policy of pacification. Tribal leaders, such as Feng-ang, with their children all came to submit, and the entire southern region was settled. When they calculated the gains, established authority and created offices, they had added ninety-six commanderies in all, with more than six hundred thousand households. He was summoned by imperial edict and his efforts praised. He was granted the title of Pacification Commissioner for Ling-nan and acting Commander-in-Chief for K'uei-chou.

"He felt that Ling-hai was rustic and distant, and for a long time had not seen a proper display of Virtue, so that unless he manifested awesomeness and military majesty, and displayed the rites and righteousness, he wouldn't have the means to transform their customs. Thus he led the army on a southern tour. Wherever they went he inquired about the sick and suffering, and saw the elders and aged in his courtyard. He proclaimed the Emperor's beneficent intentions, and near and far submitted in fear.

"Fu Kung-shih occupied Tan-yang in rebellion. The emperor appointed Hsiao-kung as Commander-in-Chief, and summoned Ching to the court where he received the general strategy, and was appointed Vice Commander under Hsiao-kung. When they marched east on their punitive expedition, Li Shih-chi and the others, seven general officers, all received appointment as Area Commanders. Kung-shih dispatched Feng Hui-liang with thirty thousand naval forces to invest Tang-t'u, and Ch'en Cheng-t'ung with twenty thousand infantry and cavalry to invest the Ch'ing-lin mountains. From Mt. Liang they linked their forces in order to sever the road to Chiang, and built crescent-shaped walls stretching out more than ten kilometers from north to south in order to extend their flanks.

"The emperor's generals all voiced one opinion: 'They have strong soldiers and unbroken palisades. Even without engaging in battle they will wear out our army. If you directly seize Tan-yang and empty his stronghold, then Hui-liang and the others will surrender by themselves.' Ching said: 'It is not so.

While those two armies are elite units, the ones under Kung-shih's personal command are also spirited troops. Since they have already secured Shih-t'ou mountain, their stronghold can not yet be breached. If we remain we will not gain our objective, but we must shun retreat. For the stomach and back to suffer overwhelming worries isn't a completely successful plan. Moreover, Hui-liang and Cheng-t'ung are experienced rebels of more than a hundred battles. They do not fear combat in the wilds. Right now they are maintaining the security of their position, clinging to Kung-shih's strategy. If we do the unexpected, provoking them and attacking their fortifications, we will certainly destroy them. Hui-liang will be drawn out, and Kung-shih captured.'

"Hsiao-kung listened to him. Ching, leading Huang Chun-han and the others, advanced along water and land routes. After a bitter battle they killed and wounded more than ten thousand men. Hui-liang and the others fled, so Ching, in command of light cavalry, went to Tan-yang. Kung-shih was afraid, but although his forces were still numerous, they were incapable of fighting, so he fled. They captured him, and the region south of the Yangtze River was at peace.

"When the Branch Department of State Affairs was established for the Southeast Circuit, Ching was made Minister for the Ministry of War. He was granted a thousand pieces of silk, a hundred female slaves, and a hundred horses. When the Branch Department of State Affairs was discontinued, he was made Acting Chief Administrator for the Yang-chou Superior Area Command. The emperor sighed and said, 'Ching, could the ancient generals Han, Pai, Wei, and Hun have done any more than you in the vital affairs of Hsien and Kung-shih!'

"In the eighth year [625 CE] the Turks made an incursion into T'ai-yüan. Ching, as Commander-in-Chief of the Campaign Army, encamped with ten thousand men from the Chiang and Huai armies in the T'ai-ku region. At this time all the other generals suffered numerous defeats, while Ching alone returned with his army intact. For a short while he was appointed Acting Commander-in-Chief for An-chou Prefecture.

"When T'ang T'ai-tsung ascended the throne Li Ching was appointed as Minister of the Ministry of Justice, his accomplishments were recorded, and he was enfeoffed with four hundred households, concurrently acting as Secretariat Director.

"A portion of the Turks separated and revolted, so the Emperor planned a strategy to advance and take them. As Minister of the Ministry of War, Li Ching acted as Commander-in-Chief for the Campaign Army of the Ting-hsiang Circuit, leading three thousand crack cavalry through Ma-i to race to the O-yang mountains. Hsieh-li K'o-han was astonished: 'If the entire T'ang army has not been mobilized, how would Ching dare to bring his single army here?' Thereupon the soldiers were repeatedly frightened. Ching let loose his agents to sow discord among the K'o-han's trusted confidants. At night he launched a sudden attack against Ting-hsiang and destroyed it. The khan managed to escape and fled to Ch'i-k'ou.

"For his accomplishments Ching was advanced and enfeoffed as Duke of Tai-kuo. The Emperor said: 'Li Ling crossed the desert with five thousand infantrymen, but in the end surrendered to the Hsiung-nu. His achievements were still recorded on bamboo and silk. With three thousand cavalrymen Ching trampled through blood and took their court prisoner, subsequently taking Ting-hsiang. Antiquity does not have its like. It's enough to wash away my shame at Wei River!'

"The khan went to secure Mount T'ieh, then dispatched an emissary to acknowledge his offense, requesting that his state could become an inner vassal. Ching, as the Commander-in-Chief of the Ting-hsiang Circuit, was sent out to receive him. The Emperor also dispatched the Chief Minister of the Court for State Ceremonies, T'ang Chien, and General An Hsiu-jen to act as officers for the pacification. Ching, who knew the khan's submission was doubtful, spoke with Lieutenant-general Chang Kung-chin: 'The Imperial Emissary is, on the contrary, a prisoner, so the khan must feel secure. If ten thousand cavalrymen, carrying twenty days' rations, stage a sudden attack from Pai-tao, we will certainly obtain what we desire.' Kung-chin said: 'The Emperor has already agreed to the surrender, and the administrators are with them. What about that?' Ching said: 'The opportunity cannot be lost.

This is the way Han Hsin destroyed Ch'i. For someone like T'ang Chien, what is there to regret?'

"He directed the army on an urgent advance. Whenever they encountered enemy patrols, they took the soldiers prisoner and had them follow. Only when they were seven kilometers from his headquarters did the khan realize it. The tribesmen were terrified and scattered, and Ching's army killed more than ten thousand, making prisoners of a hundred thousand men and women. They captured his son, Tieh-luo-shih, and killed his wife, the princess of Yi-ch'eng. The khan fled, but was captured and presented to the Emperor by the Assistant Commander-in-Chief of the Campaign Army for the T'a-tung Circuit, Chang Pao-hsiang. Thereby the T'ang enlarged its territory from north of Mount Yi to the Great Desert.

"The Emperor thereupon declared a general pardon throughout the realm, and bestowed five days of festivities on the people. The Censor-in-Chief Hsiao Yü accused Ching of disregarding the laws while commanding the army, allowing the troops to plunder extensively, losing a great many rarities and treasures for the state. The Emperor summoned Ching and upbraided him. Ching didn't offer any argument, but bowed his head to the ground and acknowledged his offense. The Emperor slowly said, 'In the Sui, when General Shih Wan-sui destroyed Ta-t'ou K'o-han he was not rewarded, but was executed. I will not do that. I pardon your offenses, and take note of your achievements.' Then he advanced him to be Left Grand Master for Splendid Happiness, presented him with a thousand pieces of silk, and increased his fief to five hundred households. When this had been done he said, 'Previously people slandered and criticized you, but now I have realized the truth.' Then he bestowed an additional two thousand pieces of material, and transferred him to be Vice Director on the Right for State Affairs. Whenever Ching participated in discussions he was very respectful, as if he couldn't speak, and was considered profound and sincere.

"At the time the Emperor dispatched emissaries to the sixteen circuits to travel about investigating the customs of the people, and appointed Ching to be Commissioner for the

Metropolitan Circuit. It happened that he suffered from a foot disease, so he beseeched the Emperor to release him from this duty. The Emperor dispatched the Vice Director of the Secretariat, Ts'en Wen-pen, to proclaim to him: 'From antiquity, those that knew how to stop after attaining riches and honor have probably been few. Although you are ill and weary, still exert yourself to go on. Now if you consider the welfare of the state, I will deeply admire it. If you want to complete your elegant objectives, and become a model for the age, you must accept.' Then he bestowed upon him the privilege of an Acting Lord Specially Advanced remaining in residence, and gave him a thousand pieces of silk and a superior carriage with two horses. For his salary the Emperor continued his previous emoluments as an officer for the state and domain. Whenever his illness abated somewhat he would go to the Secretariat-Chancellery one day out of three as a Grand Counselor for the Secretariat-Chancellery, and was accorded the privilege of using the staff of spiritual longevity.

"A short time later the T'u-yü-hun invaded the border. The Emperor queried his attendants, 'Is Ching able to again assume the post of general?' Ching went to see Fang Hsüan-ling and said, 'Even though I am old, I can still undertake one more campaign.' The Emperor was elated, and appointed him as the Commander-in-Chief of the Campaign Army for the West Seas Circuit. Five other generals, with their armies—Tao-tsung, King of Ch'eng; Hou Chün-chi; Li Ta-liang; Li Tao-yen; and Kao Tseng-sheng—were all made subordinate to him. When the army arrived at the city of Fu-ssu, the T'u-yü-hun had already burned all the grass and withdrawn to secure the Ta-fei River valley. The generals all advised that since the spring grass had not yet sprouted, and the horses were weak, they could not do battle. Ching decided that their strategy would be to make a deep penetration. Subsequently they passed beyond Mount Chi-shih, and engaged in more than several major battles. They killed and captured great numbers, destroying their states, and most of the inhabitants surrendered. Fu-yün, Qughan of the T'u-yü-hun, being depressed, hung himself. Ching then established

Fu-yün's son, Mu-jung Sun, also known as King Ta-ning, in authority and returned home.

"Early in the campaign Kao Tseng-sheng's army, traveling by way of salt-marsh roads, arrived late. Ching upbraided him somewhat, so that after they returned Kao reviled him. Together with the Aide for Kuang-chou, T'ang Feng-i, he accused Ching of plotting to revolt. Officers investigated the charge but found it unsubstantiated. Tseng-sheng and the others were judged guilty of making false accusations. Ching then closed his doors and dwelt in seclusion, refusing the visits of both guests and relatives.

"The Emperor changed his enfeoffment to Duke of Wei-kuo. His wife died. The Emperor instructed that the grave should be built in the style indicated by stories about Wei and Huo, making the towers like Mount T'ieh and Mount Chi-shih, to manifest his accomplishments. He was advanced to Commander Unequaled in Honor.

"The Emperor wanted to attack Liao, so he summoned Ching to come to the court, and said: 'In the south you pacified Wu, in the north destroyed the Turks, in the west settled the T'u-yü-hun. Only Kao-li [Koguryo] has not submitted. Do you also have any inclination about this?' He replied, 'In the past I relied upon the awesomeness of Heaven to achieve some small measure of merit. Now although I am weak from my illness, if your Majesty is truly unwilling to release me, my sickness will be healed.' The Emperor took pity on his old age and did not press the assignment.

"In the twenty-third year [649 CE] his illness became acute. The Emperor favored him with a visit at his official residence, and wept. 'You have been my lifelong friend, and have labored for the state. Now your illness has become severe, I sorrow for you.' He died at age seventy-nine and was granted the posthumous titles of Minister of Education and Auxiliary Regional Area Commander-in-Chief. As a loyal minister he was interred on the side of the Imperial burial grounds at Chao-ling, and bestowed the posthumous title *Ching Wu*."

The book itself differs markedly from the earlier classics, being more of a survey of the former works, together with a wide-ranging discussion and appreciation of their theories and contradictions. Illustrated by historical examples from their campaign experiences, these discussions apparently reveal the predominant strategies and tactics of their era. Although most historians consider the book to be a forgery of either the late T'ang or Northern Sung, arguments have also been advanced that it, like other compendiums summarizing the thought and actions of the period, is at least based upon an actual protowork or recorded notes.

Part One
FUNDAMENTALS

1

The Nature of Warfare

Warfare is the greatest affair of state, the basis of life and death, the Tao to survival or extinction. It must be thoroughly pondered and analyzed.

The Art of War, 1

The T'ai Kung said to King Wu: "Today the Shang King knows about existence, but not about perishing. He knows pleasure, but not disaster. Now existence doesn't lie in existence, but in thinking about perishing. Pleasure doesn't lie in pleasure, but in contemplating disaster."

Six Secret Teachings, 12

The Sage takes his signs from the movements of Heaven and Earth; who knows his principles? He accords with the Tao of yin and yang, and follows their seasonal activity. He follows the cycles of fullness and emptiness of Heaven and Earth, taking them as his constant. All things have life and death in accord with the form of Heaven and Earth. Thus it is said that if one fights before seeing the situation, even if he is more numerous, he will certainly be defeated.

One who excels at warfare will await events in the situation without making any movement. When he sees he can be victorious he will arise; if he sees he cannot be victorious he will desist. Thus it is said he doesn't have any fear, he doesn't vacillate. Of the many harms that can beset an army, vacillation is the greatest. Of disasters that can befall an army, none surpasses doubt.

Six Secret Teachings, 26

In antiquity taking benevolence as the foundation and employing righteousness to govern constituted uprightness. However, when uprightness failed to attain the desired objectives they resorted to authority. Authority comes from warfare, not from harmony among men. For this reason if one must kill people to give peace to the people, then killing is permissible. If one must attack a state out of love for their people, then attacking it is permissible. If one must stop war with war, although it is war it is permissible. Thus benevolence is loved, righteousness is willingly submitted to, wisdom is relied upon, courage is embraced, and credibility is trusted. Within, the government gains the love of the people, the means by which it can be preserved. Outside, it acquires awesomeness, the means by which it can wage war.

Ssu-ma Fa, 1

Even though a state may be vast, those who love warfare will inevitably perish. Even though calm may prevail under Heaven, those who forget warfare will certainly be endangered.

Ssu-ma Fa, 1

Perceiving a victory that does not surpass what the masses could know is not the pinnacle of excellence. Wresting victories for which All under Heaven proclaim your excellence is not the pinnacle of excellence. Thus lifting an autumn hair cannot be considered great strength; seeing the sun and moon cannot be considered acute vision; hearing the sound of thunder cannot be considered having sensitive ears.

Those that the ancients referred to as excelling at warfare conquered those who were easy to conquer. Thus the victories of those that excelled in warfare were not marked by fame for wisdom or courageous achievement. Thus their victories were free from errors. One who is free from errors directs his measures toward certain victory, conquering those who are already defeated.

The Art of War, 4

If it is not advantageous, do not move. If objectives cannot be attained, do not employ the army. Unless endangered do not engage in warfare. The ruler cannot mobilize the army out of personal anger. The general cannot engage in battle because of personal frustration. When it is advantageous, move; when not advantageous, stop. Anger can revert to happiness, annoyance can revert to joy, but a vanquished state cannot be revived, the dead cannot be brought back to life. Thus the unenlightened ruler is cautious about it, the good general respectful of it. This is the Tao for bringing security to the state and preserving the army intact.

The Art of War, 12

Being victorious in battle is easy, but preserving the results of victory is difficult. Thus it is said that among the states under Heaven that engage in warfare those who garner five victories will meet with disaster; those with four victories will be exhausted; those with three victories will become hegemons; those with two victories will be kings; and those with one victory will become emperors. For this reason those who have conquered the world through numerous victories are extremely rare, while those who thereby perished are many.

Wu-tzu, 1

Now the military does not rely on an unvarying strategic configuration of power. This is the Tao transmitted from the Former Kings. Victory in warfare is the means by which to preserve vanquished states and continue severed generations. Not being victorious in warfare is the means by which to diminish territory and endanger the altars of state. For this reason military affairs cannot but be investigated. Yet one who takes pleasure in the military will perish, and one who finds profit in victory will be insulted. The military is not something to take pleasure in, victory not something through which to profit.

Military Methods, 2

The army's victory lies in selecting the troops. Its courage lies in the regulations. Its skill lies in the strategic configuration of power. Its sharpness lies in trust. Its power lies in the Tao. Its wealth lies in a speedy return. Its strength lies in giving rest to the people. Its injury lies in frequent battles.

Military Methods, 5

The implementation of Virtue is the army's great resource. Trust is the army's clear reward. One who detests warfare is the army's true kingly implement. Taking the masses is the basis for victory.

Military Methods, 5

Control of the army is as secretive as the depths of Earth, as dark and obscure as the heights of Heaven, and is given birth from the nonexistent. Therefore it must be opened. The great is not frivolous, the small is not vast.

One who is enlightened about prohibitions, pardons, opening, and stopping up will attract displaced people, and bring unworked lands under cultivation.

When the land is broad and under cultivation the state will be wealthy; when the people are numerous and well ordered the state will be governed. When the state is wealthy and well governed, although the people do not remove the blocks from the chariots, nor expose their armor, their awesomeness instills order on All under Heaven. Thus it is said: "The army's victory stems from the court." When one is victorious without exposing his armor, it is the ruler's victory; when victory comes after deploying the army, it is the general's victory.

Wei Liao-tzu, 2

The army cannot be mobilized out of personal anger. If victory can be foreseen then the troops can be raised. If victory cannot be foreseen, then the mobilization should be stopped.

Wei Liao-tzu, 2

When the soaring birds have all been slain then good bows are stored away. When enemy states have been extinguished ministers in charge of planning are lost. Here "lost" doesn't mean they lose their lives, but that the ruler has taken away their awesomeness and removed their authority. He enfeoffs them in court, at the highest ranks of his subordinates, in order to manifest their merit. He presents them with excellent states in the central region in order to enrich their families, and bestows beautiful women and valuable treasures upon them in order to please their hearts.

Now once the masses have been brought together they cannot be hastily separated. Once the awesomeness of authority has been granted it cannot be suddenly shifted. Returning the forces and disbanding the armies after the war are critical stages in preservation and loss. Thus weakening the commanding general through appointment to new positions, taking his authority by granting him a state, is referred to as a hegemon's strategy. Thus the hegemon's actions incorporate a mixed approach of Virtue and power. Preserving the altars of state, gathering those of character and courage, both are encouraged by the strategic power of the Middle Strategy. Thus to exercise such power the ruler must be very secretive.

Huang Shih-kung, 2

The Sage King does not take any pleasure in using the army. He mobilizes it to execute the violently perverse and punish the rebellious. Now using the righteous to execute the unrighteous is like releasing the Yangtze and Yellow Rivers to douse a torch, or pushing a person tottering at the edge of an abyss. Their success is inevitable! Thus when action should be taken one who hesitates and is quiet, without advancing, seriously injures all living beings. Weapons are inauspicious instruments, and the Tao of Heaven abhors them. However when their employment is unavoidable it accords with the Tao of Heaven. Now men in the Tao are like fish in water. If they have water they will live; if not they will die. Thus the ruler must constantly be afraid and not dare lose the Tao.

Huang Shih-kung, 3

One who abandons what is nearby to plan for what is distant will labor without success. One who abandons the distant to plan for the nearby will be at ease and attain lasting results. A government marked by ease has many loyal ministers. A government marked by labor has many resentful people. Thus it is said, "One who concentrates upon broadening his territory will waste his energies; one who concentrates upon broadening his Virtue will be strong." One who is able to hold what he possesses will be secure; one who is greedy for what others have will be destroyed. A government that verges on being destroyed will entangle later generations in the misfortune. One who enacts policies beyond proper measure will, even though successful, inevitably be defeated. Indulging oneself while instructing others is contrary to natural order; rectifying yourself and transforming others accords with the Tao. Contrariness is a summons to chaos; according with is the essence of order.

Huang Shih-kung, 9

2
The Tao of
Rulership

If one sees good but is dilatory in doing it; if the time for action arrives and one is doubtful; if you know something is wrong but you sanction it—it is in these three that the Tao stops. If one is soft and quiet, dignified and respectful, strong yet genial, tolerant yet hard—it is in these four that the Tao begins. Accordingly, when righteousness overcomes desire one will flourish; when desire overcomes righteousness one will perish. When respect overcomes dilatoriness it is auspicious; when dilatoriness overcomes respect one is destroyed.

Six Secret Teachings, 5

Heaven gives birth to the four seasons, Earth produces the myriad things. Under Heaven there are the people, and the Sage acts as their shepherd. Thus the Tao of spring is birth and the myriad things begin to flourish. The Tao of summer is growth, the myriad things mature. The Tao of autumn is gathering, the myriad things are full. The Tao of winter is storing away, the myriad things are still. When they are full they are stored away; after they are stored away they again revive. No one knows where it ends, no one knows where it begins. The Sage accords with it, and models himself on Heaven and Earth. Thus when the realm is well ordered, his benevolence and sagacity are hidden. When All under Heaven are in turbulence, his benevolence and sagacity flourish. This is the true Tao.

Six Secret Teachings, 8

Once when Marquis Wu was planning government affairs none of his numerous ministers could equal him. After dismissing the court he had a happy, self-satisfied look. Wu Ch'i entered and said, "Once in antiquity when King Chuang of Ch'u was planning state affairs he discovered none of his ministers could equal his talents. After he had dismissed the court he wore a troubled countenance. Duke Shen inquired, 'Why does your lordship have a troubled countenance?' He replied, 'I have heard it said that there is no lack of Sages in the world, and no shortage of Worthies in a state. One who can get them to be his teacher will be a king, while one who has them as his friends can become a hegemon. Now I am not talented, yet none of my ministers can even equal me in ability. Our state of Ch'u is in deep trouble.' This is what the King of Ch'u found troublesome, yet you are pleased by it. I therefore dare to be fearful!" Marquis Wu immediately looked embarrassed.

Wu-tzu, 1

The state must have the righteousness of the forms of etiquette, trust, familiarity, and love, and then it can exchange hunger for surfeit. The state must first have the customs of filiality, parental love, honesty, and shame, and then it can exchange death for life. When the ancients led the people they invariably placed the rites and trust first, and afterward ranks and emoluments. They put honesty and shame first, and punishments and fines afterward; close relationships and love first, and imposed constraints on their persons afterward.

Wei Liao-tzu, 4

Now the Tao for governing the state is to rely on Worthies and the people. If you trust the Worthies as if they were your belly and heart, and employ the people as if they were your four limbs, then all your plans will be accomplished. If your measures follow upon each other as naturally as the four limbs, or the way the joints of the bones cooperate with each other, this is the Tao of Heaven, the natural. There is no gap in such skill.

The essence of the army and state lies in investigating the mind of the people and putting into effect the hundred duties of government. Bring peace to those who are in danger. Give happiness to those who are afraid. Return those who rebel. Be indulgent to those who have grievances. Investigate the complaints of those who have legal suits. Raise up the lowly. Repress the strong. Destroy the enemy. Enrich the greedy. Use those that have desires. Conceal the fearful. Attract strategists. Investigate slanderers. Reproach the insulting. Eliminate the rebellious. Stifle those who act willfully. Diminish the arrogant. Summon those who turn their allegiance toward you. Give life to those who submit. Release those who surrender.

Huang Shih-kung, 1

When a ruler's actions are cruelly violent, his subordinates will be hasty to implement harsh measures. When the taxes are onerous, impositions numerous, and fines and punishments endless, while the people mutually injure and steal from each other, this is referred to as a "lost state."

Huang Shih-kung, 1

If administrative officials form parties and cliques, each advancing those with whom they are familiar; the state summons and appoints the evil and corrupt, while insulting and repressing the benevolent and worthy; officials turn their backs on the state and establish their personal interests; and men of equal rank disparage each other, this is termed "the source of chaos."

Huang Shih-kung, 1

When the officials are many but the people few; there is no distinction between the honored and lowly; the strong and weak insult each other; and no one observes the prohibitions or adheres to the laws, then these effects will extend to the ruler, and the state will reap the misfortune.

Huang Shih-kung, 1

When the ruler regards the good as good but doesn't advance them, while he hates the evil but doesn't dismiss them;

when the worthy are hidden and covered, while the unworthy hold positions, then the state will suffer harm.

Huang Shih-kung, 1

When the ruler's relatives and the powerful families are strong and large, forming parties and occupying positions of authority, so that the lowly and mean insult the honored, growing more powerful with the passing of time, while the ruler cannot bear to dismiss them, then the state will suffer defeat from it.

Huang Shih-kung, 1

3
The People

The T'ai Kung said: "All under Heaven is not one man's domain. All under Heaven means just that, *all* under Heaven. Anyone who shares profit with all the people under Heaven will gain the world. Anyone who monopolizes its profits will lose the world. Heaven has its seasons, Earth its resources. Being capable of sharing these in common with the people is true humanity. Wherever there is true humanity, All under Heaven will give their allegiance.

"Sparing the people from death; eliminating the hardships of the people; relieving the misfortunes of the people; and sustaining the people in their extremities, is Virtue. Wherever there is Virtue, All under Heaven will give their allegiance.

"Sharing worries, pleasures, likes, and dislikes with the people constitutes righteousness. Where there is righteousness the people will go.

"In general, people hate death and take pleasure in life. They love Virtue and incline to profit. The ability to produce profit accords with the Tao. Where the Tao resides All under Heaven will give their allegiance."

Six Secret Teachings, 1

King Wen said to the T'ai Kung: "I would like to learn about the affair of administering the state. If I want to have the ruler honored and the people settled, how should I proceed?"

T'ai Kung: "Just love the people."

King Wen: "How does one love the people?"

T'ai Kung: "Profit them, do not harm them. Help them to succeed, not defeat them. Give them life, do not slay them. Grant, do not take away. Give them pleasure, do not cause them to suffer. Make them happy, do not cause them to be angry."

King Wen: "May I dare ask you to explain the reasons for these?"

T'ai Kung: "When the people do not lose their fundamental occupations you have profited them. When the farmers do not lose the agricultural seasons you have completed them. When you reduce punishments and fines, you give them life. When you impose light taxes you give to them. When you keep your palaces, mansions, terraces, and pavilions few, you give them pleasure. When the officials are pure and neither irritating nor troublesome, you make them happy.

"But when the people lose their fundamental occupations you harm them. When the farmers lose the agricultural seasons you defeat them. When they are innocent but you punish them, you kill them. When you impose heavy taxes you take from them. When you construct numerous palaces, mansions, terraces, and pavilions, thereby wearing out the people's strength, you make it bitter for them. When the officials are corrupt, irritating, and troublesome, you anger them.

"Thus one who excels at administering a state governs the people as parents govern their beloved children, or as an older brother acts toward his beloved younger brother. When they see their hunger and cold they are troubled for them. When they see their labors and suffering they grieve for them.

"Rewards and punishments should be implemented as if being imposed upon yourself. Taxes should be imposed as if taking from yourself. This is the Way to love the people."

Six Secret Teachings, 3

The T'ai Kung, addressing King Wen, said: "If you suffer the same illness as other people, and you all aid each other; if you have the same emotions and complete each other; the same hatreds and assist each other; and the same likes and seek them together—then without any armored soldiers you will win; without any battering rams you will have attacked; and without moats and ditches you will have defended.

"The greatest wisdom is not wise; the greatest plans not planned; the greatest courage not courageous; the greatest gain not profitable. If you profit All under Heaven, All under Heaven will be open to you. If you harm All under Heaven, All under Heaven will be closed. All under Heaven is not the property of one man, but of All under Heaven. If you take All under Heaven as if pursuing some wild animal, then All under Heaven will want to carve it up like a piece of meat. If you all ride in the same boat to cross over the water, after completing the crossing you will all have profited. However if you fail to make the crossing then you will all suffer the harm. If you act as if you're all on the same vessel the empire will be open to your aim, and none will be closed to you.

"He who does not take from the people, takes the people. He who does not take from the people, the people will profit. He who does not take from the states, the states will profit. He who does not take from All under Heaven, All under Heaven will profit. Thus the Tao lies in what cannot be seen, affairs lie in what cannot be heard, and victory lies in what cannot be known. How marvelous! How subtle!"

Six Secret Teachings, 13

The Tao is the means by which one turns back to the foundation and returns to the beginning. Righteousness is the means by which to put affairs into action and realize accomplishments. Plans are the means by which to keep harm distant and gain profit. The essence provides the constraints by which to preserve duty and conserve achievements. Now if behavior does not accord with the Tao, and actions do not accord with righteousness, but instead one dwells in magnificence and enjoys nobility, disaster will inevitably befall him.

For this reason the Sage rests the people in the Tao, orders them with righteousness, moves them with the forms of propriety, and consoles them with benevolence. Cultivate these four virtues and you will flourish. Neglect them and you will decline.

Thus when Ch'eng T'ang extirpated the evil tyrant Chieh, Chieh's people rejoiced, and when King Wu of Chou attacked the vile King Chou of the Shang dynasty, the people of Shang did not condemn him. Because their actions accorded with Heaven and Man they were able to succeed.

Wu-tzu, 1

Now one who can sustain the imperiled under Heaven can control the security of All under Heaven. One who can remove the distress of those under Heaven will be able to enjoy the pleasure of governing All under Heaven. One who can rescue those under Heaven suffering from misfortune will be able to gain the prosperity of All under Heaven. Therefore when the ruler's munificence extends to the people, worthy men will give their allegiance. When his munificence reaches the multitudinous insects, then Sages will ally with him. Whomever the Worthy give their allegiance to, his state will be strong. Whomever the Sages support, under him the six directions will be unified. One seeks the Worthy through Virtue, one attracts Sages with the Tao. If the Worthy depart the state will become weak; if the Sages depart the state will grow depraved. Weakness is a step on the road to danger, depravity is a sign of doom.

The government of a Worthy causes men to submit with their bodies. The government of a Sage causes men to submit with their minds. When their bodies submit the beginning can be planned; when their minds submit the end can be preserved. Their physical submission is attained through the forms of propriety; their mental submission is attained through music.

What I refer to as music is not the sound of musical instruments—the stones, metal bells, strings, and bamboo pipes. Rather I refer to people taking pleasure in their families, clans, occupations, capitals and towns, orders of government, the Tao, and Virtue. One who rules the people in this fashion creates music in order to bring measure to their activities, to ensure that they do not lose their essential harmony. Thus the virtuous ruler uses music to give pleasure to the people; the debauched ruler uses music to give pleasure to himself. One

The wise must contemplate the intermixture of gain and loss. If they discern advantage in difficult situations, their efforts can be trusted. If they discern harm in prospective advantage, difficulties can be resolved.

The Art of War, 8

The essential principle for the army is that those fifty miles apart do not rescue each other. How much more so is this the case when the nearest are a hundred miles apart, the farthest several hundred miles. These are the extremes for weighing the army's possibilities. Thus the *Tactics* states: "If your provisions are unlike theirs, do not engage them in protracted battles. If your masses are unlike theirs, do not engage them in battle. If your numbers are unlike theirs, do not contend with them across a broad front. If your training is unlike theirs, do not oppose them in their strength." When these five criteria are clear, the army will be able to forcefully advance unhindered.

Military Methods, 28

Before punishment has been applied to the enemy, before the soldiers have clashed, the means by which one seizes the enemy are five: Discussing the way to victory in the court; discussing the general receiving his mandate; discussing crossing the borders; discussing making the moats deep and fortifications high; and discussing mobilizing, deploying, and applying punitive measures to the enemy. In these five cases first evaluate the enemy and afterward move. In this way you can attack their voids and seize them.

Wei Liao-tzu, 4

Now one must make decisions early and determine plans beforehand. If plans are not first determined, if intentions are not decided early, then neither advancing nor retreating will be ordered. When doubts arise defeat is certain. Thus an orthodox army values being first, an unorthodox army values being afterward. Sometimes being first, sometimes being afterward, this is the way to control the enemy. Generals throughout the ages who have not known this method, after receiving their commission to go forward, were first to launch an attack, relying upon courage alone. There were none who were not defeated.

Wei Liao-tzu, 18

In general, whenever about to mobilize the army you must first investigate the strategic balance of power both within and without the borders in order to calculate whether to mount a campaign. You must know whether the army is well prepared or suffers from inadequacies; whether there is a surplus or shortage of foodstuffs. You must determine the routes for advancing and returning. Only thereafter can you mobilize the army to attack the chaotic and be certain of being able to enter his state.

Wei Liao-tzu, 22

5
Preparations

Increasing the army and making the formations solid; multiplying its strength and constantly training the troops; relying upon exploiting the strength of things; perceiving the nature of things; and responding to sudden events, is what is meant by "effecting preparations."

Fast chariots and fleet infantrymen, bows and arrows, and a strong defense, are what is meant by "increasing the army." Secrecy, silence, and great internal strength are what is meant by "making formations solid." Upon this basis, being able to advance, and being able to withdraw, is what is meant by "multiplying strength." At times of little activity the upper ranks instruct and constantly drill the lower ranks. This is what is meant by "training the troops in formations." When there are appropriate offices for both command and administration, it is termed "relying upon exploiting the strength of things." When in accord with this things are perceived and managed, it is referred to as "simplifying administration."

Ssu-ma Fa, 3

Move only after all affairs have been prepared. Thus one whose walled city is small but defense solid has accumulated resources. One whose troops are few but army is strong has righteousness. Now mounting a defense without anything to rely upon, or engaging in battle without righteousness, no one under Heaven would be able to be solid and strong.

Military Methods, 2

An army that is unable to discern good fortune and misfortune in the as-yet-unformed does not understand preparations.

Military Methods, 22

The Former Kings concentrated on five military affairs: When the store of accumulated foodstuffs is not substantial, the soldiers do not set out. When rewards are not generous, the people are not stimulated. When martial warriors are not selected, the masses will not be strong. When weapons and implements are not prepared, their strength will not be great. When punishments and rewards are not appropriate, the masses will not respect them. If one emphasizes these five, then at rest the army will be able to defend any place it secures, and in motion it will be able to attain its objectives.

Wei Liao-tzu, 4

In general, what is the Way to govern men? I say that without the five grains you have nothing to fill their stomachs, without silk and hemp nothing to cover their form. Thus to fill their stomachs there are grains, and to cover their form there is thread. Husbands work at weeding and plowing, wives at weaving. If the people do not have secondary occupations then there will be goods accumulated in the storehouses. The men should not engrave nor make decorative carving, the women should not embroider nor do decorative stitching.

Carved wooden vessels emit secretions, engraved metal utensils smell offensive. The Sage drinks from an earthen vessel, and eats from an earthen vessel. Thus when clay is formed to make utensils there's no waste under Heaven. Today people think the nature of metal and wood is not cold, for they embroider their clothes with them. The original nature of horses and oxen is to eat grass and drink water, but they give them beans and grains. This is governing what has lost its foundation, and it would be appropriate to establish regulations to control it.

If in the spring and summer the men go out to the southern fields, and in the fall and winter the women work at weaving cloth, the people will not be impoverished. Today, when their short coarse clothing does not even cover their bodies, nor the dregs of wine and husks of grain fill their stomachs, the foundation of government has been lost.

In antiquity the land was not classified as fertile or barren, the people were not classified as diligent or lazy. How could the ancients have attained this, how could we have lost it now? The men do not finish plowing their fields, the women daily break their shuttles, so how could they not be hungry and cold? Probably the administration of the ancients was fully effected, while that of today stops before thorough implementation.

Now what I term governing well means causing the people not to have any selfish interests. If the people do not have selfish interests then All under Heaven will be one family. In the absence of private plowing and weaving they will suffer the cold together, they will experience hunger together. Then even if they have ten sons they will not have the expense of even an extra bowl of rice, while if they have one son their expenses will not be reduced by even one bowl. Thus where would there be any clamoring and drunken indulgence to ruin the good people?

When the people stimulate each other to frivolity and extravagance, the misfortunes of the desiring mind and of the competition to seize things arise. Perversity begins with one fellow, and then the people seek to selfishly accumulate some extra food and have some stored wealth. If the people then commit a single offense, and you arrest them and impose corporeal punishments to control them, how is one acting as the ruler of the people? Those that excel at governing take hold of the regulations, causing the people not to have any selfish interests. When those below do not dare to be selfish, there will not be any who commit evil.

Return to the foundation, accord with principle, have all issue forth from one Tao, and then the desiring mind will be eliminated. Competition will be stopped, the jails will be empty, the fields full, and the grains plentiful. You will settle the people and embrace the distant. Then outside your borders there will not be any difficulty under Heaven, while within the state there will be neither violence nor turbulence. This is the perfection of administration.

Wei Liao-tzu, 11

6

The History of Warfare

As for the administrative measures of the Former Kings: They accorded with the Tao of Heaven; they established what was appropriate to Earth. They put the virtuous among the people into office, rectified names, and governed things. They established the states, defined the hierarchy of feudal positions, and apportioned emoluments according to rank. The feudal lords were pleased and embraced them. Those beyond the seas came to submit. Punishments were eliminated and the army rested. These were the attainments of Sagely Virtue.

Next came the Worthy Kings: They ordered the rites, music, laws, and measures, and then created the five punishments, raising armored troops to chastise the unrighteous. They made inspection tours of the feudal lands, investigated the customs of the four quarters, assembled the feudal lords, and investigated differences. If any of the feudal lords had disobeyed orders; disordered the constant; turned his back on Virtue; or contravened the seasons of Heaven, endangering meritorious rulers, then they would publicize it among all the feudal lords, making it evident that he had committed an offense. They then announced it to August Heaven, and to the sun, moon, planets, and constellations. They prayed to the Gods of Earth, the spirits of the Four Seasons, mountains, rivers, and at the Great Altar of state. Then they offered sacrifice to the Former Kings. Only thereafter would the prime minister charge the army before the feudal lords, saying; "A certain state has acted contrary to the Tao. You will participate in the rectification campaign on such a year, month, and day. On that date the army will reach the offending state and assemble with the Son of Heaven to apply the punishment of rectification."

The prime minister and other high officials would issue the following orders to the army: "When you enter the offender's territory do not do violence to his gods; do not hunt his wild animals; do not destroy earthworks; do not set fire to buildings; do not cut down forests; do not take the six domesticated animals, grains, or implements. When you see their elderly or very young return them without harming them. Even if you encounter adults, unless they engage you in combat, do not treat them as enemies. If an enemy has been wounded provide medical attention and return him."

When they had executed the guilty, the king, together with the feudal lords, corrected and rectified the government and customs of the state. They raised up the worthy, established an enlightened ruler, and corrected and restored their feudal position and obligations.

The ways by which the kings and hegemons governed the feudal lords were six: With territory they gave shape to the feudal lords. With government directives they pacified the feudal lords. With the rites and good faith they drew the feudal lords close to them. With men of wisdom and strength they pleased the feudal lords. Through strategists they constrained the feudal lords. With weapons and armor they forced the submission of the feudal lords.

By sharing misfortune with them, by sharing benefits with them, they united the feudal lords. They had the smaller states serve the larger ones in order to bring the feudal lords into harmony.

They assembled them in order to announce nine prohibitions. Those who take advantage of weak states or encroach upon sparsely populated ones will have their borders reduced on all sides. Those who murder a Worthy or harm the people will be attacked and deposed. Those who are brutal within their state and encroach upon others outside it will be purged. Those whose fields turn wild and whose people scatter will be reduced. Those who rely on the fastness of natural advantages to disobey orders will be invaded. Those who harm or kill their relatives will be rectified. Those who depose or slay their ruler will be exterminated. Those who oppose orders and resist the government will be isolated. Those who are chaotic and rebellious both within and without their borders, who act like animals, will be extinguished.

Ssu-ma Fa, 1

In antiquity they did not pursue a fleeing enemy more than a hundred paces, nor follow a retreating enemy more than three days, thereby making clear their observance of the forms of proper conduct. They did not exhaust the incapable, and had sympathy for the wounded and sick, thereby making evident their benevolence. They awaited the completion of the enemy's formation and then drummed the attack, thereby making clear their good faith. They contended for righteousness, not profit, thereby manifesting their righteousness. Moreover they were able to pardon those who submitted, thereby making evident their courage. They knew the end, they knew the beginning, thereby making clear their wisdom. These six virtues were taught together at appropriate times, being taken as the Tao of the people's guidelines. This was the rule from antiquity.

Ssu-ma Fa, 1

At the time when Yao possessed All under Heaven there were seven tribes who dishonored the king's edicts and did not put them into effect. There were the two Yi in the east, and four in the central states. It was not possible for Yao to be at ease and attain the profit of governing All under Heaven. He was victorious in battle and his strength was established; therefore, All under Heaven submitted.

In antiquity Shen Nung did battle with the Fu and Sui; the Yellow Emperor did battle with Ch'ih Yu at Shu-lü; Yao attacked Kung Kung; Shun attacked Ch'e and drove off the Three Miao; T'ang deposed Chieh; King Wu attacked Chou; and the Duke of Chou obliterated the remnant state of Shang-yen when it rebelled.

Thus it is said that if someone's virtue is not like that of the Five Emperors, his ability does not reach that of the Three Kings, nor his wisdom match that of the Duke of Chou—and yet he says, "I want to accumulate benevolence and righteousness, practice the rites and music, and wear flowing robes and thereby prevent conflict and seizure"—it is not that Yao and Shun did not want this, but they could not attain it. Therefore they mobilized the military to constrain the evil.

Military Methods, 2

Now the Three August Ones never spoke, but their transformations flowed throughout the Four Seas. Thus the world had no one to whom to attribute the accomplishments.

The Emperors embodied Heaven and took Earth as their model. They spoke and issued orders, and the world attained Great Peace. Ruler and minister yielded the credit for this to each other, while all within the Four Seas were transformed without the common people being conscious of how the changes came about. Therefore in employing subordinates they did not rely on the forms of propriety or rewards. There was the beauty of accomplishments and no harm.

Kings governed men by means of the Tao, causing their hearts to be compliant and their wills to be submissive, while also establishing restrictive measures and making preparations against decline. All the feudal lords within the Four Seas assembled at their courts, and the duty of kingship was not neglected. Even though they made military preparations they never suffered the misfortune of warfare. Rulers did not doubt their subordinates, while subordinates had faith in their rulers. The state was settled, the ruler secure, and bureaucrats could resign with righteousness, so they also were able to have beauty without harm.

The hegemons governed their officers by virtue of authority, bonding them through trust, motivating them with rewards. When that trust declined the officers grew distant, and when rewards became inadequate they would not submit to orders.

Huang Shih-kung, 2

Part Two
THE TAO OF WARFARE

7

The Tao of Warfare

King Wu asked the T'ai Kung, "What is the Tao for aggressive warfare?"

The T'ai Kung replied: "Strategic power is exercised in accord with the enemy's movements. Changes stem from the confrontation between the two armies. Unorthodox and orthodox tactics are produced from the inexhaustible resources of the mind. Thus the greatest affairs are not discussed, and the employment of troops is not spoken about. Moreover, words which discuss ultimate affairs are not worth listening to. The employment of troops is not so definitive as to be visible. They go suddenly, they come suddenly. Only someone who can exercise sole control, without being governed by other men, is a military weapon.

"If your plans are heard about, the enemy will make counterplans. If you are perceived, they will plot against you. If you are known, they will put you in difficulty. If you are fathomed, they will endanger you.

"Thus one who excels in warfare does not await the deployment of forces. One who excels at eliminating the misfortunes of the people manages them before they appear. Conquering the enemy means being victorious over the formless. The superior fighter does not engage in battle. Thus one who fights and attains victory in front of naked blades is not a good general. One who makes preparations after the battle has been lost is not a superior Sage! One whose wisdom is the same as the masses is not a general for the state. One whose skill is the same as the masses is not a State Artisan.

"In military affairs nothing is more important than certain victory. In employing the army nothing is more important than obscurity and silence. In movement nothing is more important than the unexpected. In planning nothing is more important than not being knowable."

Six Secret Teachings, 26

In antiquity the form and spirit governing civilian affairs would not be found in the military realm; those appropriate to the military realm would not be found in the civilian sphere. If the form and spirit appropriate to the military realm enter the civilian sphere the Virtue of the people will decline. When the form and spirit appropriate to the civilian sphere enter the military realm, then the Virtue of the people will weaken. In the civilian sphere words are cultivated and speech languid. In court one is respectful and courteous, and cultivates himself to serve others. Unsummoned, he does not step forth; unquestioned, he does not speak. It is difficult to advance but easy to withdraw.

In the military realm one speaks directly and stands firm. When deployed in formation one focuses on duty and acts decisively. Those wearing battle armor do not bow; those in war chariots need not observe the forms of propriety; those manning fortifications do not scurry. In times of danger one does not pay attention to seniority. Thus the civilian forms of behavior and military standards are like inside and outside; the civil and martial are like left and right.

Ssu-ma Fa, 2

In general, to wage war: employ spies against the distant; observe the near; act in accord with the seasons; take advantage of the enemy's material resources; esteem good faith; abhor the doubtful. Arouse the soldiers with the fervor of righteousness. Undertake affairs at the appropriate time. Employ people with kindness. When you see the enemy, remain quiet; when you see turbulence, do not be hasty to respond. When you see danger and hardship do not forget the masses.

Within the state be generous and foster good faith. Within the army be magnanimous and martial. When the blades clash, be decisive and adroit. Within the state there should be harmony, within the army there should be standards. When the blades clash, investigate the battlefield situation. Within the state display cooperation; within the army display uprightness; in battle display good faith.

Ssu-ma Fa, 3

In general, warfare is a question of having Heaven, material resources, and excellence.

When the day and time for battle have been appropriately fixed and it is not necessary to change them; when augury by the tortoise shell presages victory; and when events proceed in subtle, mysterious fashion, this is termed "having Heaven."

When the masses have material resources, the state has them. When they thereby produce what is profitable, this is termed "having resources."

When the men are practiced in the relative advantages of the formations, and they fully exhaust the strength of things in preparation for battle, this is referred to as "attaining excellence."

When the people are encouraged to fulfill their responsibilities, they are termed "men who take pleasure in warfare."

Ssu-ma Fa, 3

In general, warfare is a question of the strategic balance of power, combat is a matter of courage. The deployment of formations is a matter of skill. Employ what your men want, effect what they are capable of; abolish what they do not want and are incapable of. Do the opposite of this to the enemy.

Ssu-ma Fa, 3

In general, with regard to the people: rescue them with benevolence; engage in battle with righteousness; make decisions through wisdom; fight with courage; exercise sole authority through credibility; encourage them with profits; and gain victory through achievements. Thus the mind must embody benevolence and actions should incorporate righteousness. Relying on the nature of things is wisdom; relying on the great is courage; relying on longstanding relations leads to good faith. Yielding results in harmony, and the men of themselves will be deferential. If men attribute failings to themselves, they will compete to be worthy. When men are pleased in their hearts they will exhaust their strength.

Ssu-ma Fa, 4

In general, as for the Tao of warfare: positions should be strictly defined; administrative measures should be severe; strength should be nimble; the soldier's *ch'i* (spirit) should be constrained; the minds of the officers and people should be unified.

Ssu-ma Fa, 4

Warfare is the greatest affair of state, the basis of life and death, the Tao to survival or extinction. It must be thoroughly pondered and analyzed. Therefore, structure it according to the following five factors, evaluate it comparatively through estimations, and seek out its true nature. The first is termed the Tao, the second Heaven, the third Earth, the fourth generals, and the fifth the laws for military organization and discipline.

The Tao causes the people to be fully in accord with the ruler. Thus they will die with him; they will live with him and not fear danger. Heaven encompasses yin and yang, cold and heat, and the constraints of the seasons. Earth encompasses far and near, difficult and easy, expansive and confined, fatal and tenable terrain. The general encompasses wisdom, credibility, benevolence, courage, and strictness. The laws for military organization and discipline encompass organization and regulations, the Tao of command, and the management of logistics.

There are no generals who have not heard of these five. Those who understand them will be victorious; those who do not understand them will not be victorious.

The Art of War, 1

When employing the army in battle, a victory that is long in coming will blunt their weapons and dampen their ardor. If you attack cities, their strength will be exhausted. If you expose the army to a prolonged campaign, the state's resources will be inadequate.

When the weapons have grown dull and spirits depressed, when our strength has been expended and resources consumed, then the feudal lords will take advantage of our exhaustion to arise. Even though you have wise generals, they will not be able to achieve a good result.

Thus in military campaigns I have heard of awkward speed but have never seen any skill in lengthy campaigns. No country has ever profited from protracted warfare. Those who do not thoroughly comprehend the dangers inherent in employing the army are incapable of truly knowing the potential advantages of military actions.

The Art of War, 2

In general, the method for employing the military is this: Preserving the enemy's state capital is best, destroying their state capital second-best. Preserving their army is best, destroying their army second-best. Preserving their battalions is best, destroying their battalions second-best. Preserving their companies is best, destroying their companies second-best. Preserving their squads is best, destroying their squads second-best. For this reason attaining one hundred victories in one hundred battles is not the pinnacle of excellence. Subjugating the enemy's army without fighting is the true pinnacle of excellence.

The Art of War, 3

Thus the highest realization of warfare is to attack the enemy's plans; next is to attack their alliances; next to attack their army; and the lowest is to attack their fortified cities. This tactic of attacking fortified cities is adopted only when unavoidable. Preparing large movable protective shields, armored assault wagons, and other equipment and devices will require three months. Building earthworks will require another three months to complete. If the general cannot overcome his impatience but instead launches an assault wherein his men swarm over the walls like ants, he will kill one-third of his officers and troops, and the city will still not be taken. This is the disaster that results from attacking fortified cities.

Thus one who excels at employing the military subjugates other people's armies without engaging in battle, captures other people's fortified cities without attacking them, and destroys other people's states without prolonged fighting. He must fight under Heaven with the paramount aim of "preservation." Thus his weapons will not become dull, and the gains can be preserved. This is the strategy for planning offensives.

The Art of War, 3

Thus it is said that one who knows the enemy and knows himself will not be endangered in a hundred engagements. One who does not know the enemy but knows himself will sometimes be victorious, sometimes meet with defeat. One who knows neither the enemy nor himself will invariably be defeated in every engagement.

The Art of War, 3

Thus there are five factors from which victory can be known: One who knows when he can fight, and when he cannot fight, will be victorious. One who recognizes how to employ large and small numbers will be victorious. One whose upper and lower ranks have the same desires will be victorious. One who, fully prepared, awaits the unprepared will be victorious. One whose general is capable and not interfered with by the ruler will be victorious. These five are the Tao for knowing victory.

The Art of War, 3

In antiquity those that excelled in warfare first made themselves unconquerable in order to await the moment when the enemy could be conquered. Being unconquerable lies with yourself; being conquerable lies with the enemy. Thus one who excels in warfare is able to make himself unconquerable, but cannot necessarily cause the enemy to be conquerable.

Thus it is said a strategy for conquering the enemy can be known but yet not possible to implement.

The Art of War, 4

Thus the army is established by deceit, moves for advantage, and changes through segmenting and reuniting. Thus its speed is like the wind, its slowness like the forest; its invasion and plundering like a fire; unmoving, it is like the mountains. It is as difficult to know as the darkness; in movement it is like thunder.

The Art of War, 7

If the enemy opens the door, you must race in. Attack what they love first. Do not fix any time for battle, assess and react to the enemy in order to determine the strategy for battle. For this reason at first be like a virgin at home; later—when the enemy opens the door—be like a fleeing rabbit. The enemy will be unable to withstand you.

The Art of War, 11

In antiquity those who were referred to as excelling in the employment of the army were able to keep the enemy's forward and rear forces from connecting; the many and few from relying on each other; the noble and lowly from coming to each other's rescue; the upper and lower ranks from trusting each other; the troops to be separated, unable to reassemble, or when assembled, not to be well ordered. They moved when it was advantageous, halted when it was not advantageous.

The Art of War, 11

When you mobilize the army and form strategic plans, you must be unfathomable.

The Art of War, 11

It is the nature of the army to stress speed; to take advantage of the enemy's absence; to travel unanticipated roads; and to attack when they are not alert.

The Art of War, 11

Marquis Wu inquired: "I would like to hear about the Tao for making battle formations invariably stable, defenses inevitably solid, and victory in battle certain."

Wu Ch'i replied, "This can immediately be made clear, but why ask only about this? If you are able to have worthy men hold high positions, and the unworthy occupy low positions, then your battle formations will already be stable. If the people are settled in their farming and homes, and attached to their local authorities, then your defenses will already be solid. When the hundred surnames all acclaim my lord and condemn neighboring states, then in battle you will already be victorious."

Wu-tzu, 1

There are five aspects to constantly being victorious. One who obtains the ruler's sole authority will be victorious. One who knows the Tao will be victorious. One who gains the masses will be victorious. One whose left and right are in harmony will be victorious. One who analyzes the enemy and estimates the terrain will be victorious.

There are five aspects to constantly not being victorious. A general who is hampered by the ruler will not be victorious. One who does not know the Tao will not be victorious. A perverse general will not be victorious. One who does not use spies will not be victorious. One who does not gain the masses will not be victorious.

Military Methods, 5

Victory lies in exhausting trust, making rewards clear, selecting the troops, and taking advantage of the enemy's weakness. This is referred to as King Wu's treasure.

Military Methods, 5

In the region between Heaven and Earth nothing is more noble than man. Warfare is not a matter of a single factor. If the seasons of Heaven, the advantages of Earth, and the harmony of men, these three, are not realized, even though one might be victorious there will be disaster. For this reason they must be mutually relied upon to engage in battle; thereafter only when it is unavoidable engage in warfare. Thus if one accords with the seasons to engage in warfare, it will not be necessary to employ the masses again. If one engages in battle without any basis and gains a minor victory, it is due to astrological influences.

Military Methods, 6

If in ten battles someone is victorious six times, it is due to the stars. If in ten battles someone is victorious seven times, it is due to the sun. If in ten battles someone is victorious eight times, it is due to the moon. If in ten battles someone is victorious nine times, the moon has sustained him. If in ten battles someone is victorious ten times, the general excels, but it leads to misfortune.

Military Methods, 6

Being unexpected and relying on suddenness are the means by which to conduct unfathomable warfare.

Military Methods, 14

If the mailed troops are counted by the hundreds of thousands, while the people have a surplus of grain that they are unable to eat, they have an excess. If the number of troops dwelling in a state is numerous, but the number employed is few, then the standing forces are excessive and those employed in combat insufficient. If there are several hundred thousand mailed soldiers going forth a thousand by a thousand, those who are referred to as excelling at warfare excel at cutting and severing them, just as if a hand happened to wipe them away. One who can divide up the enemy's soldiers, who can repress the enemy's soldiers, will have enough men even with the smallest amounts. One who can not divide up the enemy's soldiers, who cannot repress the enemy's soldiers, will be insufficient even if several times more numerous.

Is it that the more numerous will be victorious? Then calculate the numbers and engage in battle. Is it that the richest will win? Then measure the grain supplies and engage in battle. Is it that the sharpest weapons and stoutest armor will win? Then it will be easy to foretell victory. Since this is not the case, the rich still do not dwell in security; the poor do not yet dwell in danger; the numerous have not yet attained victory; the few are not yet defeated. Now what determines victory or defeat, security or danger, is the Tao.

If the enemy's men are more numerous but you can cause them to become divided and unable to rescue each other; those that suffer attacks unable to know about each other; moats that are deep and fortifications that are high unable to be taken as secure; stout armor and sharp weapons unable to be taken as strength; and courageous, strong warriors unable to protect their general, then your victory will have realized the Tao. Thus enlightened rulers and generals who know the Tao will certainly first calculate whether they can attain success before the battle, so they will not lose any opportunity for achievement after engaging in battle. Thus if when the army goes forth it achieves success, while when it returns it is unharmed, the commander is enlightened about military affairs.

Military Methods, 19

Those who excel in warfare, even when the enemy's forces are strong and numerous, can force them to divide and separate, unable to rescue each other, and suffer enemy attacks without mutually knowing about it. Thus ditches that are deep and ramparts that are high will be unable to provide security; chariots that are sturdy and weapons that are sharp unable to create awesomeness; and warriors of courage and strength unable to make one strong. Those who excel in warfare control the ravines and evaluate the narrows, incite the Three Armies, and take advantage of contracting and expanding. Enemy troops that are numerous they can make few. Armies fully supplied and well provisioned they can make hungry. Those securely emplaced, unmoving, they can cause to become tired. Those who have gained All under Heaven they can cause to become estranged. When the Three Armies are united, they can cause them to become rancorous.

Military Methods, 20

Wherever the army ventures, whether it is along byways that wind about like sheep's intestines, along roads as bumpy as a saw's teeth, curling about the mountains, or entering a valley, it will be victorious. Whether deployed in a square formation or deployed in a round formation it will be victorious. A heavy army is like the mountains, like the forests, like the rivers and great streams. A light force is like a roaring fire; like earthen walls it presses upon them, like clouds it covers them. They cause the enemy's troops to be unable to disperse, and those that are dispersed to be unable to reassemble. Those on the left are unable to rescue those on the right, those on the right are unable to rescue those on the left.

The weapons are like a mass of trees, the effects of the crossbows like a goat's horns. Every man, without exception, steps high and displays his courage. Casting off all doubts, fervent and determined, they go forth decisively!

Wei Liao-tzu, 2

In general, in employing the military there are those who gain victory through the Tao; those that gain victory through awesomeness; and those that gain victory through strength. Holding careful military discussions and evaluating the enemy, causing the enemy's *ch'i* (spirit) to be lost and his forces to scatter, so that even if his disposition is complete he will not be able to employ it, this is victory through the Tao.

Being precise about laws and regulations, making rewards and punishments clear, improving weapons and equipment, causing the people to have minds totally committed to fighting, this is victory through awesomeness.

Destroying armies and slaying generals, mounting barbicans and firing crossbows, overwhelming the populace and seizing territory, returning only after being successful, this is victory through strength. When kings and feudal lords know these, the three ways to victory will be complete.

Wei Liao-tzu, 4

Land is the means for nourishing the populace; fortified cities the means for defending the land; combat the means for defending the cities. Thus if one concentrates upon plowing the people will not be hungry; if one concentrates upon defense the land will not be endangered; if one concentrates upon combat the cities will not be encircled. These three were the fundamental concerns of the Former Kings, and among them military affairs were the most urgent.

Wei Liao-tzu, 4

There are armies that are victorious in the court; those that achieve victory in the plains and fields; and those that attain victory in the marketplace. There are those who fight and gain victory; those that submit and are lost; and those that are fortunate not to be defeated, as in cases where the enemy is unexpectedly frightened, and victory is gained by a turn of events. This sort of victory "by turn of events" is said not to be a complete victory. What is not a complete victory lacks any claim to having effected a tactical imbalance in power. Thus the enlightened ruler, on the day for attack, will concentrate upon having the drums and horns sound in unison and regulating their armed might. Without seeking victory he will then be victorious.

Wei Liao-tzu, 5

Among armies there are those who abandon their defenses, abolish their awesomeness, and are yet victorious because they have methods. There are those who have early established the use of their weapons, so that their response to the enemy is all-encompassing, and their general leadership is perfected.

Wei Liao-tzu, 5

Those who are unguarded in their discussion can be clandestinely listened to. Those who come forth to insult and taunt your forces without proper discipline can be destroyed. Those whose attack is like water rushing forth, like lightning striking, can throw their army into chaos. You must settle those of your troops who are in crisis, eliminate their worries, and decide matters through wisdom. Be superior to the enemy through discussions in the court; be more majestic and severe than they through discussions on bestowing the mandate of command; and arouse their fighting spirit through discussions of crossing the enemy's borders. Then the enemy state can be forced to submit without fighting.

Wei Liao-tzu, 12

Weapons are inauspicious implements. Conflict is a contrary Virtue. All affairs must have their foundation. Therefore when a true king attacks the brutal and chaotic he takes benevolence and righteousness as the foundation for it. At the present time the warring states then establish their awesomeness, resist their enemies, and plot against each other. Thus they cannot abandon their armies.

The military takes the martial as its trunk, and takes the civil as its seed. It makes the martial its exterior, and the civil the interior. One who can investigate and fathom the two will know victory and defeat. The civil is the means to discern benefit and harm, discriminate security and danger. The martial is the means to contravene a strong enemy, to forcefully attack and defend.

Wei Liao-tzu, 23

No Doubt

Quick & Decisive

Multiple Plans

Flank/Fallback

8

Doubt and Timeliness

King Wen asked the T'ai Kung: "How does one preserve the state's territory?"

The T'ai Kung said: "Do not dig valleys deeper to increase hills. Do not abandon the foundation to govern the branches. When the sun is at midday you should dry things. If you grasp a knife you must cut. If you hold an axe you must attack.

"If, at the height of day, you do not dry things in the sun this is termed losing the time. If you grasp a knife but do not cut anything, you will lose the moment for profits. If you hold an axe but do not attack, then bandits will come.

"If trickling streams are not blocked they will become great rivers. If you don't extinguish the smallest flames, what will you do about a great conflagration? If you do not eliminate the two-leaf sapling, how will you use your axe when the tree has grown?"

Six Secret Teachings, 7

One who excels at warfare will await events in the situation without making any movement. When he sees he can be victorious he will arise; if he sees he cannot be victorious he will desist. Thus it is said he doesn't have any fear, he doesn't vacillate. Of the many harms that can beset an army, vacillation is the greatest. Of disasters that can befall an army, none surpasses doubt.

Six Secret Teachings, 26

One who excels in warfare will not lose an advantage when he perceives it, nor be doubtful when he meets the moment. One who loses an advantage or lags behind the time for action will, on the contrary, suffer from disaster. Thus the wise follow the time and do not lose an advantage; the skillful are decisive and have no doubts. For this reason when there is a sudden clap of thunder there isn't time to cover the ears; when there's a flash of lightning there isn't time to close the eyes. Advance as if suddenly startled, employ your troops as if deranged. Those who oppose you will be destroyed, those who come near will perish. Who can defend against such an attack?

Six Secret Teachings, 26

Now if someone is victorious in battle and succeeds in attack but does not exploit the achievement, it is disastrous, and his fate should be termed "wasteful and tarrying." Thus it is said the wise general ponders it, the good general cultivates it.

The Art of War, 12

In general, on the battlefield, soon to become a graveyard, if the soldiers are committed to fight to the death they will live, whereas if they seek to stay alive they will die. A good general will act as if in a sinking boat or trapped in a burning building—there's not enough time for the wise to make plans nor the courageous to get angry. Only engaging the enemy will do! Thus it is said that the greatest harm that can befall the army's employment stems from hesitation, while the disasters that strike the Three Armies are born in doubt.

Wu-tzu, 3

When the army sees the good but is dilatory; when the time comes but it is doubtful; when it expels perversity but is unable to dwell in the results, this is the Tao of stopping. To be lustful yet scrupulous; to be a dragon yet respectful; to be weak yet strong; to be pliant yet firm, this is the Tao of arising. If you implement the Tao of stopping, then even Heaven and Earth will not be able to make you flourish. If you implement the Tao of arising, then even Heaven and Earth will not be able to obstruct you.

Military Methods, 22

If an army employs great force but the achievements are small, it does not understand time. An army that frequently suffers from regret trusts the doubtful.

Military Methods, 22

Where the Worthy go they have no enemies before them. Thus officers can be deferred to, but they cannot be arrogant. The general can be pleased, but cannot be troubled. Plans can be complex, but they cannot be doubted. When the officers are arrogant their subordinates will not be submissive. When the general is troubled his subordinates and troops will not trust each other. When plans are doubted the enemy will be roused to confidence. If one proceeds to mount an attack under these conditions chaos will result.

Huang Shih-kung, 1

When the masses are doubtful there are no settled states. When the masses are deluded there are no governed people. When doubts are settled and the deluded returned, then the state can be secure. When one order is contravened then a hundred orders will be disobeyed. When one evil act is done a hundred evils will form. Thus if you put good into effect amidst a compliant people, and impose harsh measures on wicked people, orders will be implemented without any discontent.

Employing the discontented to govern the discontented is termed "contrary to Heaven." Having the vengeful control the vengeful, an irreversible disaster will result. Govern the people by causing them to be peaceful. If one attains peace through purity, then the people will have their places, and the world will be tranquil.

Huang Shih-kung, 3

The T'ai-tsung said: "The T'ai Kung has stated, 'When infantrymen engage chariots and cavalry in battle, they must take advantage of hillocks, funeral mounds, ravines, and defiles.' Moreover, Sun-tzu said, 'Terrain that looks like fissures in the Heavens, hillocks, funeral mounds, and old fortifications should not be occupied by the army.' What about this contradiction?"

Li Ching said: "The successful employment of the masses lies in their being of one mind. Unification of mind lies in prohibiting omens and dispelling doubts. Should the commanding general have anything about which he is doubtful or fearful, emotions will waver. When their emotions waver, the enemy will take advantage of the chink to attack. Thus when securing an encampment or occupying terrain, it should be convenient to human affairs, that's all. Terrain such as precipitous gorges, deep canyons, ravines, and passes with high sides, natural prisons, and heavily overgrown areas are not suitable for human activity. Thus military strategists avoid leading troops into them, to prevent the enemy from gaining an advantage over us. Hillocks, funeral mounds, and old fortifications are not isolated terrain or places of danger. If we gain them it will be advantageous, so how would it be appropriate to turn around and abandon them? What the T'ai Kung discussed is the very essence of military affairs."

The T'ai-tsung said: "I think that among implements of violence none is more terrible than the army. If mobilizing the army is advantageous to human affairs, how can one, for the sake of avoiding evil omens, be doubtful? If in the future any of the generals fails to take appropriate action because of yin and yang or other baleful indications, my lord should repeatedly upbraid and instruct them."

Questions and Replies, 3

9

Military and Political Intelligence

In general, when you venture deep beyond the enemy's borders you must investigate the configuration and strategic advantages of the terrain, and concentrate upon seeking out and improving the advantages. Rely upon mountains, forests, ravines, rivers, streams, woods, and trees to secure defense. Carefully guard passes and bridges, and moreover be certain you know the advantages of terrain conveyed by the various cities, towns, hills, and funeral mounds. In this way the army will be solidly entrenched. The enemy will not be able to sever our supply routes, nor be able to occupy positions cutting across our front and rear.

Now the rule for commanding an army is always to first dispatch scouts far forward so that when you are two hundred miles from the enemy you will already know their location. If the strategic configuration of the terrain is not advantageous, then use the Martial Attack chariots to form a mobile rampart and advance. Also establish two rear-guard armies to the rear, the further one a hundred miles away, the nearer fifty miles away. Thus, when there is a sudden alarm or urgent situation, both front and rear will know about it, and the Three Armies will always be able to complete their deployment into a solid formation, never suffering any destruction or harm.

Six Secret Teachings, 39

One who does not know the plans of the feudal lords cannot prepare alliances beforehand. Someone unfamiliar with the mountains and forests, gorges and defiles, the shape of marshes and wetlands cannot advance the army. One who does not employ local guides cannot gain advantages of terrain.

The Art of War, 7

If I know our troops can attack, but do not know the enemy cannot be attacked, it is only halfway to victory. If I know the enemy can be attacked, but do not realize our troops cannot attack, it is only halfway to victory.

Knowing that the enemy can be attacked, and knowing that our army can effect the attack, but not knowing the terrain is not suitable for combat, is only halfway to victory. Thus one who truly knows the army will never be deluded when he moves, never be impoverished when initiating an action.

Thus it is said if you know them and know yourself, your victory will not be imperiled. If you know Heaven and know Earth, your victory can be complete.

The Art of War, 10

The prosecution of military affairs lies in according with and learning in detail the enemy's intentions. If one then focuses his strength toward the enemy, strikes a thousand miles away, and kills their general, it is termed "being skillful and capable in completing military affairs."

The Art of War, 11

When you send forth an army of a hundred thousand on a campaign, marching them out a thousand miles, the expenditures of the common people and the contributions of the feudal house will be one thousand pieces of gold per day. Those inconvenienced and troubled both within and without the border, who are exhausted on the road or unable to pursue their agricultural work, will be seven hundred thousand families.

Armies remain locked in a standoff for years to fight for victory on a single day, yet generals begrudge bestowing ranks and emoluments of one hundred pieces of gold and therefore do not know the enemy's situation. This is the ultimate inhumanity. Such a person is not a general for the people, an assistant for a ruler, or the arbiter of victory.

The Art of War, 13

The means by which enlightened rulers and sagacious generals moved and conquered others, that their achievements surpassed the masses, was advance knowledge.

Advance knowledge cannot be gained from ghosts and spirits, inferred from phenomena, or projected from the measures of Heaven, but must be gained from men for it is the knowledge of the enemy's true situation.

The Art of War, 13

Thus there are five types of spies to be employed: local spy, internal spy, turned spy (double agent), dead (expendable) spy, and the living spy. When all five are employed together and no one knows their Tao, this is termed "spiritual methodology." They are a ruler's treasures.

Local spies: employ people from the local district. Internal spies: employ their people who hold government positions. Double agents: employ the enemy's spies. Expendable spies: are employed to spread disinformation outside the state. Provide our expendable spies with false information and have them leak it to enemy agents. Living spies return with their reports.

Thus of all the Three Armies' affairs no relationship is closer than with spies; no rewards are more generous than those given to spies, no affairs are more secret than those pertaining to spies.

The Art of War, 13

Unless someone has the wisdom of a Sage, he cannot use spies; unless he is benevolent and righteous, he cannot employ spies; unless he is subtle and perspicacious, he cannot perceive the substance in intelligence reports. It is subtle, subtle! There are no areas in which one does not employ spies.

The Art of War, 13

You must search for enemy agents who have come to spy on us. Tempt them with profits, instruct and retain them. Thus double agents can be obtained and employed. Through knowledge gained from them, you can recruit both local and internal spies. Through knowledge gained from them, the expendable spy can spread his falsehoods; can be used to misinform the enemy. Through knowledge gained from them, our living spies can be employed as times require.

The ruler must know these five aspects of espionage work. This knowledge inevitably depends on turned spies; therefore, you must be generous to double agents.

The Art of War, 13

In antiquity, when the Yin arose, they had I Chih in the Hsia. When the Chou arose, they had Lü Yin in the Shang. Thus enlightened rulers and sagacious generals who are able to get intelligent spies will invariably attain great achievements. This is the essence of the military, what the Three Armies rely on to move.

The Art of War, 13

T'ien Chi said: "Are authority, strategic power, plans, and deception urgent matters for the military?"

Sun Pin said: "They are not. Now authority is the means by which to assemble the masses. Strategic power is the means by which to cause the soldiers to invariably fight. Plans are the means by which to cause the enemy to be unprepared. Deception is the means by which to put the enemy into difficulty. They can be employed to facilitate victory, but they are not urgent affairs."

T'ien Chi angrily flushed: "These six are all employed by those who excel in military affairs, and yet you, sir, say they are not urgent. Then what matters are urgent?"

Sun Pin said: "Evaluating the enemy, estimating the difficulties of terrain, invariably investigating both near and far . . . is the Tao of the general. Invariably attacking where they do not defend, this is the army's urgency."

Military Methods, 3

10

Economics and Logistics

The ruler must focus upon developing wealth within his state. Without material wealth he has nothing with which to be benevolent. If he does not bespread beneficence he will have nothing with which to bring his relatives together. If he estranges his relatives it will be harmful. If he loses the common people he will be defeated.

Six Secret Teachings, 7

One who excels in employing the military does not conscript the people twice or transport provisions a third time. If you obtain your equipment from within the state and rely on seizing provisions from the enemy, then the army's foodstuffs will be sufficient.

The state is impoverished by the army when it transports provisions far off. When provisions are transported far off, the hundred surnames are impoverished. Those in proximity to the army will sell their goods expensively. When goods are expensive, the hundred surnames' wealth will be exhausted. When their wealth is exhausted, they will be extremely hard-pressed to supply their village's military impositions.

When their strength has been expended and their wealth depleted, then the houses in the central plains will be empty. The expenses of the hundred surnames will be some seven-tenths of whatever they have. The ruler's irrecoverable expenditures—such as ruined chariots, exhausted horses, armor, helmets, arrows and crossbows, halberdtipped and speartipped large, movable protective shields, strong oxen, and large wagons—will consume six-tenths of his resources.

Thus the wise general will concentrate on securing provisions from the enemy. One bushel of the enemy's foodstuffs is worth twenty of ours; one picul of fodder is worth twenty of ours.

The Art of War, 2

Combat between armies is advantageous; combat between masses is dangerous. If the entire army contends for advantage, you will not arrive in time. If you reduce the army's size to contend for advantage, your baggage and heavy equipment will suffer losses.

For this reason if you abandon your armor and heavy equipment to race forward day and night without encamping, covering two days' normal distance at a time, marching forward a hundred miles to contend for gain, the Three Armies' generals will be captured. The strong will be first to arrive, while the exhausted will follow. With such tactics only one in ten will reach the battle site. If one contends for gain fifty miles away, it will cause the general of the Upper Army to stumble, and by following such tactics half the men will reach the objective. If you contend for gain at thirty miles, then two-thirds of the army will reach the objective. Accordingly, if the army does not have baggage and heavy equipment it will be lost; if it does not have provisions it will be lost; if it does not have stores it will be lost.

The Art of War, 7

Numerous supply sources and dispersed provisions are the means to facilitate victory.

Military Methods, 14

The army has its squads of ten and five, and the methods of dividing and reuniting. Before engaging in battle duties are assigned, and designated units should occupy the strategic locations, passes, and bridges. When the pennant for uniting to engage in battle is raised, they should all assemble. The main army sets out with a fixed daily ration and their combat equipment all complete. The orders are issued and they move; anyone who does not follow orders is executed.

Now determine and assign forces to the strategic points within the four borders of the state. After the advance army and vanguard have already set out, the people within the borders are not able to move about. Those who have received the king's commands, who have been given and carry the proper tallies and tokens, are called "officers acting in accord with their duties." Officers who are not acting in accord with their duties but yet move about should be executed. When the pennant for uniting to engage in battle is raised, these officers, acting in accord with their duties, travel about and are employed to ensure that affairs are mutually regulated. Accordingly, one who wants to wage warfare must first secure the interior.

Wei Liao-tzu, 20

Part Three

THE TAO OF COMMAND

11

Rulership

King Wen inquired of the T'ai Kung: "The world is replete with a dazzling array of states—some full, others empty, some well ordered, others in chaos. How does it come to be thus? Is it that the moral qualities of these rulers are not the same? Or that the changes and transformations of the seasons of Heaven naturally cause it to be thus?"

The T'ai Kung said: "If the ruler lacks moral worth, then the state will be in danger and the people in turbulence. If the ruler is a Worthy or Sage, then the state will be at peace and the people well ordered. Fortune and misfortune lie with the ruler, not with the seasons of Heaven."

Six Secret Teachings, 2

The T'ai Kung: "Former generations referred to Emperor Yao, in his kingship over the realm in antiquity, as a worthy ruler. When Yao was king of the world he did not adorn himself with gold, silver, pearls, and jade. He didn't wear brocaded, embroidered, or elegantly decorated clothes. He did not look at strange, odd, rare, or unusual things. He didn't treasure items of amusement nor listen to licentious music. He didn't whitewash the walls around the palace or the buildings, nor decoratively carve the beams, square and round rafters, and pillars. He didn't even trim the reeds that grew all about his courtyards. He used a deerskin robe to ward off the cold, while simple clothes covered his body. He ate coarse millet and unpolished grains, and thick soups from rough vegetables. He did not, through the untimely imposition of labor service, injure the people's seasons for agriculture and sericulture. He reduced his desires and constrained his will, managing affairs by nonaction.

"He honored the positions of the officials who were loyal, upright, and upheld the laws, and made generous the salaries of those who were pure and scrupulous and loved people. He loved and respected those among the people who were filial and compassionate, and he comforted and encouraged those who exhausted their strength in agriculture and sericulture. Pennants distinguished the virtuous from the evil, being displayed at the gates of the village lanes. He tranquilized his heart and rectified the constraints of social forms. With laws and measures he prohibited evil and artifice.

"Among those he hated, if anyone had merit he would invariably reward him. Among those he loved, if anyone were guilty of an offense he would certainly punish him. He preserved and nurtured the widows, widowers, orphans, and solitary elderly, and gave aid to the families who had suffered misfortune and loss.

"What he allotted to himself was extremely meager, the taxes and services he required of the people extremely few. Thus the myriad peoples were prosperous and happy, and did not have the appearance of suffering from hunger and cold. The hundred surnames revered their ruler as if he were the sun and moon, and gave their emotional allegiance as if he were their father and mother."

Six Secret Teachings, 2

King Wen: "How should the ruler act in his position?"

T'ai Kung: "He should be composed, dignified, and quiet. His softness and self-constraint should be established first. He should excel at giving and not be contentious. He should empty his mind and tranquilize his intentions, awaiting events with uprightness."

King Wen inquired: "How should the ruler listen to affairs?"

The T'ai Kung replied: "He should not carelessly allow them, nor go against opinion and oppose them. If he allows them in this fashion, he will lose his central control; if he opposes them in this way, he will close off his access.

"He should be like the height of a mountain which, when looked up to, cannot be perceived, or the depths of a great abyss which, when measured, cannot be fathomed. Such spiritual and enlightened Virtue is the pinnacle of uprightness and tranquility."

King Wen inquired: "What should the ruler's wisdom be like?"

The T'ai Kung: "The eye values clarity, the ear values sharpness, the mind values wisdom. If you look with the eyes of All under Heaven, there is nothing you will not see. If you listen with the ears of All under Heaven, there is nothing you will not hear. If you think with the minds of All under Heaven, there is nothing you will not know. When you receive information from all directions just like the spokes converging on the hub of a wheel, your clarity will not be obfuscated."

Six Secret Teachings, 4

The T'ai Kung said: "One who exercises kingship over the people recognizes 'six thieves': First, if your subordinates build large palaces and mansions, pools and terraces, and amble about enjoying the pleasures of scenery and female musicians, it will injure the king's Virtue.

"Second, when the people are not engaged in agriculture and sericulture, but instead give rein to their tempers and travel about as bravos, disdaining and transgressing the laws and prohibitions, not following the instructions of the officials, it harms the king's transforming influence.

"Third, when officials form cliques and parties, obfuscating the worthy and wise, obstructing the ruler's clarity, it injures the king's authority.

"Fourth, when the knights are contrary-minded and conspicuously display 'high moral standards,' taking such behavior to be powerful expression of their *ch'i* (spirit), and have private relationships with other feudal lords, slighting their own ruler, it injures the king's awesomeness.

"Fifth, when subordinates disdain titles and positions, are contemptuous of the administrators, and are ashamed to face hardship for their ruler, it injures the efforts of the meritorious subordinates.

"Sixth, when the strong clans encroach upon others, seizing what they want, insulting and ridiculing the poor and weak, it injures the work of the common people."

Six Secret Teachings, 9

King Wen asked the T'ai Kung: "How does it happen that a ruler may exert himself to advance the Worthy, but is unable to obtain any results from such efforts, and in fact the world grows increasingly turbulent, even to the point that he is endangered or perishes?"

The T'ai Kung: "If one advances the Worthy but does not employ them, this is attaining the name of 'advancing the Worthy' but lacking the substance of 'using the Worthy.' "

King Wen asked: "Whence comes the error?"

The T'ai Kung: "The error lies in wanting to employ men who are popularly praised rather than obtaining true Worthies."

King Wen: "How is that?"

The T'ai Kung said: "If the ruler takes those that the world commonly praises as being Worthies, and those that they condemn as being worthless, then the larger cliques will advance and the smaller ones will retreat. In this situation groups of evil individuals will associate together to obscure the Worthy. Loyal subordinates will die even though innocent. And perverse subordinates will obtain rank and position through empty fame. In this way, as turbulence continues to grow in the world, the state cannot avoid danger and destruction."

King Wen asked: "How does one advance the Worthy?"

T'ai Kung replied: "Your general and chancellor should divide the responsibility, each of them selecting men based upon the names of the positions. In accord with the name of the position, they will assess the substance required. In selecting men, they will evaluate their abilities, making the reality of their talents match the name of the position. When the name matches the reality you will have realized the Tao for advancing the Worthy."

Six Secret Teachings, 10

When bestowing your beneficence upon the people you cannot begrudge the expense. The people are like cows and horses. Frequently make gifts of food and clothing, and follow up by loving them.

Six Secret Teachings, 17

The duty of the Son of Heaven must be to concentrate upon modeling on Heaven and Earth and observing the measures of the Former Sages. The duty of officers and common men must be to respectfully serve their parents, and to be upright with their ruler and superiors. Even though there is an enlightened ruler, if the officers are not first instructed, they cannot be used.

When the ancients instructed the people they would invariably establish the relationships and fixed distinctions of noble and common, causing them not to encroach upon each other; the virtuous and righteous not to exceed each other; the talented and technically skilled not to occlude each other; and the courageous and strong not to clash with each other. Thus their strength was united and their thoughts were in harmony.

Ssu-ma Fa, 2

The Tao, Virtue, benevolence, righteousness, and the forms of propriety—these five—are one body. The Tao is what men tread; Virtue is what men gain; benevolence is what men approach; righteousness is what men consider appropriate; and the forms of propriety are what people embody. You cannot lack any one of them.

Thus rising in the early morning, sleeping at night, are constraints of the forms of propriety. Punishing brigands and taking revenge are decisions of righteousness. The compassionate heart is an expression of benevolence. Gaining what you want yourself, and gaining it for other people, is the path of Virtue. Ensuring that people are equal and do not lose their place, this is the transformation of the Tao.

Huang Shih-kung, 3

12

Power and Authority

King Wen asked the T'ai Kung: "How does the ruler of the state and leader of the people come to lose his position?"

The T'ai Kung said: "He is not cautious about whom he has as associates."

Six Secret Teachings, 6

Do not loan the handles of state—the power to grant rewards and inflict punishments—to other men. If you loan the handles of state to other men then you will lose your authority.

Do not loan sharp weapons to other men. If you loan sharp weapons to other men, you will be hurt by them, and will not live out your allotted span of years.

Do not allow other men to snatch away your awesomeness. Rely on your wisdom, follow the constant. Those that submit and accord with you treat generously with Virtue. Those that oppose you break with force. If you respect the people and are decisive, then All under Heaven will be peaceful and submissive.

Six Secret Teachings, 7

I have heard that in antiquity those who excelled in employing the army could bear to have half their officers and soldiers killed. The next could kill thirty percent, and the lowest ten percent. The awesomeness of one who could sacrifice half of his troops affected all within the Four Seas. The strength of one who could sacrifice thirty percent could be applied to the

actions, but esteem violent behavior, so that the people insult the minor officials—this is termed "diminished awesomeness." If the conditions of diminished awesomeness prevail the people will not be victorious.

Ssu-ma Fa, 2

As to the Seven Administrative Affairs: the first is termed men; the second, uprightness; the third, language; the fourth, skill; the fifth, fire; the sixth, water; the seventh, weapons. Glory, profit, shame, and death are referred to as the Four Preservations.

Being tolerant and congenial, while yet accumulating awesomeness, is the way to prevent transgressions and change intentions. In all cases this is the Tao.

Only benevolence can attract people; however, if one is benevolent but not trustworthy, then on the contrary he will vanquish himself. Treat men as men, be upright with the upright, employ appropriate language, and use fire only where it should be used.

Ssu-ma Fa, 3

In general the Tao for imposing order on chaos consists of: first, benevolence; second, credibility; third, straightforwardness; fourth, unity; fifth, righteousness; sixth, change wrought by authority; seventh, centralized authority.

The Tao for establishing the laws consists of: first, acceptance of constraints; second, the laws; third, the establishment of the talented and upright; fourth, urgency in administration; fifth, distinguishing them with insignia; sixth, ordering the colors; seventh, no nonstandard uniforms among the officers.

As for the army, when the power of the law lies solely with oneself it is termed "centralized." When those below the ruler all fear the law it is termed "law." When the army does not listen to minor affairs; when in battle it does not concern itself with small advantages; and on the day of conflict it successfully completes its plans in subtle fashion, it is termed "the Tao."

Ssu-ma Fa, 3

As for warfare: when upright methods do not prove effective then centralized control of affairs must be undertaken. If the people do not submit to Virtue, then laws must be imposed. If they do not trust each other, they must be unified. If they are dilatory, move them; if they are doubtful, change their doubts. If the people do not trust the ruler, then whatever is promulgated must not be revised. This has been the administrative rule from antiquity.

Ssu-ma Fa, 3

If you are respectful the troops will be satisfied. If you lead in person they will follow. When orders are annoying they will be ignored. When commands are issued in proper measure they will be seriously regarded. When the drumbeat is rapid they will move quickly; when the drumbeat is more measured they will move accordingly. When their uniforms are light they will feel quick; if lustrous they will feel stalwart.

Ssu-ma Fa, 4

In general, commanding a large number is like commanding a few. It is a question of dividing up the numbers. Fighting with a large number is like fighting with a few. It is a question of configuration and designation.

Bestow rewards not required by law, impose exceptional governmental orders. Direct the masses of the Three Armies as though commanding one man. Press affairs upon them. Do not explain the purpose to them. Compel them with prospects for profit, but do not inform them about the potential harm.

One who excels at employing the army leads them by the hand as if they were only one man, so they cannot avoid it.

The Art of War, 5, 11

If orders are consistently implemented to instruct the people, then the people will submit. If orders are not consistently implemented to instruct the people, then the people will not submit. One whose orders are consistently carried out has established a mutual relationship with the people.

The Art of War, 9

At the moment the general has designated with them, it will be as if they ascended a height and abandoned their ladders. The general advances with them deep into the territory of the feudal lords and then releases the trigger. He commands them as if racing a herd of sheep—they are driven away, driven back, but no one knows where they are going.

The Art of War, 11

Marquis Wu asked, "What measures will ensure the soldiers will be victorious?"

Wu Ch'i replied, "Control is foremost."

Marquis Wu again asked, "It is not large numbers?"

"If the laws and orders are not clear, rewards and punishments not trusted—when sounding the gongs will not cause them to halt, nor beating the drum to advance—then even if you had a million men, of what use would they be? What is meant by control is that when stationary they observe the forms of propriety, and when in action they are awesome. When they advance they cannot be withstood; when they withdraw they cannot be pursued. Their advancing and withdrawing are measured, the left and right flanks respond to the signal flags. Even if broken off from the main order they preserve their formations, even if scattered they will reform lines. They will hold together in peace, they will hold together in danger. Their number can be assembled together, but cannot be forced apart. They can be employed, but they cannot be exhausted. No matter where you dispatch them, no one under Heaven will be able to withstand them. They are called 'the troops of a father and son.' "

Wu-tzu, 3

In general, warfare has four vital points: *ch'i* (spirit), terrain, affairs, and strength. When the masses of the Three Armies, the million soldiers of the forces, are strategically deployed in appropriate formations according to varying degrees of strength by one man, this is termed the "vital point of *ch'i*." When the road is narrow and the way perilous; when famous mountains present great obstacles; and if ten men defend a place a thousand cannot pass, this is termed a "vital point of earth." Being good at controlling clandestine operatives; with a few light troops harassing the enemy, causing them to scatter; and forcing rulers and ministers to feel mutual annoyance, higher and lower ranks to reproach each other, this is termed the "vital point of affairs." When the chariots have solid axles and secure pins; the boats well-suited rudders and oars; the officers are thoroughly familiar with the fighting formations; and the horses practiced in pursuit and maneuvers, this is termed the "vital point of strength." One who knows these four is qualified to be a general. However his awesomeness, Virtue, benevolence, and courage must be sufficient to lead his subordinates and settle the masses. Furthermore he must frighten the enemy and resolve doubts. When he issues orders no one will dare disobey them. Wherever he may be, rebels will not dare oppose him. Gaining him the state will grow strong; losing him the state will perish. This is what is referred to as a good general.

Wu-tzu, 4

King Wei said: "How can we cause the people to always listen to orders?"

Sun Pin said: "Always be sincere."

Military Methods, 3

If the general's employment of his mind is not in harmony with the army, even though the formation's lightness and heaviness are correct, and the front and rear are appropriate, they still will not conquer the enemy.

Military Methods, 10

Even if an arrow's lightness and heaviness are correct, the front and rear are appropriate, the crossbow drawn straight, and the shooting of the arrow at one, if the archer is not correct, it still will not hit the target. If the lightness and heaviness of the troops are correct, the front and rear appropriate, and the general in harmony with the army, but the ruler does not excel, they still will not conquer the enemy. Thus it is said for the crossbow to hit the objective it must realize these four. For the army to be successful there must be the ruler, the general, and the troops, these three. Thus it is said that an army conquering an enemy is no different from a crossbow hitting a target. This is the Tao of the military. If the model of the arrow is complied with, the Tao will be completed. When someone understands the Tao, the army will be successful, and the ruler will be famous.

Military Methods, 10

In the military, regulations must first be established. When regulations are established first, the soldiers will not be disordered. When the soldiers are not disordered, punishments will be clear. If wherever the gongs and drums direct them a hundred men all contend; to penetrate the enemy's ranks and cause chaos among his formations a thousand men all strive; and to overturn the enemy's army and kill his generals ten thousand men raise their blades in unison, no one under Heaven will be able to withstand them in battle.

People do not take pleasure in dying nor do they hate life, but if the commands and orders are clear, and the laws and regulations carefully detailed, you can make them advance. When, before combat, rewards are made clear, and afterward punishments are made decisive, then when the troops issue forth they will be able to realize an advantage, and when they move they will be successful.

Wei Liao-tzu, 3

One who excels at employing the army is able to seize men and not be seized by others. This seizing is a technique of mind. Orders unify the minds of the masses. When the masses are not understood, the orders will have to be changed frequently. When they are changed frequently, then, even though orders are issued the masses will not have faith in them.

Thus the rule for giving commands is that small errors should not be changed, minor doubts should not be publicized. Thus when those above do not issue doubtful orders, the masses will not listen to two different versions. When actions do not have any questionable aspects, the multitude will not have divided intentions. There has never been an instance where the people did not believe the mind of their leader and were able to attain their strength. It has never been the case that one was unable to realize their strength and yet attain their deaths in battle.

Wei Liao-tzu, 4

Thus those who engage in combat must take leading in person as their foundation in order to incite the masses and officers, just as the mind controls the four limbs. If their minds are not incited, then the officers will not die for honor. When the officers will not die for honor then the masses will not do battle.

Wei Liao-tzu, 4

The military is victorious through being quiet; a state is victorious through being united. One whose strength is divided, whose mind has doubts, will be turned against. Now when one's strength is weak, advancing and retreating will not be bold, and pursuing an enemy will not result in capturing anyone. Generals, commanders, officers, and troops should be a single body both in action and at rest. But if the commander's mind is already doubtful, and the troops inclined to rebellion, then even though a plan has been decided upon they will not move, or if movement has been initiated they cannot be controlled. When different mouths speak empty words; the general lacks the proper demeanor; and the troops have not had constant tests during training, if they set out to attack they will inevitably be defeated. This is what is referred to as a hasty, belligerent army. It is inadequate for engaging in warfare.

Now the general is the mind of the army, while all those below are the limbs and joints. When the mind moves in complete sincerity, then the limbs and joints are invariably strong. When the mind moves in doubt, then the limbs and joints are invariably contrary. Now if the general does not govern his mind, the troops will not move as his limbs. Then even though the army might be victorious, it will be a lucky victory, not the result of the tactical imbalance of power in the attack.

Wei Liao-tzu, 5

Now the people do not have two things they fear equally. If they fear us then they will despise the enemy; if they fear the enemy they will despise us. The one who is despised will be defeated; the one who establishes his awesomeness will be victorious. In general, when the general is able to implement the Tao to awesomeness, his commanders will fear him. When the commanders fear their general, the people will fear their commanders. When the people fear their commanders, then the enemy will fear the people. For this reason those who would know the Tao of victory and defeat must first know about the balance of power of "fearing" and "despising."

Now one who is not loved and cherished in the minds of his men cannot be employed by me; one who is not respected and feared in the minds of his men cannot be appointed by me. Love follows from below, awesomeness is established from above. If they love their general they will not have divided minds; if they are awestruck by their general they will not be rebellious. Thus excelling at generalship is merely a question of love and awesomeness.

Wei Liao-tzu, 5

Awesomeness lies in not making changes. Beneficence lies in according with the seasons. Perceptivity lies in promptly responding to affairs. Success in warfare lies in controlling *ch'i* (spirit). Skill in attacks lies in fathoming externals. Defense lies in manipulating external appearance. Not being excessive lies in measuring and counting. Not encountering difficulty lies in foresight and preparation. Being cautious lies in respecting the small. Wisdom lies in controlling the large. Eliminating harm lies in being decisive. Gaining the masses lies in deferring to other men.

Regret arises from relying upon what is doubtful. Evil lies in excessive executions. Prejudiced views come from frequently following one's own desires. Inauspicious events arise from detesting to hear about one's errors. Extravagance lies in exhausting the people's resources. Unenlightenment consists in accepting advice that separates you from reality. Being insubstantial stems from lightly initiating movements. Stubbornness and ignorance lie in separating yourself from the Worthy. Misfortune lies in loving profits. Harm lies in drawing common men near. Disaster lies in lacking any place to defend. Danger lies in lacking clear commands and orders.

Wei Liao-tzu, 7

To retain men in service straight from their mobilization to the time when their armor and helmets have become worminfested, they must be men whom we can employ. This is like a bird of prey pursuing a sparrow that flies into a man's arms or enters someone's dwelling. It's not that the bird is casting away its life, but that to the rear there is something to fear.

Wei Liao-tzu, 8

When Wu Ch'i engaged Ch'in in battle, before the armies clashed, one man, unable to overcome his courage, went forth to slay two of the enemy and return with their heads. Wu Ch'i immediately ordered his decapitation. An army commander remonstrated with him, saying "This is a skilled warrior. You cannot execute him." Wu Ch'i said, "There is no question that he is a skilled warrior. But it's not what I ordered." He had him executed.

Wei Liao-tzu, 8

The commander-in-chief's method focuses upon winning the minds of the valiant; rewarding and providing salaries to the meritorious; and having his will penetrate to the masses. Thus if he has the same likes as the masses there is nothing he will not accomplish. If he has the same dislikes as the masses there is nothing he will not overturn. Governing the state and giving security to one's family is a question of gaining the people. Losing the state and destroying one's family is a question of losing the people. All living beings want to realize their ambitions.

Huang Shih-kung, 1

Thus I say everyone covets strength, but rare are those capable of preserving the subtle. If someone can preserve the subtle he can protect his life. The Sage preserves it in order to respond to the slightest change in affairs. If he releases it then it will extend throughout the Four Seas. If he rolls it up it will not fill a cup. He dwells in it but without a house. He guards it but without city walls. He stores it away in his breast, and enemy states submit.

The *Military Pronouncements* states: "The soft can control the hard, the weak can control the strong." The soft is Virtue. The hard is a brigand. The weak is what the people will help, the strong is what resentment will attack. The soft has situations in which it is established; the hard has situations in which it is applied; the weak has situations in which it is employed; and the strong has situations in which it is augmented. Combine these four and control them appropriately.

The *Military Pronouncements* states: "If one can be soft and hard his state will be increasingly glorious! If one can be weak and strong, his state will be increasingly illustrious! If purely soft and purely weak, his state will inevitably decline. If purely hard and purely strong, his state will inevitably be destroyed."

Huang Shih-kung, 1

The *Military Pronouncements* states: "The basis of the general's awesomeness is his commands and orders. The basis of complete victory in battle is military administration. The reason officers treat battle lightly is the employment of commands." Thus the general never rescinds an order. Rewards and punishments must be as certain as Heaven and Earth, for then the general can employ the men. When the officers and soldiers follow orders the army can cross the border.

Now the one who unifies the army and wields its strategic power is the general. The ones that bring about conquest and defeat the enemy are the masses. Thus a disordered general cannot be employed to preserve an army, while a rebellious mass cannot be used to attack an enemy. If this sort of general attacks a city it cannot be taken, while if this type of army lays siege to a town it will not fall. If both are unsuccessful then the officer's strength will be exhausted. If it is exhausted then the general will be alone and the masses will be rebellious. If they try to hold defensive positions they will not be secure, while if they engage in battle they will turn and run. They are referred to as an "old army."

When the troops are "old" then the general's awesomeness will not be effective. When the general lacks awesomeness then the officers and troops will disdain punishment. When they disdain punishment the army will lose its organization into squads of five. When the army loses its squads of five the officers and soldiers will abandon their positions and run off. When they flee the enemy will take advantage of the situation. When the enemy seizes the opportunity to profit from this situation the army will inevitably perish.

Huang Shih-kung, 1

The *Military Pronouncements* states: "The exemplary general, in his command of the army, governs men as he would want to be treated himself. Spreading his kindness and extending his beneficence, the strength of his officers is daily renewed. In battle they are like the wind arising, their attack is like the release of a pent-up river." Thus our army can be seen but not withstood, can be submitted to but not be conquered. If you lead the men in person your soldiers will become the most valiant under Heaven.

Huang Shih-kung, 1

The *Military Pronouncements* states: "A state about to mobilize its army concentrates first upon making its beneficence ample. A state about to attack and seize another concentrates upon first nurturing the people." Conquering the many with only a few is a question of beneficence. Conquering the strong with the weak is a question of people. Thus the good general, in nurturing his officers, treats them no differently than himself. Therefore he is able to direct the Three Armies as if they were of one mind, and then his victory can be complete.

Huang Shih-kung, 1

The T'ai-tsung said: "I observe that the thousand chapters and ten thousand sentences of the military writings do not go beyond 'Use many methods to cause them to make errors,' this single statement."

After a long while Li Ching said: "Truly, it is as you have wisely said. In ordinary situations involving the use of the military, if the enemy does not make an error in judgment, how can our army conquer them? It may be compared with chess where the two enemies begin equal in strength. As soon as someone makes a mistake, truly no one can rescue him. For this reason, in both ancient and modern times, victory and defeat have proceeded from a single error, so how much more would this be the case with many mistakes?"

Questions and Replies, 3

14
Unity

King Wu asked the T'ai Kung: "What is the Tao of the military?"

The T'ai Kung said: "In general, as for the Tao of the military, nothing surpasses unity. The unified can come alone, can depart alone. The Yellow Emperor said: 'Unification approaches the Tao and touches upon the spiritual.' Its employment lies in the subtle; its conspicuous manifestation lies in the strategic configuration of power; its completion lies with the ruler. Thus the Sage Kings termed weapons evil implements, but when they had no alternative, they employed them."

Six Secret Teachings, 12

Horses, oxen, chariots, weapons, relaxation, and an adequate diet are the army's strength. Instructions are simply a matter of preparation; warfare is only a question of constraints. The army's commanding general is the body, the companies are the limbs, and the squads of five the thumb and fingers.

Ssu-ma Fa, 3

In general, regarding victory: when the Three Armies are united as one man they will conquer.

Ssu-ma Fa, 4

The *Military Administration* states: "Because they could not hear each other they made gongs and drums; because they could not see each other they made pennants and flags." Gongs, drums, pennants, and flags are the means to unify the men's ears and eyes. When the men have been unified the courageous will not be able to advance alone, the fearful will not be able to retreat alone. This is the method for employing large numbers. Thus in night battles make the fires and drums numerous, and in daylight battles make the flags and pennants numerous in order to change the men's ears and eyes.

The Art of War, 7

An army that is unable to overcome great adversity is unable to unite the people's minds.

Military methods, 22

One who is unified will be victorious; one who is beset by dissension will be defeated. When formations are tight they are solid; when the front is dispersed it can attain its objectives.

Wei Liao-tzu, 23

15

Generals and Generalship

Military matters are not determined by the ruler's commands; they all proceed from the commanding general. When the commanding general approaches an enemy and decides to engage in battle, he is not of two minds. In this way there is no Heaven above, no Earth below, no enemy in front, and no ruler to the rear. For this reason the wise make plans for him, the courageous fight for him. Their spirit soars to the blue clouds, they are swift like galloping steeds. Even before the blades clash, the enemy surrenders submissively.

Six Secret Teachings, 21

The general is the supporting pillar of state. If his talents are all-encompassing, the state will invariably be strong. If the supporting pillar is marked by fissures, the state will invariably grow weak.

The Art of War, 3

Thus there are three ways by which an army is put into difficulty by a ruler: he does not know that the Three Armies should not advance but instructs them to advance or does not know that the Three Armies should not withdraw and orders a retreat. This is termed "entangling the army." He does not understand the Three Armies' military affairs but directs them in the same way as his civil administration. Then the officers will become confused. He does not understand the Three Armies' tactical balance of power but undertakes responsibility for command. Then the officers will be doubtful. When the Three Armies are already confused and doubtful, the danger of the feudal lords taking advantage of the situation arises. This is referred to as "a disordered army drawing another on to victory."

The Art of War, 3

If the Tao of Warfare indicates certain victory, even though the ruler has instructed that combat should be avoided, if you must engage in battle it is permissible. If the Tao of Warfare indicates you will not be victorious, even though the ruler instructs you to engage in battle, not fighting is permissible.

Thus a general who does not advance to seek fame, nor fail to retreat to avoid being charged with the capital offense of retreating, but seeks only to preserve the people and gain advantage for the ruler is the state's treasure.

The Art of War, 10

One who does not obtain the ruler's trust does not act as his general.

Military Methods, 5

Now when the commanding general takes up the drum, brandishes the drumsticks, and approaches danger for a decisive battle, so that the soldiers meet and the naked blades clash—if he drums the advance and they respond to wrest the victory, then he will be rewarded for his achievements and his fame will be established. If he drums the advance but they fail, then he himself will die and the state will perish. For this reason survival and extinction, security and danger all lie at the end of the drumstick! How can one not value the general?

Wei Liao-tzu, 8

Now the commanding general is not governed by Heaven above, nor controlled by Earth below, nor governed by men in the middle. Thus weapons are evil implements. Conflict is a contrary virtue. The post of general is an office of death. Thus only when it cannot be avoided does one employ them. There is no Heaven above, no Earth below, no ruler to the rear, and no enemy in the front. The unified army of one man is like the wolf and tiger, like the wind and rain, like thunder and lightning. Shaking and mysterious, All under Heaven are terrified by it.

Wei Liao-tzu, 8

When the commanding general receives his mandate he forgets his family. When he commands the army and they encamp in the field he forgets those close to him. When he takes up the drumsticks and drums the advance he forgets himself.

Wei Liao-tzu, 8

When Wu Ch'i approached the time for battle his attendants offered their swords. Wu Ch'i said, "The general takes sole control of the flags and drums, and that's all. Approaching hardship he decides what is doubtful, controls the troops, and directs their blades. Such is the work of the general. Bearing a single sword, that is not a general's affair."

Wei Liao-tzu, 8

In general, a general is an officer of the law, the ruler of the ten thousand things. It cannot be the personal domain of one man. When it is not the personal domain of one man the ten thousand things will all come of themselves and be governed there, the ten thousand things will all come and be commanded there.

Wei Liao-tzu, 9

When the army is mobilized and advances into the field, the sole exercise of power lies with the general. If in advancing or withdrawing the court interferes, it will be difficult to attain success.

Huang Shih-kung, 2

PERSONAL BEHAVIOR AND EXAMPLE

Now when the army is toiling on the march the general must establish himself as an example. In the heat he does not set up an umbrella; in the cold he doesn't wear heavier clothes. On difficult terrain he must dismount and walk. Only after the army's well is finished does he drink. Only after the army's food is cooked does he eat. Only after the army's ramparts are complete does he rest. He must personally experience the same toil and respite. In this fashion even though the army is in the field for a long time, it will be neither old nor exhausted.

Wei Liao-tzu, 4

When Wu Ch'i engaged Ch'in in battle, wherever he encamped the army did not flatten the paths between the fields. Young saplings provided protective covering against the frost and dew. Why did he act like this? Because he didn't place himself higher than other men. If you want men to die you don't require them to perform perfunctory acts of respect. If you want men to exhaust their strength you don't hold them responsible for performing the rites. Thus in antiquity an officer wearing a helmet and armor didn't bow, showing people that he is not troubled by anything. To annoy people yet require them to die, to exhaust their strength, from antiquity until today has never been heard of.

Wei Liao-tzu, 8

Now those who command the army must share tastes and attitudes with the officers and men, and confront both safety and danger with them, for then the enemy can be attacked. Thus the army will attain full victory, and the enemy will be completely destroyed. In antiquity, when outstanding generals commanded armies, there was once a case where the commander was presented with a cask of sweet wine. The general had it poured into the river and shared the drinking of the wine with the officers and men as it flowed downstream. Now a cask of wine is unable to flavor a river of water, but the officers of the Three Armies were all motivated to fight to the death because the flavor and taste reached them personally.

The *Military Pronouncements* states: "When the army's wells have not yet been completed the general does not mention thirst. When the encampment has not yet been secured the general does not speak about fatigue. When the army's cook stoves have not yet been lit the general does not speak about hunger. In the winter he doesn't wear a fur robe; in the summer he doesn't use a fan; and in the rain he doesn't set up an umbrella." This is termed the proper form of behavior for a general.

He is with them in safety, he is united with them in danger. Thus his troops can be combined but cannot be forced apart. They can be employed but can not be tired out. With his beneficence he ceaselessly gathers them together, with his plans he constantly unites them. Thus it is said that when you cultivate beneficence tirelessly, with one you can take ten thousand.

Huang Shih-kung, 1

ESSENTIAL TALENTS AND CHARACTER TRAITS

Generals have five critical talents and ten excesses. What are referred to as the five talents are courage, wisdom, benevolence, trustworthiness, and loyalty. If he is courageous he cannot be overwhelmed. If he is wise he cannot be forced into turmoil. If he is benevolent he will love his men. If he is trustworthy he will not be deceitful. If he is loyal he won't be of two minds.

What are referred to as the ten errors are as follows: being courageous and treating death lightly; being hasty and impatient; being greedy and loving profit; being benevolent but unable to inflict suffering; being wise but afraid; being trustworthy and liking to trust others; being scrupulous and incorruptible but not loving men; being wise but indecisive; being resolute and self-reliant; and being fearful while liking to entrust responsibility to other men.

One who is courageous and treats death lightly can be destroyed by violence. One who is hasty and impatient can be destroyed by persistence. One who is greedy and loves profit can be bribed. One who is benevolent but unable to inflict suffering can be worn down. One who is wise but fearful can be distressed. One who is trustworthy and likes to trust others can be deceived. One who is scrupulous and incorruptible but doesn't love men can be insulted. One who is wise but indecisive can be suddenly attacked. One who is resolute and self-reliant can be confounded by events. One who is fearful and likes to entrust responsibility to others can be tricked. Thus, as Sun-tzu said, "Warfare is the greatest affair of state, the Tao of survival or extinction." The fate of the state lies in the hands of the general. The general is the support of the state, a man that the former kings all valued. Thus in commissioning a general you cannot but carefully evaluate and investigate his character.

Six Secret Teachings, 19

One who does not know how to plan for aggressive warfare cannot be spoken with about the enemy. One who cannot divide and move his troops about cannot be spoken with about unorthodox strategies. One who does not have a penetrating understanding of both order and chaos cannot be spoken with about changes.

Six Secret Teachings, 27

The general encompasses wisdom, credibility, benevolence, courage, and strictness.

The Art of War, 1

It is essential for a general to be tranquil and obscure, upright and self-disciplined, and able to stupefy the eyes and ears of the officers and troops, keeping them ignorant. He alters his management of affairs and changes his strategies to keep other people from recognizing them. He shifts his position and traverses indirect routes to keep other people from being able to anticipate him.

The Art of War, 11

Now the commanding general of the Three Armies should combine both military and civilian abilities. The employment of soldiers requires uniting both hardness and softness. In general, when people discuss generalship they usually focus on courage. However, courage is but one of a general's many characteristics, for the courageous will rashly join battle with the enemy. To rashly join battle with an enemy without knowing the advantages and disadvantages is not acceptable. Now the affairs which the general must pay careful attention to are five: First, regulation. Second, preparation. Third, commitment. Fourth, caution. And Fifth, simplification. Regulation is governing the masses just as one controls a few. Preparation is going out the city gate as if seeing the enemy. Commitment means entering combat without any concern for life. Caution means that even after conquering one maintains the same control and attitude as if just entering a battle. Simplification means the laws and orders are kept to a minimum, and are not abrasive.

To accept the mandate of command without ever declining, destroy the enemy, and only afterward speak about returning is the proper form of behavior for a general. Thus when the army goes forth his only thought should be of the glory that death will bring, not the shame of living.

Wu-tzu, 4

When someone whose wisdom is inadequate commands the army it is conceit. When someone whose courage is inadequate commands the army it is bravado. When someone does not know the Tao nor has engaged in a sufficient number of battles commands the army it becomes a matter of luck.

To ensure the security of a state of ten thousand chariots; to bring glory to the ruler of ten thousand chariots; and to preserve the lives of the people of a state of ten thousand chariots, only a general who knows the Tao is capable. Above he knows the Tao of Heaven; below he knows the patterns of Earth; within the state he has gained the hearts of the people; outside it he knows the enemy's true condition; and in deploying his forces he knows the principles for the eight formations. If he perceives victory he engages in battle; if he does not perceive it he remains quiet. This is the general of a true king.

Military Methods, 7

The crossbow is the general. When the crossbow is drawn, if the stock is not straight, or if one side of the bow is strong and one side weak and unbalanced, then in shooting the arrow the two arms will not be at one. Then even though the arrow's lightness and heaviness are correct, the front and rear are appropriate, it still will not hit the target.

Military Methods, 10

As for the commanding general: above he is not governed by Heaven, below he is not controlled by Earth, in the middle he is not governed by men. He should be composed so that he cannot be stimulated to anger. He should be pure so that he cannot be inveigled by wealth. Now if the mind is deranged by emotion, the eyes are blind, and the ears are deaf—to lead men with these three perversities is difficult!

Wei Liao-tzu, 2

Now the general is the fate of the state. If he is able to manage the army and attain victory the state will be secure and settled. The Military Pronouncements states: "The general should be able to be pure; able to be quiet; able to be tranquil; able to be controlled; able to accept criticism; able to judge disputes; able to attract and employ men; able to select and accept advice; able to know the customs of states; able to map mountains and rivers; able to discern defiles and difficulty; and able to control military authority."

Thus it is said that the wisdom of the benevolent and Worthy, the thoughts and plans of the Sages and illuminated, the words of the wood carriers, the discussions in court, and the affairs of ascension and decline, all of these are what the general should hear about.

Huang Shih-kung, 1

FLAWS AND WEAKNESSES

If the general is not benevolent, then the Three Armies will not be close to him. If the general is not courageous, then the Three Armies will not be fierce. If the general is not wise, then the Three Armies will be greatly perplexed. If the general is not perspicacious, then the Three Armies will be confounded. If the general is not quick-witted and acute, then the Three Armies will lose the moment. If the general is not constantly alert the Three Armies will waste their preparations. If the general is not strong and forceful, then the Three Armies will fail in their duty.

Thus the general is their Master of Fate. The Three Armies are ordered with him, and they are disordered with him. If one obtains a Worthy to serve as general the army will be strong and the state will prosper. If one doesn't obtain a Worthy as general, the army will be weak and the state will perish.

Six Secret Teachings, 27

Generals have five dangerous character traits: One committed to dying can be slain. One committed to living can be captured. One easily angered and hasty to act can be insulted. One obsessed with being scrupulous and untainted can be shamed. One who loves the people can be troubled.

Now these five dangerous traits are excesses in a general, potential disaster for employing the army. The army's destruction and the general's death will invariably stem from these five, so they must be investigated.

The Art of War, 8

There are six types of ill-fated armies: running off, lax, sinking, crumbling, chaotic, and routed. Now these six are not disasters brought about by Heaven and Earth but by the general's errors.

Now if, when their strategic power is equal, one attacks ten, this is called "running off."

If the troops are strong but the officers are weak, it is termed "lax." If the officers are strong but the troops weak, it is termed "sinking." If the higher officers are angry and insubordinate, engaging the enemy themselves out of unrestrained anger while the general does not yet know their capability, it is termed "crumbling."

If the general is weak and not strict, unenlightened in his instructions and leadership; the officers and troops lack constant duties; and their deployment of troops into formation is askew, it is termed "chaotic."

If the general, unable to fathom the enemy, engages a large number with a small number, attacks the strong with the weak while the army lacks a properly selected vanguard, it is termed "routed."

Now these six are the Tao of defeat. Any general who undertakes responsibility for command cannot but investigate them.

The Art of War, 10

In general the essentials of battle are as follows: you must first attempt to divine the enemy's general and evaluate his talent. In accord with the situation, exploit the strategic imbalance of power, then you will not labor but still achieve results. A commanding general who is stupid and trusting can be deceived and entrapped. One who is greedy and unconcerned about reputation can be given gifts and bribed. One who easily changes his mind and lacks real plans can be labored and distressed. If the upper ranks are wealthy and arrogant, while the lower ranks are poor and resentful, they can be separated and divided. If their advancing and withdrawing are often marked by doubt and the troops have no one to rely on, they can be shocked into running off. If the officers despise the commanding general and are intent on returning home, by blocking off the easy roads and leaving the treacherous ones open they can be attacked and captured. If the terrain over which they advance is easy, but the road for withdrawal difficult, they can be forced to come forward. If the way to advance is difficult, but the road for retreating easy, they can be pressed and attacked. If they encamp on low wetlands, where there is no way for the water to drain off, if heavy rain should fall several times they can be flooded and drowned. If they make camp in a wild marsh or fields dense with a heavy tangle of grass and stalks, should violent winds frequently arise you can burn the fields and destroy them. If they remain encamped for a long time, the generals and officers growing lax and lazy, the army becoming unprepared, you can sneak up and spring a surprise attack.

Wu-tzu, 4

Sun Pin, in discussing the characteristics of generals, said: "The first is called trust, the second loyalty, the third daring.

What loyalty? To the ruler. What trust? In rewards. What daring? To eliminate the bad. If someone is not loyal to the ruler, you cannot risk employing him in the army. One whose rewards are not trusted in the hundred surnames will not be regarded as Virtuous. One who does not dare eliminate the bad will not be respected by the hundred surnames."

Military Methods, 5

The general cannot but be righteous. If he is not righteous then he will not be severe. If he is not severe then he will not be awesome. If he is not awesome then the troops will not die for him. Thus righteousness is the head of the army.

The general cannot but be benevolent. If he is not benevolent then the army will not conquer. If the army does not conquer it will lack achievement. Thus benevolence is the belly of the army.

The general cannot be without Virtue. If he lacks Virtue then he will not have any strength. If he lacks strength the advantages of the Three Armies will not be realized. Thus Virtue is the hands of the army.

The general cannot be without credibility. If he is not trusted then his orders will not be implemented. If his orders are not implemented, then the army will not be unified. If the army is not unified then it will not attain fame. Thus credibility is the feet of the army.

The general cannot but know victory. If he does not know victory . . . the army will not be decisive. Thus decisiveness is the tail of the army.

Military Methods, 23

First, he is incapable but believes himself to be capable. Second, arrogance. Third, greedy for position. Fourth, greedy for wealth. Sixth, light. Seventh, obtuse. Eighth, has little courage. Ninth, courageous but weak. Tenth, has little credibility. Fourteenth, rarely decisive. Fifteenth, slow. Sixteenth, indolent. Seventeenth, oppressive. Eighteenth, brutal. Nineteenth, selfish. Twentieth, induces confusion. When the defects are numerous the losses will be many.

Military Methods, 25

If the general can think of his officers as if thirsty, his plans will be followed. But if the general stifles advice the valiant will depart. If plans are not followed the strategists will rebel. If good and evil are treated alike the meritorious officers will grow weary. If the general relies solely upon himself his subordinates will shirk all responsibility. If he brags his assistants will have few attainments. If he believes slander he will lose the hearts of the people. If he is greedy treachery will be unchecked. If he is preoccupied with women then the officers and troops will become licentious. If the general has a single one of these faults the masses will not submit. If he is marked by two of them the army will lack order. If by three of them his subordinates will abandon him. If by four the disaster will extend to the entire state!

Huang Shih-kung, 1

If the general doesn't carefully contemplate his course of action his strategists will abandon him. If the general isn't courageous the officers and troops will be terrified. If the general moves the army recklessly it will not be imposing. If he transfers his anger to the innocent the whole army will be afraid. As the *Military Pronouncements* states, "Contemplation and courage are what the general values; movement and anger are what the general employs." These four are the general's clear precepts.

Huang Shih-kung, 1

16
Military Organization, Administration, and Discipline

King Wu asked the T'ai Kung: "When the king commands the army he must have 'legs and arms' [top assistants] and 'feathers and wings' [aides] to bring about his awesomeness and spiritualness. How should this be done?"

The T'ai Kung said: "Whenever one mobilizes the army it takes the commanding general as its fate. Its fate lies in a penetrating understanding of all aspects, not in clinging to one technique. In accord with their abilities assign duties, each one taking charge of what they are good at, constantly changing and transforming with the times, to create the essential principles and order. Thus the general has seventy-two 'legs and arms' and 'feathers and wings' in order to respond to the Tao of Heaven. Prepare their number according to method, being careful that they know its orders and principles. When you have all the different abilities and various skills, then the myriad affairs will be complete."

Six Secret Teachings, 18

In general, as for the Tao of Warfare: rank and appoint men to office who understand the Tao and display righteousness. Establish companies and squads. Order the rows and files. Set the correct spacing between the horizontal and vertical. Investigate whether names and realities correspond.

Ssu-ma Fa, 4

In general, to command troops, make formations advantageous, and unify the mailed soldiers, establish offices as appropriate to the body. Implement orders with colored insignia; have the chariots carry pennants to distinguish the relationships of things; arrange the rows; organize the troops by hamlets and neighborhoods; confer leadership in accord with the towns and villages; settle doubts with flags and pennons; disseminate orders with gongs and drums; unify the soldiers with tight marching; and form them into close order, shoulder to shoulder.

Military Methods, 14

For five men there is a squad leader, for ten men a lieutenant, for a hundred men a company captain, for a thousand men a battalion commander, and for ten thousand men a general. This organization is already all-encompassing, already perfected. If a man dies in the morning another will replace him that morning; if a man dies in the evening, another will replace him that evening. The wise ruler weighs the tactical balance of power with the enemy, evaluates the generals, and only thereafter mobilizes the army.

Wei Liao-tzu, 5

Within the army the regulations for organization should be as follows: five men comprise a squad of five, with all the members being mutually responsible for each other. Ten men comprise a double squad of ten, with all the members being mutually responsible for each other. Fifty men compose a platoon, with all the members being mutually responsible for each other. A hundred men comprise a company, with all the members being mutually responsible for each other.

If a member of the squad of five violates an order or commits an offense, should the others report it their punishment will be remitted. If they know about it but do not report it, then the entire squad will be punished. If a member of the double squad of ten violates an order or commits an offense, should the others report it their punishment will be remitted. If they know about it but do not report it, then the entire double squad will be punished. If a member of a platoon violates an order or commits an offense, should the others report it their punishment will be remitted. If they know about it but do not report it, then the entire platoon will be punished. If a member of a company violates an order or commits an offense, should the others report it their punishment will be remitted. If they know about it but don't expose him, the entire company will be punished.

All the officers, from the level of the double squad of ten up to the generals of the right and left, superiors and inferiors, are mutually responsible for each other. If someone violates an order or commits an offense, those that report it will be spared from punishment, while those who know about it but do not report it will all share the same offense.

Now when the members of the squads of five and ten are mutually bonded, and the upper and lower ranks mutually linked, no perversity will remain undiscovered, no offense will remain unreported. Fathers will not be able to cover for their sons, older brothers will not be able to conceal their younger brothers. How much less so will the people of the state, living and eating together, be able to violate orders and conceal each other?

Wei Liao-tzu, 14

Generals have different flags, companies have different emblems. The Army of the Left wears their emblems on the left shoulder; the Army of the Right wears their emblems on the right shoulder; the Central Army wears their emblems on the front of the chest. Record their emblems, as "a certain armored soldier," and "a certain officer." From front to rear, for each platoon of five lines, the most honored emblems are placed on the head, the others accordingly lower and lower.

Wei Liao-tzu, 21

17
Evaluating People

King Wen asked: "How does one go about carefully selecting people using the 'six preservations' of benevolence, righteousness, loyalty, trust, courage, and planning?"

The T'ai Kung: "Make them rich and observe whether they do not commit offenses. Give them rank and observe whether they do not become arrogant. Entrust them with responsibility and see whether they won't change. Employ them and see whether they won't conceal anything. Endanger them and see whether they aren't afraid. Give them the management of affairs and see whether they aren't perplexed.

"If you make them rich but they do not commit offenses, they are benevolent. If you give them rank and they do not grow arrogant, they are righteous. If you entrust them with office and they do not change, they are loyal. If you employ them and they do not conceal anything, they are trustworthy. If you put them in danger and they are not afraid, they are courageous. If you give them the management of affairs and they are not perplexed, they are capable of making plans."

Six Secret Teachings, 6

The T'ai Kung said: "One who exercises kingship over the people recognizes 'seven harms.' First, men without knowledge or strategic planning ability are generously rewarded and honored with rank. Therefore the strong and courageous who regard war lightly take their chances in the field. The king must be careful not to employ them as generals.

"Second, they have reputation but lack substance. What they say is constantly shifting. They conceal the good and point out deficiencies. They view advancement and dismissal as a question of skill. The king should be careful not to make plans with them.

"Third, they make their appearance simple, wear ugly clothes, speak about actionless action in order to seek fame, and talk about non-desire in order to gain profit. They are artificial men, and the king should be careful not to bring them near.

"Fourth, they wear strange caps and belts, and their clothes are overflowing. They listen widely to the disputations of others and speak speciously about unrealistic ideas, displaying them as a sort of personal adornment. They dwell in poverty and live in tranquility, deprecating the customs of the world. They are cunning people, and the king should be careful not to favor them.

"Fifth, with slander, obsequiousness, and pandering they seek office and rank. They are courageous and daring, treating death lightly, out of their greed for salary and position. They are not concerned with major affairs, but move solely out of avarice. With lofty talk and specious discussions they please the ruler. The king should be careful not to employ them.

"Sixth, they have buildings elaborately carved and inlaid. They promote artifice and flowery adornment to the injury of agriculture. You must prohibit them.

"Seventh, they create magical formulas and weird techniques, practice sorcery and witchcraft, advance unorthodox ways, and circulate inauspicious sayings, confusing and befuddling the good people. The king must stop them.

"Now when the people do not exhaust their strength they are not our people. If the officers are not sincere and trustworthy, they are not our officers. If the ministers do not offer loyal remonstrance, they are not our ministers. If the officials are not even-handed, pure, and love the people, they are not our officials. If the chancellor can not enrich the state and strengthen the army, harmonize yin and yang, and ensure security for the ruler of the state of ten thousand chariots—and moreover properly control the ministers, set names and realities, make clear rewards and punishments, and give pleasure to the people—he is not our chancellor."

Six Secret Teachings, 9

King Wu asked the T'ai Kung: "If a king wants to raise an army, how should he go about selecting and training heroic officers, and determining their moral qualifications?"

The T'ai Kung said: "There are fifteen cases where a knight's external appearance and internal character do not cohere. These are: He appears to be a Worthy, but actually is immoral. He seems warm and conscientious, but is a thief. His countenance is reverent and respectful, but his heart is insolent. Externally he is incorruptible and circumspect, but he lacks respect. He appears perceptive and sharp, but lacks such talent. He appears profound, but lacks all sincerity. He appears adept at planning, but is indecisive. He appears to be decisive and daring, but is incapable. He appears guileless, but is not trustworthy. He appears confused and disoriented, but on the contrary is loyal and substantial. He appears to engage in specious discourse, but is a man of merit and achievement. He appears courageous, but is afraid. He seems severe and remote, but on the contrary easily befriends men. He appears forbidding, but on the contrary is quiet and sincere. He appears weak and insubstantial, yet when dispatched outside the state there is nothing he does not accomplish, no mission that he does not execute successfully.

"Those whom the world disdains the Sage values. Ordinary men do not know these things, only great wisdom can discern the edge of these matters. This is because the knight's external appearance and internal character do not visibly cohere."

King Wu asked: "How does one know this?"

The T'ai Kung replied: "There are eight forms of evidence by which you may know it. First, question them and observe the details of their reply. Second, verbally confound and perplex them and observe how they change. Third, discuss things that you have secretly learned to observe their sincerity. Fourth, clearly and explicitly question them to observe their virtue. Fifth, appoint them to positions of financial responsibility to observe their honesty. Sixth, test them with beautiful women to observe their uprightness. Seventh, confront them with difficulties to observe their courage. Eighth, get them drunk to observe their deportment. When all eight have been fully explored, then the Worthy and unworthy can be distinguished."

Six Secret Teachings, 20

The ruler of a strong state must evaluate his people. Among the people those who have courage and strength should be assembled into one unit. Those who take pleasure in advancing into battle and exerting their strength to manifest their loyalty and courage should be assembled into another unit. Those who can climb high and traverse far, who are nimble and fleet, should be assembled into a unit. Officials of the king who have lost their positions and want to show their merit to their ruler should be assembled into a unit. Those who abandoned their cities or left their defensive positions and want to eradicate the disgrace should also be assembled into a unit. These five will constitute the army's disciplined, elite troops. With three thousand such men, from within one can strike out and break any encirclement, or from without break into any city and slaughter the defenders.

Wu-tzu, 1

18
Employing People

The Tao for employing the military and affecting the people is authority and the steelyard. Authority and the steelyard are the means by which to select the Worthy and choose the good. Yin and yang are the means by which to assemble the masses and engage the enemy. First you must correct the balance, then the weights, and then they will have already attained the standard. This is referred to as being inexhaustible. Evaluate talent and performance by weighing them with the standard, solely to determine what is appropriate.

Military Methods, 11

Employ the wise, courageous, greedy, and stupid. The wise take pleasure in establishing their achievements. The courageous love to put their will into effect. The greedy fervently pursue profits. The stupid have little regard for death. Employ them through their emotions, for this is the military's subtle exercise of authority.

Huang Shih-kung, 2

Do not allow your disputatious officers to discuss the enemy's good points because they may delude the masses. Do not allow the benevolent to control the finances, for they will dispense too much and become attached to the lower ranks.

Huang Shih-kung, 2

19

Motivating Warriors

King Wu asked the T'ai Kung: "When we attack I want the masses of the Three Armies to contend with each other to scale the wall first, and compete with each other to be in the forefront when we fight in the field. When they hear the sound of the gongs to retreat they will be angry, and when they hear the sound of the drums to advance they will be happy. How can we accomplish this?"

The T'ai Kung said: "A general has three techniques for attaining victory."

King Wu asked: "May I ask what they are?"

The T'ai Kung: "If in winter the general does not wear a fur robe, in summer does not carry a fan, and in the rain does not set up a canopy, he is called a 'general of proper form.' Unless the general himself submits to these observances he will not have the means to know the cold and warmth of the officers and soldiers.

"If, when they advance into ravines and obstacles, or encounter muddy terrain, the general always takes the first steps he is termed a 'general of strength.' If the general does not personally exert his strength he has no means to know the labors and hardships of the officers and soldiers.

"If only after the men are settled in their encampment does the general retire; only after all the cooks have finished their cooking does he go in to eat; and if the army does not light fires to keep warm he also does not have one, he is termed a 'general who stifles desire.' Unless the general himself practices stifling his desires, he has no way to know the hunger and satiety of the officers and troops.

"The general shares heat and cold, labor and suffering, hunger and satiety with the officers and men. Therefore when the masses of the Three Armies hear the sound of the drum they are happy, and when they hear the sound of the gong they are angry. When attacking a high wall or crossing a deep lake, under a hail of arrows and stones, the officers will compete to be first to scale the wall. When the naked blades clash the officers will compete to be the first to go forward. It's not because they like death and take pleasure in being wounded, but because the general knows their feelings of heat and cold, hunger and satiety, and clearly displays his knowledge of their labor and suffering."

Six Secret Teachings, 23

Warfare that is invariably in accord with righteousness is the means by which to incite the masses and be victorious over the enemy.

Six Secret Teachings, 27

Whenever affairs are well executed they will endure; when they accord with ancient ways they can be effected. When the oath is clear the men will be strong, and you will extinguish the effects of baleful omens and auspicious signs.

The Tao for eliminating baleful omens is as follows. One is called righteousness. Charge the people with good faith, approach them with strength, establish the foundation of kingly government, and unify the strategic power of All under Heaven. There will not be any men who are not pleased, so this is termed "doubly employing the people."

Ssu-ma Fa, 3

In general, if in warfare you are victorious, share the achievement and praise with the troops. If you are about to reengage in battle then make their rewards exceptionally generous and the punishments heavier. If you failed to direct them to victory accept the blame yourself. If you must fight again, swear an oath and assume a forward position. Do not repeat your previous tactics. Whether you win or not, do not deviate from this method, for it is referred to as the "True Principle."

Ssu-ma Fa, 4

In antiquity those who planned government affairs would invariably first instruct the hundred surnames and gain the affection of the common people.

There are four disharmonies. If there is disharmony in the state you cannot put the army into the field. If there is disharmony within the army, you cannot deploy into formations. If you lack harmony within the formations, you cannot advance into battle. If you lack cohesion during the conduct of the battle, you cannot score a decisive victory.

For this reason when a ruler who has comprehended the Tao is about to employ his people he will first bring them into harmony, and only thereafter embark on great affairs. He will not dare rely solely upon his own plans, but will certainly announce them formally in the ancestral temple, divine their prospects by the great tortoiseshell, and seek their confirmation in the Heavens and seasons. Only if they are all auspicious will he proceed to mobilize the army.

Because the people know the ruler values their lives and is sorrowed by their deaths, when such circumstances arise and they must confront danger with him, the officers will consider death while advancing glorious, but life gained through retreating disgraceful.

Wu-tzu, 1

In general, to govern the state and order the army you must instruct them with the forms of propriety, stimulate them with righteousness, and cause them to have a sense of shame. For when men have a sense of shame, in the greatest degree it will be sufficient to wage war, while in the least degree it will suffice to preserve the state.

Wu-tzu, 1

If you treat them deferentially, then the officers will die for you; the officers will die, but their names will be transmitted. If you encourage them with fundamental pleasures, they will die for their native places. If you importune them with family relationships, they will die for the ancestral graves. If you honor them with feasts, they will die for food and drink. If you have them dwell in tranquility, they will die in the urgency of defense. If you inquire about their febrile diseases, they will die for your solicitude.

Military Methods, 12

In order to stimulate the soldiers, the people's material welfare cannot but be ample. The ranks of nobility, the degree of relationship in death and mourning, the activities by which the people live, cannot but be made evident. One must govern the people in accord with their means to life, and make distinctions clear in accord with the people's activities. The fruits of the field and their salaries, the feasting of relatives through the rites of eating and drinking, the mutual encouragement in the village ceremonies, mutual assistance in death and the rites of mourning, sending off and greeting the troops—these are what stimulate the people.

Wei Liao-tzu, 4

Now the essence of employing the army lies in respecting the forms of propriety and making salaries generous. When the proper forms of propriety are followed wise officers will be attracted. When salaries are generous righteous officers will regard death lightly. Thus if when granting salaries to the Worthy you do not begrudge the expense, and when rewarding the able are not dilatory, then the strength of your subordinates will be united, while your enemy's state will be reduced as the capable abandon him.

The Way to employ men is to honor them with rank and supply them generously with material goods, for then the officers will come of their own accord. Welcome them according to the forms of propriety, stimulate them with righteousness, and then the officers will die for the state.

Huang Shih-kung, 1

Pure, incorruptible officers cannot be enticed with rank and salary. Self-constrained, righteous officers cannot be coerced with awesomeness or punishment. Thus when the enlightened ruler seeks the Worthy he must observe what will attract them. To attract pure, incorruptible officers he perfects his observance of the forms of propriety. To attract self-constrained, righteous officers he perfects himself in the Tao. Only thereafter will they be attracted and the ruler's reputation preserved.

The Sage and Perfected Man perceive the sources of flourishing and decline, understand the beginnings of success and defeat, have attained true knowledge of the crux of governing and turbulence, and know the measure of coming and going. Such men, even if in poverty, will not hold a position in a doomed state. Though lowly they will not eat the rice of a turbulent country. They conceal their names and cling to the Tao. When the proper time comes they move, reaching the pinnacle which a subject can attain. When they encounter Virtue that accords with them they will establish extraordinary achievements. Thus their Tao is lofty, and their names will be praised in later generations.

Huang Shih-kung, 3

To welcome Worthies a thousand miles away the road is far; to bring in the unworthy the road is quite near. For this reason the enlightened ruler abandons the near and takes the distant. Therefore he is able to complete his achievements. He honors worthy men, and his subordinates all exhaust their energies.

If you dismiss one good man, then a myriad good acts will decline. If you reward one evil man, then a myriad evils will be drawn to you. When the good are rewarded and the evil suffer punishment, the state will be secure and the multitudes of good people will come.

Huang Shih-kung, 3

20
Psychology of Warfare

As for the Tao of warfare: After you have aroused the people's *ch'i* (spirit), and moreover enacted administrative measures, encompass them with a benign countenance, and lead them with your speeches. Upbraid them in accord with their fears, assign affairs in accord with their desires. When you have crossed the enemy's borders and taken control of his territory, appoint people to the tasks of government. These are termed "methods of war."

Ssu-ma Fa, 3

In general, in warfare act in accord with whether the troops have the spirit to be victorious or not. Accord with Heaven, accord with men.

Ssu-ma Fa, 4

In general, when the horses and chariots are sturdy, the armor and weapons advantageous, then even a light force can penetrate deeply. If you esteem equality, then no one will strive for great results. If you value taking charge, then many will die for the cause. If you value life, then there will be many doubts; if you honor death itself, then they will not be victorious.

In general, men will die for love, out of anger, out of fear of awesomeness, for righteousness, and for profit. In general it is the Tao of warfare that when they are well instructed, men will regard death lightly. When they are constrained by the Tao, they will die for the upright.

Ssu-ma Fa, 4

When men have minds set on victory, all they see is the enemy. When men have minds filled with fear, all they see is their fear. When these two minds intersect and determine action, it is essential that the advantages as perceived by each are as one. It is the commander's duty to create this unification. Only from the perspective of authority can it be seen.

Ssu-ma Fa, 4

In general, in battle one endures through strength and gains victory through spirit. One can endure with a solid defense, but will achieve victory through being endangered. When the heart's foundation is solid, a new surge of *ch'i* (spirit) will bring victory. With armor one is secure; with weapons one attains victory.

Ssu-ma Fa, 4

Writing letters of final farewell is referred to as "breaking off all thoughts of life." Selecting the elite and ranking the weapons is termed "increasing the strength of the men." Casting aside the implements of office and carrying only minimal rations is termed "opening the men's thoughts." From antiquity this has been the rule.

Ssu-ma Fa, 5

Thus what motivates men to slay the enemy is anger; what stimulates them to seize profits from the enemy is material goods. Thus in chariot encounters, when ten or more chariots are captured, reward the first to get one. Change their flags and pennants to ours; intermix and employ them with our own chariots. Treat the captured soldiers well in order to nurture them for our use. This is referred to as "conquering the enemy and growing stronger."

The Art of War, 2

The *ch'i* of the Three Armies can be snatched away; the commanding general's mind can be seized. For this reason in the morning their *ch'i* is ardent; during the day their *ch'i* becomes indolent; at dusk their *ch'i* is exhausted. Thus one who excels at employing the army avoids their ardent *ch'i* and strikes when it is indolent or exhausted. This is the way to manipulate *ch'i*.

The Art of War, 7

Cast them into positions from which there is nowhere to go and they will die without retreating. If there is no escape from death, the officers and soldiers will fully exhaust their strength.

When the soldiers and officers have penetrated deeply into enemy territory, they will cling together. When there is no alternative, they will fight.

For this reason even though the soldiers are not instructed, they are prepared; without seeking it, their cooperation is obtained; without covenants they are close together; without issuing orders they are reliable. Prohibit omens, eliminate doubt so that they will die without other thoughts. Thus it is the nature of the army to defend when encircled; to fight fervently when unavoidable; and to follow orders when compelled by circumstances.

The Art of War, 11

In general, the Tao of the invader is this: When the troops have penetrated deeply, they will be unified, but where only shallowly, they will be inclined to scatter. For this reason on dispersive terrain I unify their will. When the army has left the state, crossed the enemy's border, and is on campaign, it is "isolated terrain." When the four sides are open, this is "focal terrain." On focal terrain I solidify our alliances. When you have advanced deeply, it is "heavy terrain." On heavy terrain I ensure a continuous supply of provisions. If you have penetrated only shallowly, it is "light terrain." On light terrain I have them group together. If you have strongholds behind you and constrictions before you, it is "encircled terrain." On encircled terrain I obstruct any openings. If there is no place to go, it is "fatal terrain." On fatal terrain I show them that we will not live.

Cast them into hopeless situations and they will be preserved; have them penetrate fatal terrain and they will live. Only after the masses have penetrated dangerous terrain will they be able to craft victory out of defeat.

The Art of War, 11

I have heard that men have strengths and weaknesses, that their *ch'i* (spirit) flourishes and ebbs. Now if there is a murderous villain hidden in the woods, even though a thousand men pursue him they all look around like owls, and glance about like wolves. Why? They are afraid that violence will erupt and harm them personally. Thus one man oblivious to life and death can frighten a thousand.

Wu-tzu, 6

When you form the army and assemble the masses, concentrate upon stimulating their *ch'i* (spirit). When you again decamp and reassemble the army, concentrate upon ordering the soldiers and sharpening their *ch'i.* When you approach the border and draw near the enemy, concentrate upon honing their *ch'i.* When the day for battle has been set, concentrate upon making their *ch'i* decisive. When the day for battle is at hand, concentrate upon expanding their *ch'i.*

Military Methods, 13

If a warrior wields a sword to strike people in the marketplace, among ten thousand people there will not be anyone who doesn't avoid him. If I say it's not that only one man is courageous, but that the ten thousand are unlike him, what is the reason? Being committed to dying and being committed to seeking life are not comparable. If you listen to my techniques, you will find they are sufficient to cause the masses of the Three Armies to become a brigand committed to dying. No one will stand before them, no one will follow them. They will be able to come and go alone, being the army of a king or hegemon.

Wei Liao-tzu, 3

Now the means by which the general fights is the people; the means by which the people fight is their *ch'i* (spirit). When their *ch'i* is substantial they will fight; when their *ch'i* has been snatched away they will run off.

Wei Liao-tzu, 4

Ensure that the members of the squads of five and ten are like relatives, the members of the companies and their officers like friends. When they stop they will be like a solid encircling wall, when they move like the wind and rain. The chariots will not wheel to the rear, the soldiers will not turn about. This is the Way to establish the foundation for combat.

Wei Liao-tzu, 4

One who occupies ravines lacks the mind to do battle. One who lightly provokes a battle lacks fullness of *ch'i* (spirit). One who is belligerent in battle lacks soldiers capable of victory.

Wei Liao-tzu, 5

Now, in general, one who presumes upon righteousness to engage in warfare values initiating the conflict. One who contends out of personal animosity responds only when it is unavoidable. Even though hatreds have formed and troops have been mobilized, await them and value acting after them. During the conflict you must await their advance. When there is a lull you must prepare against sudden attacks.

Wei Liao-tzu, 5

Soldiers have five defining commitments: for their general, they forget their families; when they cross the border, they forget their relatives; when they confront the enemy, they forget themselves; when they are committed to die, they will live; while urgently seeking victory is the lowest. A hundred men willing to suffer the pain of a blade can penetrate a line and cause chaos in a formation. A thousand men willing to suffer the pain of a blade can seize the enemy and kill its general. Ten thousand men willing to suffer the pain of a blade can traverse under Heaven at will.

Wei Liao-tzu, 22

One whose troops fear their general far more than the enemy will be victorious. One whose troops fear the enemy far more than their general will be defeated. Thus to know who will be victorious, who defeated, weigh your general with the enemy. The enemy and your general are like a steelyard and balance. If the general is settled and quiet, the troops are well ordered; if he is brutal and hasty, they are in chaos.

Wei Liao-tzu, 23

The T'ai-tsung said: "Sun-tzu spoke about strategies by which the *ch'i* (spirit) of the Three Armies may be snatched away: 'In the morning their *ch'i* is ardent; during the day their *ch'i* becomes indolent; and at dusk their *ch'i* is exhausted. One who excels at employing the army avoids their ardent *ch'i* and strikes when it is indolent or exhausted.' How is this?"

Li Ching said: "Whoever has life and a natural endowment of blood, if they die without a second thought when the drums are sounded to do battle, it is the *ch'i* which causes it to be so. Thus methods for employing the army require first investigating our own officers and troops, stimulating our *ch'i* for victory, and only then attacking the enemy. Among Wu Ch'i's four vital points, the vital point of *ch'i* is foremost. There is no other Tao. If one can cause his men themselves to want to fight, then no one will be able to oppose their ardor. What Sun-tzu meant by the *ch'i* being ardent in the morning is not limited to those hours alone. He used the beginning and end of the day as an analogy. In general, if the drum has been sounded three times but the enemy's *ch'i* has neither declined nor become depleted, then how can you cause it to invariably become indolent or exhausted? Probably those who study the text merely recite the empty words, and are misled by the enemy. If one could enlighten them with the principles for snatching away the *ch'i*, the army could be entrusted to them."

Questions and Replies, 3

21
Rewards and Punishments

GENERAL PRINCIPLES

In general, in employing rewards one values credibility; in employing punishments one values certainty. When rewards are trusted and punishments inevitable wherever the eye sees and the ear hears, then even where they do not see or hear there is no one who will not be transformed in their secrecy. Since the ruler's sincerity extends to Heaven and Earth, and penetrates to the spirits, how much the more so to men?

Six Secret Teachings, 11

The general creates awesomeness by executing the great, and becomes enlightened by rewarding the small. Prohibitions are made effective and laws implemented by careful scrutiny in the use of punishments. Therefore if by executing one man the entire army will quake, kill him. If by rewarding one man the masses will be pleased, reward him. In executing, value the great; in rewarding, value the small. When you kill the powerful and the honored, this is punishment that reaches the pinnacle. When rewards extend down to the cowherds, grooms, and stablemen, these are rewards penetrating downward to the lowest. When punishments reach the pinnacle, and rewards penetrate to the lowest, then your awesomeness has been effected.

Six Secret Teachings, 22

In antiquity the Worthy Kings made manifest the Virtue of the people, and fully sought out the goodness of the people. Thus they did not neglect the virtuous nor demean the people in any respect. Rewards were not granted, and punishments never even tried. Shun neither granted rewards nor imposed punishments, but the people could still be employed. This was the height of Virtue. The Hsia granted rewards but did not impose punishments. This was the height of instruction. The Shang imposed punishments but didn't grant rewards. This was the height of awesomeness. The Chou used both rewards and punishments, and Virtue declined.

The Hsia bestowed rewards in court in order to make eminent the good. The Shang carried out executions in the marketplace to overawe the evil. The Chou granted rewards in court and carried out executions in the marketplace to encourage gentlemen and terrify the common man. Hence the kings of all three dynasties manifested Virtue in the same way.

Ssu-ma Fa, 2

Rewards should not be delayed beyond the appropriate time, for you want the people to quickly profit from doing good. When you punish someone do not change his position, for you want the people to quickly see the harm of doing what is not good.

Ssu-ma Fa, 2

Now the different drums, gongs, and bells are the means to awe the ear; flags and banners, pennants and standards the means to awe the eye; and prohibitions, orders, punishments, and fines the means to awe the mind. When the ear has been awestruck by sound it cannot but be clear. When the eye has been awestruck by color it cannot but be discriminating. When the mind has been awestruck by penalties, it cannot but be strict. If these three are not established, even though you have the support of the state you will invariably be defeated by the enemy. Thus it is said that wherever the general's banners are everyone will go, and wherever the general points everyone will move forward, even unto death.

Wu-tzu, 4

T'ien Chi said: "Are not rewards and punishments the most urgent matters for the military?"

Sun Pin said: "They are not. Now rewards are the means by which to give happiness to the masses and cause soldiers to forget death. Punishments are the means by which to rectify the chaotic and cause the people to fear their superiors. They can be employed to facilitate victory, but they are not urgent matters."

Military Methods, 3

When the bestowing of rewards does not extend past the day; the imposition of punishments is as quick as turning the face; and they are not affected by the man nor subject to external threats, this is the general of the army's Virtue.

Military Methods, 24

One who engages in battle but does not invariably win cannot be said to "do battle." One who attacks an enemy but does not invariably seize them cannot be said to have "attacked." If it were otherwise, their punishments and rewards were not sufficiently trusted. Credibility must be established before the moment of need; affairs must be managed before the first signs appear. Thus the masses, when once assembled, should not be fruitlessly dispersed. When the army goes forth it should not return empty-handed. They will seek the enemy as if searching for a lost son; they will attack the enemy as if rescuing a drowning man.

Wei Liao-tzu, 5

Victory in war lies in establishing awesomeness. Establishing awesomeness lies in uniting strength. Uniting strength lies in rectifying punishments. By rectifying punishments rewards are illuminated.

Wei Liao-tzu, 21

The *Military Pronouncements* states: "The army employs rewards as its external form, and punishments as its internal substance." When rewards and punishments are clear then the general's awesomeness is effected. When the proper officials are obtained then the officers and troops are obedient. When those entrusted with responsibility are Worthies, enemy states will be fearful.

Huang Shih-kung, 1

THE NATURE OF REWARDS

Honored ranks and generous rewards are the means by which to encourage obeying orders.

Six Secret Teachings, 27

Do not reward great victories, for then neither the upper nor lower ranks will boast of their achievements. If the upper ranks cannot boast they will not seem arrogant, while if the lower ranks cannot boast no distinctions will be established among the men. When neither of them boasts this is the pinnacle of deference.

Ssu-ma Fa, 2

T'ien Chi said: "When their deployment has already been determined, how can we cause the soldiers to invariably obey?"

Sun Pin said: "Be severe and show them the profits of their rewards."

Military Methods, 3

When material goods are plentiful there will be contention; when there is contention the people will not regard their superiors as Virtuous. When goods are few they will incline toward their superiors; when they incline toward them, then All under Heaven will respect them. If what the people seek is the means by which I seek their performance, this will be the basis for the military's endurance. In employing the army this is the state's treasure.

Military Methods, 11

When rewards are like the sun and moon, credibility is like the four seasons, orders are like the *fu* and *yüeh* axes, and regulations are as sharp as the famous sword Kan-chiang, I've never heard of officers and troops not following orders!

Wei Liao-tzu, 24

THE NATURE OF PUNISHMENTS

Now the Tao of the king is like that of a dragon's head. He dwells in the heights and looks out far. He sees deeply and listens carefully. He displays his form, but conceals his nature. He is like the heights of Heaven, which cannot be perceived. He is like the depths of an abyss that cannot be fathomed. Thus if he should get angry but does not, evil subordinates will arise. If he should execute but does not, great thieves will appear. If strategic military power is not exercised, enemy states will grow strong.

Six Secret Teachings, 9

Severe punishments and heavy fines are the means by which to force the weary and indolent to advance.

Six Secret Teachings, 27

In cases of great defeat do not punish anyone, for then both the upper and lower ranks will assume the disgrace falls upon them. If the upper ranks reproach themselves they will certainly regret their errors, while if the lower ranks feel the same they will certainly try to avoid repeating the offense. When the ranks all divide the responsibility for the detestable, this is the pinnacle of yielding.

Ssu-ma Fa, 2

In general, to wage war: solidify the people; analyze the advantages of terrain; impose order on the turbulent; regulate advancing and stopping; accept upright remonstrance; nourish a sense of shame; constrain the laws; and investigate punishments. Minor offenders should then be executed. If minor offenders are executed, how can major offenses arise?

Ssu-ma Fa, 3

Seize and summarily execute any deserters to stop the others from looking about to desert. Shout in order to lead them. If they are too terrified of the enemy do not threaten them with execution and severe punishments, but display a magnanimous countenance. Speak to them about what they have to live for, supervise them in their duties.

Ssu-ma Fa, 4

If you impose punishments on the troops before they have become attached, they will not be submissive. If they are not submissive, they will be difficult to employ. If you do not impose punishments after the troops have become attached, they cannot be used. Thus if you command them with the civil and unify them through the martial, this is what is referred to as "being certain to gain them."

The Art of War, 9

When the general regards his troops as young children, they will advance into the deepest valleys with him. When he regards the troops as his beloved children, they will be willing to die with him. However, if they are well treated but cannot be employed, if they are loved but cannot be commanded, or when in chaos they cannot be governed, they may be compared to arrogant children and cannot be used.

The Art of War, 10

Marquis Wu asked: "If the chariots are sturdy, the horses excellent, the generals courageous, and the soldiers strong, but when you suddenly encounter the enemy they are thrown into turmoil and break formation, what can be done?"

Wu Ch'i replied: "In general, it is a rule of battle that during daylight hours the flags, banners, pennants, and standards provide the measure, while at night the gongs, drums, pipes, and whistles provide the constraints. When 'left' is signaled they should go left; when 'right,' then right. When the drum is beaten they should advance, when the gongs sound they should halt. At the first blowing they should form ranks; at the second assemble together. Execute anyone who does not follow the orders. When the Three Armies submit to your awesomeness, and the officers and soldiers obey commands, then in combat no enemy will be stronger than you, nor will any defenses remain impenetrable to your attack."

Wu-tzu, 5

If you flog a person's back, brand his ribs, or compress his fingers in order to question him about the nature of his offense, even a state hero could not withstand this cruelty, and would falsely implicate himself.

Wei Liao-tzu, 9

If you cause the people to fear heavy punishments within the state, then outside the state they will regard the enemy lightly. Thus the Former Kings made the regulations and measures clear before making their awesomeness and punishments heavy. When punishments are heavy then they will fear them within the state. When they fear them within the state, then they will be stalwart outside it.

Wei Liao-tzu, 13

22

Instruction and Training

Only after effective instructions have been provided to the people can the state carefully select and employ them. Only after government affairs have been thoroughly ordered can the hundred offices be sufficiently provided. When instructions are thoroughly examined the people will manifest goodness. When practice becomes habit the people will embody the customs. This is the pinnacle of transformation through education.

Ssu-ma Fa, 2

All human qualities must be sought among the masses. Test and evaluate them in terms of name and action to see if they cohere, for they must excel at implementation. If they are to perform some action but do not, then you yourself should lead them. If they are to perform some action and do so, then ensure that they do not forget it. If you test them three times successfully then make their talents evident. What is appropriate to human life is termed the law.

Ssu-ma Fa, 3

In general, in warfare: it is not forming a battle array that is difficult, it is reaching the point that the men can be ordered into formation that is hard. It is not attaining the ability to order them into formation that is difficult, it is reaching the point of being able to employ them that is hard. It is not knowing what to do that is difficult, it is putting it into effect that is hard. Men from each of the four quarters have their own nature. Character differs from region to region. Through teaching they come to have regional habits, the customs of each state thus being different. Only through the Tao are their customs transformed.

Ssu-ma Fa, 4

Now men constantly perish from their inabilities, and are defeated by the unfamiliar. Thus among the methods for using the military, training and causing them to be alert are first. One man who has been trained in warfare can instruct ten men. Ten men who have studied warfare can train a hundred men. And a hundred such men can train a thousand. A thousand, ten thousand; and ten thousand who have been trained in warfare can train the entire body of the Three Armies.

Wu-tzu, 3

Zealous training and whirlwind alacrity are the means by which to counter piercing thrusts.

Military Methods, 14

Today, if the people turn their backs to the border gates and decide the issue of life and death, if they have been taught to die without hesitation, there is a reason. Training and instructions have caused the defenders to inevitably be solid; those engaged in battle to inevitably fight; perverse plans not to be put into action; perverse people not to speak; orders to be effected without any changes; the army to advance without doubt; and the light units to be like a clap of thunder, to rush at the enemy like the terrified. Raise those of merit, distinguish those of virtue, making their distinction as clear as black and white. Cause the people to follow the orders of their superiors just as the four limbs respond to the mind.

If the forward units break up the enemy's ranks, throw their formation into chaos, and crush their hardness like water bursting through, there is a basis for it. This is termed the Army's Instructions. They provide the means to open sealed borders, preserve the altars of state, eliminate disaster and harm, and complete Martial Virtue.

Wei Liao-tzu, 21

Part Four

TACTICAL ESSENTIALS

23
Measure and Constraint

A campaign army takes measure as its prime concern so that the people's strength will be adequate. Then, even when the blades clash, the infantry will not run and the chariots will not gallop. When pursuing a fleeing enemy the troops will not break formation, thereby avoiding chaos. The solidarity of a campaign army derives from military discipline that maintains order in formation, does not exhaust the strength of men or horses, and whether moving slowly or rapidly, does not exceed the measure of the commands.

Ssu-ma Fa, 2

In general, in warfare: the Three Armies should not be on the alert for more than three days; a single company should not be vigilant more than half a day; while the guard duty for a single soldier should not exceed one rest period.

Ssu-ma Fa, 4

When halting be careful about the weapons and armor. When on the march be cautious about the rows and files. When in battle be careful about advancing and stopping.

Ssu-ma Fa, 4

In general, as for warfare: If you move first it will be easy to become exhausted. If you move after the enemy, the men may become afraid. If you rest, the men may become lax; if you do not rest, they also may become exhausted. Yet if you rest very long, on the contrary, they also may become afraid.

Ssu-ma Fa, 5

In general, as for warfare: after deploying observe their actions. Watch the enemy and then initiate movement. If they are waiting, then act accordingly. Do not drum the advance, but await the moment when their masses arise. If they attack, entrench your forces and observe them.

Ssu-ma Fa, 5

In order, await the disordered; in tranquility, await the clamorous. This is the way to control the mind. With the near, await the distant; with the rested, await the fatigued; with the sated, await the hungry. This is the way to control strength. Do not intercept well-ordered flags; do not attack well-regulated formations. This is the way to control changes.

The Art of War, 7

If one forages in the fertile countryside, then the Three Armies will have enough to eat. If you carefully nurture them and do not overlabor them, their *ch'i* (spirit) will be united and their strength will be at maximum.

The Art of War, 11

In general the Tao for commanding an army on the march is to not contravene the proper measure of advancing and stopping; not miss the appropriate times for eating and drinking; and not completely exhaust the strength of the men and horses. These three are the means by which the troops can undertake the orders of their superiors. When the orders of superiors are followed, control is produced. If advancing and resting are not measured; if drinking and eating are not timely and appropriate; and if, when the horses are tired and the men weary, they are not allowed to relax in the encampment, then they will be unable to put the commander's orders into effect. When the commander's orders are thus disobeyed, when encamped they will be in turmoil, and in battle they will be defeated.

Wu-tzu, 3

The T'ai-tsung said: "What did Sun-tzu say about governing strength?"

Li Ching said: "'With the near await the distant; with the rested await the fatigued; with the sated await the hungry.' This covers the main points. One who excels at employing the army extends these three into six: 'With enticements, await their coming. In quiescence, await the impetuous. With the heavy, await the light. With the strictly disciplined, await the inattentive. With order, await the turbulent. With defense, await attacks.' When conditions are contrary to these, your strength will be insufficient. Without techniques to govern the expenditure of force, how can one direct the army?"

Questions and Replies, 2

24

Component Forces

Chariots are the feathers and wings of the army, the means to penetrate solid formations, to press strong enemies, and to cut off their flight. Cavalry are the army's fleet observers, the means to pursue a defeated army, to sever supply lines, to strike roving forces.

Now chariots and cavalry are the army's martial weapons. Ten chariots can defeat a thousand men; a hundred chariots can defeat ten thousand men. Ten cavalrymen can drive off a hundred men, and a hundred cavalrymen can run off one thousand men. These are the approximate numbers.

Six Secret Teachings, 55

The infantry values knowing changes and movement; the chariots value knowing the terrain's configuration; the cavalry values knowing the side roads and unorthodox methods. Thus these Three Armies bear the same name, but their employment differs. In general, in chariot battles there are ten types of terrain upon which death is likely, and eight upon which victory can be achieved:

If after advancing there is no way to withdraw, this is fatal terrain for chariots.

Passing beyond narrow defiles to pursue the enemy some distance, this is terrain which will exhaust the chariots.

When the land in front makes advancing easy, while that to the rear is treacherous, this is terrain that will cause hardship for the chariots.

Penetrating into narrow and obstructed areas from which escape will be difficult, this is terrain on which the chariots may be cut off.

If the land is collapsing, sinking, and marshy, with black mud sticking to everything, this is terrain which will labor the chariots.

To the left is precipitous, while to the right is easy, with high mounds and sharp hills. This is terrain contrary to the use of chariots.

Luxuriant grass runs through the fields, and there are deep watery channels throughout. This is terrain that thwarts the use of chariots.

When the chariots are few in number, the land easy, and one is not confronted by enemy infantry, this is terrain on which the chariots may be defeated.

To the rear are water filled ravines and ditches, to the left deep water, and to the right steep hills. This is terrain upon which chariots are destroyed.

It has been raining day and night for more than ten days without stopping. The roads have collapsed, so that it's not possible to advance nor to escape to the rear. This is terrain that will sink the chariots.

These ten are deadly terrain for chariots. Thus, they are the means by which the stupid general will be captured, and the wise general will be able to escape.

There are eight conditions of terrain that result in victory:

When the enemy's ranks, front and rear, are not yet settled, strike into them.

When their flags and pennants are in chaos, their men and horses frequently shifting about, then strike into them.

When some of their officers and troops advance, while others retreat; when some move to the left, others to the right, then strike into them.

When their battle array is not yet solid, while their officers and troops are looking around at each other, then strike into them.

When in advancing they appear full of doubt, and in withdrawing they are fearful, strike into them.

When the enemy's Three Armies are suddenly frightened, all of them rising up in great confusion, strike into them.

When you're fighting on easy terrain and twilight has come without being able to disengage from the battle, then strike into them.

When, after traveling far, at dusk they are encamping and their Three Armies are terrified, strike into them.

These eight constitute conditions in which the chariots will be victorious. If the general is clear about these ten injurious conditions and eight victorious possibilities, then even if the enemy surrounds him on all sides, attacking with a thousand chariots and ten thousand cavalry, he will be able to gallop to the front and race to the sides, and in ten thousand battles invariably be victorious.

Six Secret Teachings, 58

For the cavalry, there are ten situations that can produce victory, and nine that will result in defeat:

When the enemy first arrives and their lines and deployment are not yet settled, the front and rear not yet united, then strike into their forward cavalry, attack the left and right flanks. The enemy will certainly flee.

When the enemy's lines and deployment are well-ordered and solid, while their officers and troops want to fight, our cavalry should outflank them, but not go far off. Some should race away, some race forward. Their speed should be like the wind, their explosiveness like thunder, so that the daylight becomes as murky as dusk. Change our flags and pennants several times, also change our uniforms. Then their army can be conquered.

When the enemy's lines and deployment are not solid, while their officers and troops will not fight, press upon them both front and rear, make sudden thrusts on their left and right. Outflank and strike them, and the enemy will certainly be afraid.

When, at sunset, the enemy wants to return to camp, and their Three Armies are terrified, if we can outflank them on both sides, urgently strike their rear, pressing the entrance to their fortifications, not allowing them to go in, the enemy will certainly be defeated.

When the enemy, although lacking the advantages of ravines and defiles for securing their defenses, has penetrated deeply and ranged widely into distant territory, if we sever their supply lines, they will certainly be hungry.

When the land is level and easy, and we see enemy cavalry approaching from all four sides, if we have our chariots and cavalry strike into them, they will certainly become disordered.

When the enemy runs off in flight, their officers and troops scattered and in chaos, if some of our cavalry outflank them on both sides, while others obstruct them to the front and rear, their general can be captured.

When at dusk the enemy is turning back while their soldiers are extremely numerous, their lines and deployment will certainly become disordered. We should have our cavalry form platoons of ten, and regiments of a hundred; group the chariots into squads of five and companies of ten; and set out a great many flags and pennants, intermixed with strong crossbowmen. Some should strike their two flanks, others cut off the front and rear, and then the enemy's general can be taken prisoner. These are the ten situations in which the cavalry can be victorious.

There are nine situations which produce defeat:

Whenever the cavalry penetrates the ranks of the enemy but does not destroy their formation, so that the enemy feigns flight, only to turn their chariots and cavalry about to strike our rear—this is a situation in which the cavalry will be defeated.

When we pursue a fleeing enemy onto confined ground, ranging far into their territory without stopping, until they ambush both our flanks, and sever our rear—this is a situation in which the cavalry will be encircled.

When we go forward but there is no road back, we enter but there is no way out, this is referred to as "penetrating a Heavenly Well," "being buried in an Earthly Cave." This is fatal terrain for the cavalry.

When the way by which we enter is constricted, but the way out is distant, their weak forces can attack our strong ones and their few can attack our many—this is terrain on which the cavalry will be exterminated.

When there are great mountain torrents, deep valleys, tall luxuriant grass, forests and trees—these are conditions that will exhaust the cavalry.

When there is water on the left and right, while ahead are large hills, and to the rear high mountains, and the Three Armies are fighting between the bodies of water, while the enemy occupies both the interior and exterior ground—this is terrain that means great difficulty for the cavalry.

When the enemy has cut off our supply lines, and if we advance we will not have any route by which to return—this is troublesome terrain for the cavalry.

When we are sinking into marshy ground, while advancing and retreating must both be through quagmires—this is worrisome terrain for the cavalry.

When on the left there are deep water sluices, and on the right there are gullies and hillocks, but below the heights the ground appears level, good terrain for advancing, retreating, and enticing an enemy—this terrain is a pitfall for the cavalry.

These nine comprise fatal terrain for cavalry, the means by which the enlightened general will keep the enemy far off and escape, and the ignorant general will be entrapped and defeated.

Six Secret Teachings, 59

The T'ai Kung said: "When infantry engage in battle with chariots and cavalry they must rely on hills and mounds, ravines and defiles. The long weapons and strong crossbows should occupy the fore, the short weapons and weak crossbows should occupy the rear, firing and resting in turn. Even if large numbers of the enemy's chariots and cavalry should arrive, they must maintain a solid formation and fight intensely while skilled soldiers and strong crossbowmen prepare against attacks from the rear."

King Wu said: "Suppose there are not any hills or mounds, ravines or defiles. The enemy arrives, and it is both numerous and martial. Their chariots and cavalry outflank us on both sides, and they are making sudden thrusts against our front and rear positions. Our Three Armies are terrified and fleeing in chaotic defeat. What should we do?"

The T'ai Kung said: "Order our officers and troops to set up the *chevaux-de-frise* and wooden caltrops, arraying the oxen and horses by units of five in their midst, and have them establish a four-sided martial assault formation. When you see the enemy's chariots and cavalry are about to advance, our men should evenly spread out the caltrops and dig ditches around the rear, making them five feet deep and wide. It is called the 'Fate of Dragon Grass.'

"Our men should take hold of the *chevaux-de-frise* and advance on foot. The chariots should be arrayed as ramparts and pushed forward and back. Whenever they stop set them up as fortifications. Our skilled soldiers and strong crossbowmen should prepare against the left and right flanks. Afterward, order our Three Armies to fervently fight without respite."

Six Secret Teachings, 60

In general, in warfare: when the formation is already solid do not make it heavier. When your main forces are advancing, do not commit all of them, for by doing so you will be endangered.

Ssu-ma Fa, 4

Within the army you must have soldiers with the courage of tigers, the strength to easily lift tripods, and the fleetness of barbarian horses. To attack their flags and seize their generals, you must have men with such abilities. If you have men such as these, select and segregate them into special units; favor and honor them. They are referred to as the "army's fate." Those who are expert in the use of the five weapons, who are strong and quick, and are intent upon swallowing the enemy should be given rank and prominence for they can make victory decisive. If you are generous to their parents, wives, and children, encourage them with rewards, and awe them with punishments; these strong soldiers, when in formation, will solidly hold their positions for a long time. If you can discern and evaluate men such as these, you can attack a force double your strength.

Wu-tzu, 2

25
Strategic Power

King Wu asked the T'ai Kung: "In general, what are the great essentials in the art of employing the army?"

The T'ai Kung replied: "The ancients who excelled at warfare were not able to wage war above Heaven, nor could they wage war below Earth. Their success and defeat in all cases proceeded from the spiritual employment of strategic power. Those who attained it flourished; those who lost it perished."

Six Secret Teachings, 27

Exploit the advantages conferred by the tactical balance of power. Increase the enemy's excesses, seize what he loves. Then we, acting from without, can cause a response from within.

Ssu-ma Fa, 3

Those that greatly excel in warfare use the foundation; next in greatness are those that employ the ends. Warfare is taking control of strategy, preserving the subtle. The foundation and the ends are only a question of exploiting the tactical balance of power.

Ssu-ma Fa, 4

After estimating the advantages in accord with what you have heard, put it into effect with strategic power supplemented by field tactics that respond to external factors. As for strategic power, it is controlling the tactical imbalance of power in accord with the gains to be realized.

The Art of War, 1

The victorious army is like a ton compared with an ounce, while the defeated army is like an ounce weighed against a ton! The combat of the victorious is like the sudden release of a pent-up torrent down a thousand-fathom gorge. This is the strategic disposition of force.

The Art of War, 4

The strategic configuration of power is visible in the onrush of pent-up water tumbling stones along. The effect of constraints is visible in the onrush of a bird of prey breaking the bones of its target. Thus the strategic configuration of power of those that excel in warfare is sharply focused, their constraints are precise. Their strategic configuration of power is like a fully drawn crossbow, their constraints like the release of the trigger.

Intermixed and turbulent, the fighting appears chaotic, but they cannot be made disordered. In turmoil and confusion, their deployment is circular, and they cannot be defeated.

The Art of War, 5

One who excels at warfare seeks victory through the strategic configuration of power, not from reliance on men. Thus he is able to select men and employ strategic power.

The Art of War, 5

One who employs strategic power commands men in battle as if he were rolling logs and stones. The nature of wood and stone is to be quiet when stable but to move when on precipitous ground. If they are square they stop, if round they tend to move. Thus the strategic power of one who excels at employing men in warfare is comparable to rolling round boulders down a thousand-fathom mountain. Such is the strategic configuration of power.

The Art of War, 5

Now the army's disposition of force is like water. Water's configuration avoids heights and races downward. The army's disposition of force avoids the substantial and strikes the vacuous. Water configures its flow in accord with the terrain; the army controls its victory in accord with the enemy. Thus the army does not maintain any constant strategic configuration of power, water has no constant shape. One who is able to change and transform in accord with the enemy and wrest victory is termed spiritual. Thus none of the five phases constantly dominates; the four seasons do not have constant positions; the sun shines for longer and shorter periods; and the moon wanes and waxes.

The Art of War, 6

Sun Pin said: "Now being endowed with teeth and mounting horns, having claws in front and spurs in back, coming together when happy, fighting when angry, this is the Tao of Heaven, it cannot be stopped. Thus those who lack Heavenly weapons provide them themselves. This was an affair of extraordinary men. The Yellow Emperor created swords and imaged military formations upon them. Yi created bows and crossbows and imaged strategic power on them. Yü created boats and carts and imaged tactical changes on them. T'ang and Wu made long weapons and imaged the strategic imbalance of power on them."

Military Methods, 9

Armies are distinguished as being a "guest" or a "host." The guest's forces are comparatively numerous, the host's forces comparatively few. Only if the guest is double and the host half can they contend as enemies. . . . The host is the one who establishes his position first, the guest is the one who establishes his position afterward. The host ensconces himself on the terrain and relies on his strategic power to await the guest who contravenes mountain passes and traverses ravines to arrive. Now if they contravene mountain passes and traverse ravines only to retreat and thereby dare to cut their own throats rather than advancing and daring to resist the enemy, what is the reason? It is because their strategic configuration of power is not conducive to attacking and the terrain is not advantageous. If their strategic power is conducive and the terrain advantageous, then the people by themselves will advance. If their strategic power is not conducive and the terrain not advantageous, the people will retreat by themselves. Those who are referred to as excelling in warfare make their strategic power conducive and the terrain advantageous.

Military Methods, 19

The Art of War states, "A thousand men provide the means to exercise the tactical balance of power, ten thousand men constitute martial prowess. If you apply the force of tactical power to the enemy first, he will not be able to commit in strength. If you apply martial prowess first, the enemy will not be able to engage you with his full awesomeness." Thus the army values being first. If it is victorious in this, then it will conquer the enemy. If it is not victorious in this, then it will not conquer them.

Now when we go, they come; when we come, they go. These mutually produce victory and defeat. The pattern of battle is thus.

Now essential sincerity lies in spiritual enlightenment. The tactical balance of power lies in the extremities of the Tao. If you have something, pretend not to have it; if you lack something, appear to have it. Then how can the enemy trust the appearance?

Wei Liao-tzu, 12

26

The Unorthodox

Drumming an advance and setting up a great tumult are the means by which to implement unorthodox plans.

Six Secret Teachings, 27

What enable the masses of the Three Armies invariably to withstand the enemy without being defeated are the unorthodox and orthodox. If wherever the army attacks it is like a whetstone thrown against an egg, it is due to the vacuous and substantial.

In general, in battle one engages with the orthodox and gains victory through the unorthodox. Thus one who excels at sending forth the unorthodox is as inexhaustible as Heaven, as unlimited as the Yangtze and Yellow rivers. What reach an end and begin again are the sun and moon. What die and are reborn are the four seasons.

The notes do not exceed five, but the changes of the five notes can never be fully heard. The colors do not exceed five, but the changes of the five colors can never be completely seen. The flavors do not exceed five, but the changes of the five flavors can never be completely tasted. In warfare the strategic configurations of power do not exceed the unorthodox and orthodox, but the changes of the unorthodox and orthodox can never be completely exhausted. The unorthodox and orthodox mutually produce each other, just like an endless cycle. Who can exhaust them?

The Art of War, 5

The patterns of Heaven and Earth, reaching an extreme and then reversing, becoming full and then being overturned, these are yin and yang. In turn flourishing, in turn declining, these are the four seasons. Having those they conquer, having those they do not conquer, these are the five phases. Living and dying, these are the myriad things. Being capable, being incapable, these are the myriad living things. Having that which is surplus, having that which is insufficient, these are form and strategic power.

Thus as for the disciples of form, there are none that cannot be named. As for the disciples that are named, there are none that cannot be conquered. Thus the Sage conquers the myriad things with the myriad things; therefore his conquering is not impoverished.

In warfare, those with form conquer each other. There are not any forms that cannot be conquered, but none know the form (disposition) by which one conquers. The changes in the forms of conquest are coterminal with Heaven and Earth and are inexhaustible.

As for the forms of conquest, even the bamboo strips of the Ch'u and Yüeh would be insufficient for writing them down. Those that have forms (dispositions) all conquer in accord with their mode of victory. Employing one form of conquest to conquer the myriad forms (dispositions) is not possible. That by which one controls the form is singular; that by which one conquers cannot be single.

Thus when those who excel at warfare discern an enemy's strength, they know where he has a shortcoming. When they discern an enemy's insufficiency, they know where he has a surplus. They perceive victory as easily as seeing the sun and moon. Their measures for victory are like using water to conquer fire.

When form is employed to respond to form, it is orthodox. When the formless controls the formed, it is unorthodox. That the unorthodox and orthodox are inexhaustible is due to differentiation. Differentiate according to unorthodox techniques, exercise control through the five phases, engage in combat with three forces. Once differentiations have been determined things take form. Once forms have been determined they have names.

Things that are the same are inadequate for conquering each other. Thus employ the different to create the unorthodox. Accordingly, take the quiet to be the unorthodox for movement; ease to be the unorthodox for weariness; satiety to be the unorthodox for hunger; order to be the unorthodox for chaos; and the numerous masses to be the unorthodox for the few.

When action is initiated it becomes the orthodox; what has not yet been initiated is the unorthodox. When the unorthodox is initiated and is not responded to, then it will be victorious. One who has a surplus of the unorthodox will attain surpassing victories.

Thus if when one joint hurts the hundred joints are not used, it is because they are the same body. If when the front is defeated the rear is not employed, it is because they are the same form (disposition).

Thus to realize strategic power in warfare, large formations should not be severed, small formations should not be broken up. The rear should not encroach upon the front, the front should not trample the rear. Those who are advancing should have a route out, those withdrawing should have a route for advancing.

If rewards have not yet been implemented and punishments not yet employed, but the people obey their commands, it is because the people are able to implement them. If rewards are high and punishments pervasive but the people do not obey their commands, it is because the people are not able to implement the commands. In spite of disadvantageous circumstances, to make people advance unto death without turning on their heels is something that even Meng Pen would find difficult; to require it of the people is like trying to make water flow contrary to normal.

Thus to realize strategic combat power, increase the victorious; alter the defeated; rest the weary; feed the hungry. Accordingly the people will see the enemy's men but not yet perceive death; they will tread on naked blades and not turn their heels. Thus when one understands patterns of flowing water, he can float rocks and break boats. When, in employing the people, one realizes their nature, then his commands will be implemented just like flowing water.

Military Methods, 30

Those who excel at repulsing the enemy first join battle with orthodox troops, then use unorthodox ones to control them. This is the technique for certain victory.

Wei Liao-tzu, 23

If your state's Virtue and strategic configuration of power are the same as those of the enemy, so that neither state has the means to overcome the other, then you must win the minds of the valiant, share likes and dislikes with the common people, and only thereafter attack the enemy in accord with changes in the balance of power. Thus without stratagems you have no means to resolve suspicions and settle doubts. Without rumor and the unorthodox you have no means to destroy evildoers and stop invaders. Without secret plans you have no means to be successful.

Huang Shih-kung, 2

Li Ching said: "I have examined the art of war as practiced from the Yellow Emperor on down. First be orthodox, and afterward unorthodox; first be benevolent and righteous, and afterward employ the balance of power and craftiness. In general, when troops advance to the front it is orthodox, when they deliberately retreat to the rear it's unorthodox. *The Art of War* states, 'Display profits to entice them, create disorder in their forces and take them.' "

Questions and Replies, 1

The T'ai-tsung said: "When an army withdraws can it be termed unorthodox?"

Li Ching said: "It is not so. Whenever the soldiers retreat with their flags confused and disordered, the sounds of the large and small drums not responding to each other, and their orders shouted out in a clamor, this is true defeat, not unorthodox strategy. If the flags are ordered, the drums respond to each other, and the commands and orders seem unified, then even though they may be retreating and running, it's not a defeat, and must be a case of unorthodox strategy. *The Art of War* says, 'Do not pursue feigned retreats.' It also says 'Although capable, display incapability.' These all refer to the unorthodox."

Questions and Replies, 1

The T'ai-tsung said: "If I cause the enemy to perceive my orthodox as unorthodox, and cause him to perceive my unorthodox as orthodox, is this what is meant by 'displaying a form to others'? Is employing the unorthodox as orthodox, the orthodox as unorthodox, unfathomable changes and transformations, what is meant by 'being formless'?"

Li Ching bowed twice and said: "Your majesty is a spiritual Sage. You go back to the ancients, beyond what I can attain."

Questions and Replies, 1

The T'ai-tsung said: "If, as Sun-tzu said, 'dividing and combining are changes,' wherein lie the unorthodox and orthodox?"

Li Ching said: "For those who excel at employing troops there are none that are not orthodox, none that are not unorthodox, so they cause the enemy never to be able to fathom them. Thus with the orthodox they are victorious, with the unorthodox they are also victorious. The officers of the Three Armies only know the victory, none know how it is attained. Without being able to fully comprehend the changes, how could outstanding generals attain this? As for where the dividing and combining come from, only Sun-tzu was capable of comprehending it. From Wu Chi'i on no one has been able to attain it."

Questions and Replies, 1

Li Ching said: "Now orthodox troops receive their mission from the ruler, while unorthodox troops are ordered forth by the general. Sun-tzu said, 'If orders are consistently implemented so as to instruct the people, then the people will submit.' These are what are received from the ruler. Moreover he says, 'The employment of the troops cannot be spoken of beforehand,' and 'There are commands from the ruler that are not accepted.' These are what the general himself issues.

"As for generals: if they employ orthodox tactics without any unorthodox ones, they are defensive generals. If they employ unorthodox tactics without any orthodox ones, they are aggressive generals. If they employ both they are generals to preserve the state."

Questions and Replies, 1

The T'ai-tsung said: "I have looked through all the military books, but none surpass Sun-tzu. In Sun-tzu's thirteen chapters there is nothing that surpasses the 'vacuous' and 'substantial.' Now, when employing the army, if one recognizes the strategic power of the vacuous and substantial, then he will always be victorious. Our contemporary generals are only able to talk about avoiding the substantial and attacking the vacuous. When they approach the enemy, few recognize the vacuous and substantial, probably because they are unable to compel the enemy to come to them, but on the contrary are compelled by the enemy. How can this be? My lord, please discuss the essentials of all these in detail with our generals."

Li Ching said: "Instructing them first about the techniques for changing the unorthodox and orthodox into each other, and afterward telling them about the form of the vacuous and substantial, would be possible. Many of the generals do not know how to take the unorthodox to be the orthodox, and the orthodox to be the unorthodox, so how can they recognize when the vacuous is substantial, and the substantial vacuous?"

Questions and Replies, 2

The T'ai-tsung said: "According to Sun-tzu, 'Make plans against them to know the likelihood for gain and loss. Stimulate them to know their patterns of movement and stopping. Determine their disposition to know what terrain is tenable, what deadly. Probe them to know where they have an excess, where an insufficiency.' Accordingly, do the unorthodox and orthodox lie with me, while the vacuous and substantial lie with the enemy?"

Li Ching said: "The unorthodox and orthodox are the means by which to bring about the vacuous and substantial in the enemy. If the enemy is substantial, then I must use the orthodox. If the enemy is vacuous, then I must use the unorthodox. If a general does not know the unorthodox and orthodox, then even though he knows whether the enemy is vacuous or substantial, how can he bring it about? I respectfully accept your mandate, but will first instruct all the generals in the unorthodox and orthodox, and afterward they will realize the vacuous and substantial by themselves."

The T'ai-tsung said: "If we take the unorthodox as the orthodox, and the enemy realizes it is the unorthodox, then I will use the orthodox to attack him. If we take the orthodox as the unorthodox, and the enemy thinks it's the orthodox, then I will use the unorthodox to attack him. I will cause the enemy's strategic power to constantly be vacuous, and my strategic power to always be substantial. If you teach the generals these methods, it should be easy to make them understand."

Li Ching said: "A thousand essays, ten thousand sections, do not go beyond 'compel others, do not be compelled by them.' I ought to use this to teach all the generals."

Questions and Replies, 2

The T'ai-tsung said: "Li Chi spoke about male and female, square and circular tactics for ambush. Did they exist in antiquity or not?"

Li Ching said: "The male and female methods come out of the popular tradition. In actuality they refer to yin and yang, that's all. According to Fan Li's book, 'If you're last then use yin tactics, if you're first then use yang tactics. When you have exhausted the enemy's yang measures, then expand your yin to the full and seize them.' This then is the subtle mysteriousness of yin and yang according to the strategists.

"Fan Li also said, 'Establish the right as the female, increase the left to be male. At dawn and dusk accord with the Tao of Heaven.' Thus left and right, dawn and dusk, are different according to the time. They lie in the changes of the unorthodox and orthodox. Left and right are the yin and yang in man, dawn and dusk are the yin and yang of Heaven. The unorthodox and orthodox are the mutual changes of yin and yang in Heaven and man. If one wished to grasp them and not change, then yin and yang would both deteriorate. How can one preserve only the shape of the male and female? Thus when you display an appearance to an enemy, show the unorthodox, not our orthodox. When you conquer, employ the orthodox to attack the enemy, not our unorthodox. This is what is meant by the orthodox and unorthodox changing into each other.

"An 'army in ambush' does not only mean forces lying in ambush in the mountains, valleys, grass, and trees, for hiding them away is the means to effect an ambush. Our orthodox should be like the mountain, our unorthodox like thunder. Even though the enemy is directly opposite our front, no one can fathom where our unorthodox and orthodox forces are. At this point what shape do I have?"

Questions and Replies, 2

27

Manipulating the Enemy

To be the first to gain victory, initially display some weakness to the enemy and only afterward do battle. Then your effort will be half, but the achievement will be doubled.

Six Secret Teachings, 26

Display profits to entice them. Create disorder in their forces and take them. If they are substantial, prepare for them; if they are strong, avoid them. If they are angry, perturb them; be deferential to foster their arrogance. If they are rested, force them to exert themselves. If they are united, cause them to be separated. Attack where they are unprepared. Go forth where they will not expect it. These are the ways military strategists are victorious. They cannot be spoken of in advance.

The Art of War, 1

In general, whoever occupies the battleground first and awaits the enemy will be at ease; whoever occupies the battleground afterward and must race to the conflict will be fatigued. Thus one who excels at warfare compels men and is not compelled by other men.

The Art of War, 6

In order to cause the enemy to come of their own volition, extend some apparent profit. In order to prevent the enemy from coming forth, show them the potential harm. Thus if the enemy is rested you can tire him; if he is well fed you can make him hungry; if he is at rest you can move him. Go forth to positions to which he must race. Race forth where he does not expect it.

The Art of War, 6

If I determine the enemy's disposition of force while I have no perceptible form, I can concentrate my forces while the enemy is fragmented. If we are concentrated into a single force while he is fragmented into ten, then we attack him with ten times his strength. Thus we are many and the enemy is few. If we can attack his few with our many, those whom we engage in battle will be severely constrained.

The location where we will engage the enemy must not become known to them. If it is not known, then the positions they must prepare to defend will be numerous. If the positions the enemy prepares to defend are numerous, then the forces we will engage will be few. Thus if they prepare to defend the front, to the rear there will be few men. If they defend the rear, in the front there will be few. If they prepare to defend the left flank, then on the right there will be few men. If they prepare to defend the right flank, then on the left there will be few men. If there is no position left undefended, then there will not be any place with more than a few. The few are the ones who prepare against others; the many are the ones who make others prepare against them.

The Art of War, 6

In general, the strategy for employing the army is this: From the time the general receives his commands from the ruler, unites the armies, and assembles the masses, to confronting the enemy and encamping, there is nothing more difficult than military combat. In military combat what is most difficult is turning the circuitous into the straight, turning adversity into advantage. Thus if you make the enemy's path circuitous and entice them with profit, although you set out after them you will arrive before them. This results from knowing the tactics of the circuitous and the direct.

The Art of War, 7

If I dare ask, if the enemy is numerous, disciplined, and about to advance, how should we respond to them? I would say, first seize something that they love, for then they will listen to you.

The Art of War, 11

Spreading out the pennants and making the flags conspicuous are the means by which to cause doubt in the enemy. Analytically positioning fences and screens is the means by which to bedazzle and make the enemy doubtful.

Military Methods, 14

Slow movements and frequent avoidance are the means by which to entice an enemy to try to trample you.

Military Methods, 14

Creating heavily disadvantageous circumstances is the means by which to trouble and exhaust the enemy.

Military Methods, 14

Thus the army has four roads and five movements. Advancing is a road, withdrawing is a road, left is a road, right is a road. Advancing is a movement, withdrawing is a movement, left is a movement, right is a movement. Silently emplaced is also a movement. For someone to excel, these four roads must be penetrating, these five movements must be skillful. Thus when advancing he cannot be contravened to the fore, when withdrawing he cannot be cut off to the rear. To the left and right he cannot be forced into ravines. Silently remaining in position he cannot be troubled by the enemy's men. Accordingly, he causes the enemy's four roads to be impoverished, his five movements to be invariably troubled. If the enemy advances he will be pressed to the fore; if he withdraws he will be cut off to the rear. To the left and right he will be forced into ravines, while if he remains quietly encamped his army will not avoid misfortune.

Military Methods, 20

Those who excel in warfare can cause the enemy to roll up his armor and race far off; to travel two days' normal distance at a time; to be exhausted and sick but unable to rest; to be hungry and thirsty but unable to eat. An enemy emaciated in this way certainly will not be victorious! Sated, we await his hunger; resting in our emplacement, we await his fatigue; in true tranquility, we await his movement. Thus our people know about advancing but not about withdrawing. They will trample on naked blades and not turn their heels.

Military Methods, 20

As for the techniques for forcing the enemy to rush about: The first is called seizing provisions. The second is called seizing water. The third is called seizing fords. The fourth is called seizing roads. The fifth is called seizing ravines. The sixth is called seizing easy terrain. The ninth is called seizing what he solely values. In general these nine "graspings" are the means by which to force the enemy to hasten about.

Military Methods, 28

When the enemy moves observe him; when he approaches prepare for him. If the enemy is strong be deferential to make him arrogant. If the enemy is well rested then leave him. If the enemy is insulting then wait for his *ch'i* (spirit) to decline. If the enemy is explosive then soothe him. If the enemy is rebellious then treat him with righteousness. If the enemy is sincere then lead him to abandon his perverse ruler.

Accord with the enemy's actions to initiate measures and repress him. Rely upon the strategic configuration of power to destroy him. Spread false words and cause him to make errors. Set out your net to catch them.

Huang Shih-kung, 1

When neither the beginning nor end have yet become visible no one is able to know them. Heaven and Earth are spiritual and enlightened, with the myriad things they change and transform. The commander's changes and movements should not be constant. He should change and transform in response to the enemy. He does not precede affairs; when the enemy moves he immediately follows up. Thus he is able to formulate inexhaustible strategies and methods of control; can sustain and complete the awesomeness of Heaven; bring tranquility and order to the extremes of the eight directions; and gather and settle the Nine Barbarians. Such a strategist is a teacher for an emperor or true king.

Huang Shih-kung, 1

28
Deception and Deceit

Now when our two armies, opposing each other, have deployed their armored soldiers and established their battle arrays, releasing some of your troops to create chaos in the ranks is the means by which to fabricate deceptive changes.

Six Secret Teachings, 27

Disguising some men as enemy emissaries is the means by which to sever their supply lines. Forging enemy commands and orders, and wearing the same clothes as the enemy, are the means by which to be prepared for their retreat.

Six Secret Teachings, 27

Warfare is the Tao of deception. Thus although you are capable, display incapability to them. When committed to employing your forces, feign inactivity. When your objective is nearby, make it appear as if distant; when far away, create the illusion of being nearby.

The Art of War, 1

Simulated chaos is given birth from control; the illusion of fear is given birth from courage; feigned weakness is given birth from strength. Order and disorder are a question of numbers; courage and fear are a question of the strategic configuration of power; strength and weakness are a question of the deployment of forces.

Thus one who excels at moving the enemy deploys in a configuration to which the enemy must respond. He offers something that the enemy must seize. With profit he moves them, with the foundation he awaits them.

The Art of War, 5

Hidden plans and concealed deceptions are the means by which to inveigle the enemy into combat. Deliberate tactical errors and minor losses are the means by which to bait the enemy.

Military Methods, 14

29

Fundamental
Tactical Principles

Setting up ingenious ambushes and preparing unorthodox troops, stretching out distant formations to deceive and entice the enemy, are the means by which to destroy the enemy's army and capture its general.

Six Secret Teachings, 27

Being as swift as a flying arrow, attacking as suddenly as the release of a crossbow, are the means by which to destroy brilliant plans.

Six Secret Teachings, 27

Taking advantage of their fright and fear is the means by which one can attack ten. High winds and heavy rain are the means by which to strike the front and seize the rear. Taking advantage of their exhaustion and encamping at dusk is the means by which ten can attack a hundred.

Six Secret Teachings, 27

Anyone who wants to launch a strike should carefully scrutinize and investigate fourteen changes in the enemy. When any of these changes become visible, attack, for the enemy will certainly be defeated: When the enemy has begun to assemble they can be attacked. When the men and horses have not yet been fed they can be attacked. When the seasonal or weather conditions are not advantageous to them they can be attacked. When they have not secured good terrain they can be attacked. When they are fleeing they can be attacked. When they are not vigilant they can be attacked. When they are tired and exhausted they can be attacked. When the general is absent from the officers and troops they can be attacked. When they are traversing long roads they can be attacked. When they are fording rivers they can be attacked. When the troops have not had any leisure time they can be attacked. When they encounter the difficulty of precipitous ravines or are on narrow roads they can be attacked. When their battle array is in disorder they can be attacked. When they are afraid they can be attacked.

Six Secret Teachings, 52

Mount a sudden strike on their doubts. Attack their haste. Force them to constrict their deployment. Launch a sudden strike against their order. Take advantage of their failure to avoid harm. Obstruct their strategy. Seize their thoughts. Capitalize on their fears.

Ssu-ma Fa, 5

To travel a thousand miles without becoming fatigued, traverse unoccupied terrain. To ensure taking the objective in an attack, strike positions that are undefended. To be certain of an impregnable defense, secure positions that the enemy will not attack.

Thus when someone excels in attacking, the enemy does not know where to mount his defense; when someone excels at defense, the enemy does not know where to attack. Subtle! Subtle! It approaches the formless. Spiritual! Spiritual! It attains the soundless. Thus he can be the enemy's Master of Fate.

The Art of War, 6

To effect an unhampered advance, strike their vacuities. To effect a retreat that cannot be overtaken, employ unmatchable speed. Thus if I want to engage in combat, even though the enemy has high ramparts and deep moats, he cannot avoid doing battle because I attack objectives he must rescue.

If I do not want to engage in combat, even though I merely draw a line on the ground and defend it, he will not be able to engage me in battle because we thwart his movements.

The Art of War, 6

First, if he has lost the means for going and coming he can be defeated. Second, if he gathers together turbulent people and immediately employs them; if he stops retreating troops and immediately engages in battle with them; or if he lacks resources but acts as if he has resources, then he can be defeated. Third, if he constantly wrangles over right and wrong, and in planning affairs is argumentative and disputatious, he can be defeated. Fourth, if his commands are not implemented, the masses not unified, he can be defeated. Fifth, if his subordinates are not submissive and the masses not employable, he can be defeated. Sixth, if the people regard the army with bitterness, he can be defeated. Seventh, if the army is "old," he can be defeated. Eighth, if the army is thinking about home, he can be defeated. Ninth, if the soldiers are deserting, he can be defeated. Tenth, if the soldiers are disordered, he can be defeated. Eleventh, if the army has been frightened several times, he can be defeated. Twelfth, if the soldiers' route requires difficult marching and the masses suffer, he can be defeated. Thirteenth, if the army is focusing upon ravines and strong points and the masses are fatigued, he can be defeated. Fourteenth, if he engages in battle but is unprepared, he can be defeated. Fifteenth, if the sun is setting and the road is far while the masses are dispirited, he can be defeated. Seventeenth, if the masses are afraid, he can be defeated. Eighteenth, if commands are frequently changed and the masses are furtive, he can be defeated. Nineteenth, if the army is disintegrating while the masses do not regard their generals and officials as capable, he can be defeated. Twentieth, if they have been lucky several times and the masses are indolent, he can be defeated. Twenty-first, if he has numerous doubts so the masses are doubtful, he can be defeated. Twenty-second, if he hates to hear about his excesses, he can be defeated. Twenty-third, if he appoints the incapable he can be defeated. Twenty-fourth, if their *ch'i* (spirit) has been injured from being long exposed on campaign, he can be defeated. Twenty-fifth, if their minds are divided at the appointed time for battle, he can be defeated. Twenty-sixth, if he relies upon the enemy becoming dispirited, he can be defeated. Twenty-seventh, if he focuses upon harming others and relies upon ambushes and deceit, he can be defeated. Twenty-eighth, if the army's chariots lack maintenance, he can be defeated. Twenty-ninth, if he deprecates the troops and the minds of the masses are hateful, he can be defeated. Thirtieth, if he is unable to successfully deploy his forces while the route out is constricted, he can be defeated. Thirty-first, if in the army's forward ranks are soldiers from the rear ranks and they are not coordinated and unified with the forward deployment, he can be defeated. Thirty-second, if in engaging in battle he is concerned about the front and the rear is therefore empty; or, concerned about the rear, the front is empty; or, concerned about the left, the right is empty; or, concerned about the right, the left is empty—his engaging in battle being filled with worry, he can be defeated.

Military Methods, 26

Those from whom the initiative has been taken have no *ch'i* (spirit); those who are afraid are unable to mount a defense; those who have suffered defeat, have no men. They are all cases of an army lacking the Tao of the military. When you decide to go forth and have no doubts, then follow your plan. When you rob the enemy of his plans and still no one confronts you, press the attack home. If you can see clearly and occupy the high ground, then overawe them into submission. This is the pinnacle of the Tao of the military.

Wei Liao-tzu, 12

30

Evaluating the Enemy

BATTLEFIELD EVALUATIONS

King Wu asked the T'ai Kung: "Before engaging in battle I want to first know the enemy's strengths and weaknesses, to foresee indications of victory or defeat. How can this be done?"

The T'ai Kung replied, "Indications of victory or defeat will be first manifest in their spirit. The enlightened general will investigate them, for they will be evidenced in the men.

"Clearly observe the enemy's coming and going, advancing and withdrawing. Investigate their movements and periods at rest, whether they speak about portents, what the officers and troops report. If the Three Armies are exhilarated; the officers and troops fear the laws; respect the general's commands; rejoice with each other in destroying the enemy; boast to each other about their courage and ferocity; and praise each other for their awesomeness and martial demeanor—these are indications of a strong enemy.

"If the Three Armies have been startled a number of times, the officers and troops no longer maintaining good order; they terrify each other with stories about the enemy's strength; they speak to each other about the disadvantages; they anxiously look about at each other, listening carefully; they talk incessantly of ill omens, a myriad mouths confusing each other; they fear neither laws nor orders, and do not regard their general seriously—these are indications of weakness.

"When the Three Armies are well ordered; the deployment's strategic configuration of power solid, with deep moats and high ramparts; and moreover they enjoy the advantages of high winds and heavy rain, while the army is untroubled. If the signal flags and pennants point to the front; the sound of the gongs and bells rises up and is clear; and the sound of the small and large drums clearly rises—these are indications of having obtained spiritual, enlightened assistance, foretelling a great victory.

"When their formations are not solid; their flags and pennants confused and entangled with each other; they go contrary to the advantages of high wind and heavy rain; their officers and troops are terrified; and their *ch'i* (spirit) broken while they are not unified. Their war horses have been frightened and run off, their military chariots have broken axles. The sound of their gongs and bells sinks down and is murky; the sound of their drums is wet and damp. These are indications foretelling a great defeat."

Six Secret Teachings, 29

In general, as for warfare: employ large and small numbers to observe their tactical variations; advance and retreat to probe the solidity of their defenses. Endanger them to observe their fears. Be tranquil to observe if they become lax. Move to observe if they have doubts. Mount a surprise attack and observe their discipline.

Ssu-ma Fa, 5

Thus when making a comparative evaluation through estimations, seeking out its true nature, ask: Which ruler has the Tao? Which general has greater ability? Who has gained the advantages of Heaven and Earth? Whose laws and orders are more thoroughly implemented? Whose forces are stronger? Whose officers and troops are better trained? Whose rewards and punishments are clearer? From these one will know victory and defeat!

The Art of War, 1

Critically analyze them to know the estimations for gain and loss. Stimulate them to know the patterns of their movement and stopping. Determine their disposition of force, to know the tenable and fatal terrain. Probe them to know where they have an excess, where an insufficiency.

The Art of War, 6

Those who stand about leaning on their weapons are hungry. If those who draw water drink first, they are thirsty. When they see potential gain but do not know whether to advance, they are tired.

The Art of War, 9

Where birds congregate it is empty. If the enemy cries out at night, they are afraid. If the army is turbulent, the general lacks severity. If their flags and pennants move about, they are in chaos. If the officers are angry, they are exhausted.

The Art of War, 9

If they kill their horses and eat the meat, the army lacks grain. If they hang up their cooking utensils and do not return to camp, they are an exhausted invader.

The Art of War, 9

EVALUATING ENEMY COMMANDERS AND INTENTIONS

If an enemy in close proximity remains quiet, they are relying on their tactical occupation of ravines. If while far off they challenge you to battle, they want you to advance because they occupy easy terrain to their advantage.

The Art of War, 9

If large numbers of trees move, they are approaching. If there are many visible obstacles in the heavy grass, it is to make us suspicious. If the birds take flight, there is an ambush. If the animals are afraid, enemy forces are mounting a sudden attack.

The Art of War, 9

If dust rises high up in a sharply defined column, chariots are coming. If it is low and broad, the infantry is advancing. If it is dispersed in thin shafts, they are gathering firewood. If it is sparse, coming and going, they are encamping.

One who speaks deferentially but increases his preparations will advance. One who speaks belligerently and advances hastily will retreat. One whose light chariots first fan out to the sides is deploying for battle. One who seeks peace without setting any prior conditions is executing a stratagem. One whose troops race off but who deploys his army into formation is implementing a predetermined schedule. One whose troops half advance and half retreat is enticing you.

The Art of War, 9

One whose troops repeatedly congregate in small groups here and there, whispering together, has lost the masses. One who frequently grants rewards is in deep distress. One who frequently imposes punishments is in great difficulty. One who is at first excessively brutal and then fears the masses is the pinnacle of stupidity.

The Art of War, 9

One who has emissaries come forth with offerings wants to rest for a while.

The Art of War, 9

If their troops are aroused and approach our forces, only to maintain their positions without engaging in battle or breaking off the confrontation, you must carefully investigate it.

The Art of War, 9

Marquis Wu inquired: "From external observation of the enemy I would like to know their internal character, from studying their advance know at what point they will stop, in order to determine victory and defeat. May I hear about this?"

Wu Ch'i replied: "If the enemy approaches in reckless disarray, unthinking; if their flags and banners are confused and in disorder; and if the men and horses frequently look about, then one unit can attack ten of theirs, invariably causing them to be helpless.

"If the feudal lords have not yet assembled; ruler and ministers are not yet in agreement; ditches and embankments not yet complete; prohibitions and orders not yet issued; and the Three Armies clamoring, wanting to advance but being unable to, wanting to retreat but not daring to—then you can attack with half the enemy's force, and never lose in a hundred encounters."

Wu-tzu, 2

Marquis Wu asked: "When our two armies are confronting each other but I don't know their general, if I want to fathom him what methods are there?"

Wu Ch'i replied: "Order some courageous men from the lower ranks to lead some light shock troops to test him. When the enemy responds they should concentrate on running off instead of trying to gain some objective. Then analyze the enemy's advance, whether their actions, such as sitting and standing, are in unison and their organization well preserved. Whether, when they pursue your retreat, they feign being unable to catch you, or when they perceive easy gain they pretend not to realize it. A commander like this may be termed a wise general. Do not engage him in battle.

"If their troops approach yelling and screaming, their flags and pennants in confusion, while some of their units move of their own accord and others stop, some weapons held vertically, others horizontally—if they pursue our retreating troops as if they are afraid they won't reach us, or seeing advantage are afraid of not gaining it, this marks a stupid general. Even if his troops are numerous they can be taken."

Wu-tzu, 4

EVALUATING ENEMY STATES

Attack a country according to its changes. Display riches in order to observe their poverty. Display exhaustion in order to observe their illness. If the ruler is immoral and the people disaffected, in cases such as these one has a basis for attack.

Wei Liao-tzu, 22

The *Military Pronouncements* states: "The key to using the army is to first investigate the enemy's situation. Look into his granaries and armories, estimate his food stocks, divine his strengths and weaknesses, search out his natural advantages, and seek out his vacuities and fissures." Thus if the state does not have the hardship of an army in the field yet is transporting grain, it must be suffering from emptiness. If the people have a sickly cast they are impoverished.

If they are transporting provisions for a thousand miles the officers will have a hungry look. If they must gather wood and grass before they can eat, the army does not have enough food to pass one night. Accordingly if someone transports provisions a thousand miles he lacks a year's food; two thousand miles, he lacks two years' food; three thousand miles, he lacks three years' food. This is what is referred to as an empty state. When the state is empty the people are impoverished. When the people are impoverished, then the government and populace are estranged. While the enemy attacks from without, the people steal from within. This is termed a situation of "inevitable collapse."

Huang Shih-kung, 1

31

Psychological Warfare

There are twelve measures for civil offensives. First, accord with what he likes in order to accommodate his wishes. He will eventually grow arrogant, and invariably mount some perverse affair. If you can appear to follow along, you will certainly be able to eliminate him.

Second, become familiar with those he loves in order to fragment his awesomeness. When men have two different inclinations, their loyalty invariably declines. When his court no longer has any loyal ministers, the state altars will inevitably be endangered.

Third, covertly bribe his assistants, fostering a deep relationship with them. While they will bodily stand in his court, their emotions will be directed outside it. The state will certainly suffer harm.

Fourth, assist him in his licentiousness and indulgence in music in order to dissipate his will. Make him generous gifts of pearls and jade, and ply him with beautiful women. Speak deferentially, listen respectfully, follow his commands, and accord with him in everything. He will never imagine you might be in conflict with him. Our treacherous measures will then be settled.

Fifth, treat his loyal officials very generously, but reduce the gifts you provide to the ruler. Delay his emissaries; do not listen to their missions. When he eventually dispatches other men treat them with sincerity, embrace and trust them. The ruler will then again feel you are in harmony with him. If you manage to treat his formerly loyal officials very generously, his state can then be plotted against.

Sixth, make secret alliances with his favored ministers, but visibly keep his less favored outside officials at a distance. His talented people will then be under external influence, while enemy states encroach upon his territory. Few states in such a situation have survived.

Seventh, if you want to bind his heart to you, you must offer generous presents. To gather in his assistants, loyal associates, and loved ones you must secretly show them the gains they can realize by colluding with you. Have them slight their work, and then their preparations will be futile.

Eighth, gift him with great treasures and make plans with him. When the plans are successful and profit him, he will have faith in you because of the profits. This is what is termed "being closely embraced." The result of being closely embraced is that he will inevitably be used by us. When someone rules a state but is externally controlled, his territory will inevitably be defeated.

Ninth, honor him with praise. Do nothing that will cause him personal discomfort. Display the proper respect accruing to a great power, and your obedience will certainly be trusted. Magnify his honor, being the first to gloriously praise him, humbly embellishing him as a Sage. Then his state will suffer great loss!

Tenth, be submissive so that he will trust you, and thereby learn about his true situation. Accept his ideas and respond to his affairs as if you were twins. Once you have learned everything subtly gather in his power. Thus when the ultimate day arrives it will seem as if Heaven itself destroyed him.

Eleventh, block up his access by means of the Tao. Among subordinates there is no one who does not value rank and wealth, nor hate danger and misfortune. Secretly express great respect toward them, and gradually bestow valuable gifts in order to gather in the more outstanding talents. Accumulate your own resources until they become very substantial, but manifest an external appearance of shortage. Covertly bring in wise knights, and entrust them with planning great strategy. Attract courageous knights and augment their spirit. Even when they are sufficiently rich and honored continue to increase them. When your faction has been fully established you will have attained the objective referred to as "blocking his access." If someone has a state, but his access is blocked, how can he be considered as having the state?

Twelfth, support his dissolute officials in order to confuse him. Introduce beautiful women and licentious sounds in order to befuddle him. Send him outstanding dogs and horses in order to tire him. From time to time allow him great power in order to entice him to greater arrogance. Then investigate Heaven's signs and plot with the world against him.

When these twelve measures are fully employed they will become a military weapon. Thus when, as it is said, one "looks at Heaven above and investigates Earth below" and the proper signs are already visible, attack him.

Six Secret Teachings, 15

King Wu inquired of T'ai Kung: "I want to attain our aim of overthrowing the Shang, but I have three doubts. I am afraid that our strength will be inadequate to attack the strong; to estrange his close supporters within the court; and to disperse his people. What should I do?"

The T'ai Kung replied: "Accord with the situation, be very cautious in making plans, and employ your material resources. Now in order to attack the strong you must nurture them to make them even stronger, and increase them to make them even more extensive. What is too strong will certainly break; what is too extended must have deficiencies. Attack the strong through his strength. Cause the estrangement of his favored officials by using his favorites; and disperse his people by means of the people.

"Now in the Tao of planning, thoroughness and secrecy are treasured. You should become involved with him in numerous affairs, and ply him with temptations of profit. Conflict will then surely arise.

"If you want to cause his close supporters to become estranged from him, you must do it by using what they love, making gifts to those he favors, giving them what they want. Tempt them with what they find profitable, thereby making them disaffected, and cause them to be unable to attain their ambitions. Those who covet profits will be extremely happy at the prospects, and their remaining doubts will be ended.

"Now without doubt, the Tao for attacking is to first obfuscate the king's clarity, and then attack his strength, destroying his greatness and eliminating the misfortune of the people. Debauch him with beautiful women, entice him with profit. Nurture him with flavors, and provide him with the company of female musicians. Then after you have caused his subordinates to become estranged from him, you must cause the people to grow distant from him, while never letting him know your plans. Appear to support him and draw him into your trap. Don't let him become aware of what is happening, for only then can your plan be successful."

Six Secret Teachings, 17

If the Three Armies' warriors can be forced to completely lose their determination, victory can be attained and maintained. For this reason repress the left while you hit the right; then when the right is being defeated the left will not be able to rescue them. Repress the right while you hit the left; then when the left is being defeated the right will not be able to rescue them.

Military Methods, 19

Part Five

TACTICAL SPECIFICS

32

Attack and Defense

King Wu said: "Suppose two armies encounter each other. The enemy cannot come forward, and we cannot go forward. Each side goes about establishing fortifications and defenses, without daring to be the first to attack. If I want to launch a sudden attack but lack any tactical advantage, what should I do?"

The T'ai Kung said: "Make an outward display of confusion while actually being well ordered. Show an appearance of hunger while actually being well fed. Keep your sharp weapons within, and show only dull and poor weapons outside. Have some troops come together, others split up; some assemble, others scatter. Make secret plans, keep your intentions secret. Raise the height of fortifications, and conceal your elite troops. If the officers are silent, not making any sounds, the enemy will not know our preparations. Then if you want to take his western flank, attack the eastern one."

Six Secret Teachings, 12

King Wu said: "If the enemy knows my true situation and has penetrated my plans, what should I do?"

The T'ai Kung said: "The technique for military conquest is to carefully investigate the enemy's intentions and quickly take advantage of them, launching a sudden attack where unexpected."

Six Secret Teachings, 12

In general, in warfare attack where they are weak and quiet, avoid where they are strong and quiet. Attack when they are tired, avoid them when they are well trained and alert. Attack when they are truly afraid, avoid them when they display only minor fears. From antiquity these have been the rules governing the army.

Ssu-ma Fa, 4

One who cannot be victorious assumes a defensive posture; one who can be victorious attacks. In these circumstances by assuming a defensive posture, strength will be more than adequate, whereas in offensive actions it would be inadequate.

Those who excel at defense bury themselves away below the lowest depths of Earth. Those who excel at offense move from above the greatest heights of Heaven. Thus they are able to preserve themselves and attain complete victory.

The Art of War, 4

One who excels at warfare first establishes himself in a position where he cannot be defeated while not losing any opportunity to defeat the enemy. For this reason, the victorious army first realizes the conditions for victory, and then seeks to engage in battle. The vanquished army fights first, and then seeks victory.

The Art of War, 4

In general when evaluating the enemy there are eight conditions under which one engages in battle without performing divination: First, in violent winds and extreme cold, they arise early and are on the march while barely awake, breaking ice to cross streams, unfearing of any hardship.

Second, in the burning heat of midsummer, they arise late and without delay press forward in haste, through hunger and thirst, concentrating on attaining far-off objectives.

Third, the army has been out in the field for an extended period; their food supplies are exhausted; the hundred surnames are resentful and angry; and numerous baleful portents have arisen, with the superior officers being unable to quash their effects.

Fourth, the army's resources have already been exhausted; firewood and hay are scarce; the weather frequently cloudy and rainy; and even if they wanted to plunder for supplies there is nowhere to go.

Fifth, the number mobilized is not large; the terrain and water not advantageous; the men and horses both sick and worn out; and no assistance comes from their allies.

Sixth, the road is far and the sun setting; the officers and men have labored long and are fearful. They're tired and haven't eaten; having cast aside their armor they're resting.

Seventh, the generals are weak; the officials irresponsible; the officers and troops are not solid; the Three Armies are frequently frightened; and the forces lack any assistance.

Eighth, their formations are not yet settled; their encampment not yet finished; or they are traversing dangerous territory and narrow defiles, half concealed and half exposed. In these eight conditions attack them without any doubts.

Wu-tzu, 2

In employing the army to invariably attack the enemy one must ascertain the enemy's voids and strengths, and then race to take advantage of their endangered points. When the enemy has just arrived from afar and their battle formations are not yet properly deployed, they can be attacked. If they have eaten but not yet established their encampment, they can be attacked. If they are running about wildly, they can be attacked. If they have labored hard, they can be attacked. If they haven't yet taken advantage of the terrain, they can be attacked. When they have lost the critical moment and not followed up opportunities, they can be attacked. When they have traversed a great distance, and the rear guard hasn't had time to rest yet, they can be attacked. When fording rivers and only half of them have crossed, they can be attacked. In narrow and confined roads, they can be attacked. When their flags and banners move about chaotically, they can be attacked. When their formations frequently move about, they can be attacked. When a general is separated from his soldiers, they can be attacked. When they are afraid, they can be attacked. In general in circumstances such as these select crack troops to rush upon them, divide your remaining troops and continue the assault, pressing the attack swiftly and decisively.

Wu-tzu, 2

There are six circumstances in which, without performing divination, you should avoid conflict: First, the land is broad and vast, the people wealthy and numerous. Second, the government loves the people, the ruler's beneficence extends and flows to all of them. Third, rewards are trusted, punishments based upon investigation, and both are invariably implemented in a timely fashion. Fourth, people are ranked according to their military accomplishments, they award official positions to the Worthy, and employ the able. Fifth, their forces are massive, and their weapons and armor are all first rate. Sixth, they have the assistance of all their neighbors, and the support of a powerful state.

In general, in these situations you are not a match for the enemy, so without doubt avoid them. This is what is meant by "seeing possibility and advancing, knowing difficulty and withdrawing."

Wu-tzu, 2

As for remaining within the state and going forth to attack, you want those remaining behind to be "heavy." In deploying your troops you want the formations to be solid. In launching an attack you want to make the utmost effort. And in going forth to battle you want to be of one mind.

Wei Liao-tzu, 4

The reason the Former Kings are still heard about is that they entrusted the upright with responsibility and eliminated the deceitful. They always preserved their benevolent and congenial hearts, but were decisive, without delaying, in effecting punishments. One who understands the Tao of warfare will invariably first plan against the defeats which arise from not knowing where to stop. Why must one always advance to be successful? If you advance too lightly and seek to engage the enemy in battle, and should they, on the contrary, plan to stop your going forth, the enemy will control the victory. Thus *The Art of War* says, "If they seek us, pursue them; when you see them, attack. When the aggressors dare not oppose us, press the attack, and they will inevitably lose their tactical power."

Wei Liao-tzu, 12

The T'ai-tsung said: "Are the two affairs of attacking and defending in reality one method? Sun-tzu said: 'When one excels at attacking, the enemy does not know where to mount his defense. When one excels at defense, the enemy does not know where to attack.' He did not speak about the enemy coming forth to attack me, and I also attacking the enemy. If we assume a defensive posture, and the enemy also takes up a defensive position, if in attacking and defense our strengths are equal, what tactic should be employed?"

Li Ching said: "Cases like this of mutual attack and mutual defense were, in previous ages, numerous. They all said, 'One defends when strength is insufficient, one attacks when strength is more than sufficient.' Thus they referred to insufficiency as being weakness, and having an excess as strength. Apparently they didn't understand the methods for attack and defense. I recall that Sun-tzu said: 'One who cannot be victorious assumes a defensive posture; one who can be victorious attacks.' This indicates that when the enemy cannot yet be conquered I must temporarily defend myself. When we have waited until the point when the enemy can be conquered, then we attack him. It is not a statement about strength and weakness. Later generations did not understand his meaning, so when they should attack they defend, and when they should defend they attack. The two stages are distinct, so the method cannot be a single one."

The T'ai-tsung said: "I can see that the concepts of surplus and insufficiency caused later generations to be confused about strength and weakness. They probably didn't know that the essence of defensive strategy is to show the enemy an inadequacy. The essence of aggressive strategy lies in showing the enemy that you have a surplus. If you show the enemy an insufficiency, then they will certainly advance and attack. In this case, 'the enemy does not know where to attack.' If you show the enemy a surplus then they will certainly take up defensive positions. In this case, 'the enemy does not know where to mount his defense.' Attacking and defending are one method, but the enemy and I divide it into two matters. If I succeed in this matter, the enemy's affairs will be defeated. If the enemy is successful then my aims will be defeated. Gaining and losing, success or failure, our aims and the enemy's are at odds, but attacking and defending are one! If you understand that they are one, then in a hundred battles you will be victorious a hundred times. Thus it is said, 'If you know yourself and you know the enemy, in a hundred battles you will not be endangered.' This refers to the knowledge of this unity, doesn't it?"

Li Ching bowed twice and said: "Perfect indeed are the Sage's methods! Attacking is the pivotal point of defense, defending is the strategy for attack. They are both directed toward victory, that's all. If in attacking you do not understand defending, and in defending you do not understand attacking, but instead not only make them into two separate affairs, but also assign responsibility for them to separate offices, then even though the mouth recites the words of Sun-tzu and Wu-tzu, the mind has not thought about the mysterious subtleties of the discussion of the equality of attack and defense. How can the reality then be known?"

Questions and Replies, 3

The T'ai-tsung said: "The *Ssu-ma Fa* states that 'even though a state may be vast, those who love warfare will inevitably perish,' and that 'even though calm may prevail under Heaven, those who forget warfare will inevitably be endangered.' Is this also one of the ways of attacking and defending?"

Li Ching said: "If one has a state and family, how could he not discuss attacking and defending? For attacking does not stop with just attacking their cities or attacking their formations. One must have techniques for attacking their minds. Defense does not end with just the completion of the walls and the realization of solid formations. One must also preserve spirit and be prepared to await the enemy. To speak of it in the largest terms it means the Tao of rulership. To speak of it in smaller terms, it means the methods of the general. Now attacking their minds is what is referred to as knowing them. Preserving one's *ch'i* (spirit) is what is meant by knowing yourself."

The T'ai-tsung said: "True! When I was about to engage in battle, I first evaluated the enemy's mind by comparing it with my mind to determine who was more thoroughly prepared. Only after that could I know his situation. To evaluate the enemy's *ch'i* I compared it with our own to determine who was more controlled. Only then could I know myself. For this reason, 'know them and know yourself' is the great essence of the military strategists. Contemporary generals, even if they do not know the enemy, ought to be able to know themselves, so how could they lose the advantage?"

Li Ching said: "What Sun-tzu meant by 'first make yourself unconquerable' is 'know yourself.' 'Waiting until the enemy can be conquered' is 'knowing them.' Moreover, he said that 'being unconquerable lies with yourself, while being conquerable lies with the enemy.' I have not dared to neglect this admonition even for a moment."

Questions and Replies, 3

33
Defense and Fortifications

Deep moats, high ramparts, and large reserves of supplies are the means by which to sustain your position for a long time.
Six Secret Teachings, 27

A defending army should stand fast, encourage the people, and bring them into accord with their superiors. Only after seeing the invading enemy should it move. The general's mind is focused, the minds of the people are at one with his.
Ssu-ma Fa, 3

Thus the strategy for employing the army: Do not rely on their not coming, but depend upon having the means to await them. Do not rely on their not attacking, but depend upon having an unassailable position.
The Art of War, 8

T'ien Chi asked Sun Pin: "Is there a Tao for deploying the army without engaging in battle?"

Sun Pin said: "There is. Amass troops in the ravines and increase the height of your fortifications, being silently alert without moving. You must not be greedy, you must not get angry."
Military Methods, 3

T'ien Chi said: "Our troops in the field improve their positions and establish fortifications ceaselessly. How should it be done?"

Sun Pin said: "This is the question of an enlightened general. These are things that people overlook and are not urgent about. These are the means by which we urgently erect field defenses and raise our troops' determination. Employing these measures are the means by which one can respond to sudden distress, occupy defiles and passes, and survive in the midst of fatal terrain. This is the way I took P'ang Chüan and captured Imperial Prince Shen."

Military Methods, 4

Caltrops are employed as ditches and moats. Chariots are employed as fortifications. Protective enclosures on the chariots are employed as parapets. Shields are employed as battlements. Long weapons are placed next in order to rescue any breakthrough. Short spears are placed next inside them in order to act as support for the long weapons. The short weapons follow in turn in order to make it difficult for the enemy to withdraw and take advantage of their weaknesses. Crossbows are placed next in order to act as trebuchets. In the middle there are not any men, so fill it with unorthodox forces.

Once the deployment of the troops has been determined concretely establish the methods for engagement. The *Ordinances* state: "Place the crossbows behind the caltrops; only after the enemy has entered them shoot them according to the predetermined method." The top of the fortifications should be manned by equal numbers of crossbows and spear-tipped halberds. The *Methods* states: "Move only after you hear the words of the spies you dispatched."

Five miles from your defenses establish lookout posts, ordering that they be within sight of each other. If encamped on high ground, deploy them in a square array; if encamped on low ground, deploy them in a circular perimeter. At night beat the drums, in the daytime raise flags.

Military Methods, 4

Measure the fertility and barrenness of the earth, and then establish towns. To construct the city walls, determine the appropriate terrain. In accord with the city walls determine the appropriate number of men. In accord with the number of men determine the appropriate amount of grain. When all three have been mutually determined, then internally one can be solid in defense, and externally one can be victorious in battle. Being victorious in battle externally, and preparations being controlled internally, victory and preparations are mutually employed, like the halves of a tally exactly matching each other.

Wei Liao-tzu, 2

34
Relative Strength and Appropriate Tactics

FUNDAMENTAL PRINCIPLES

In general, as for the Tao of warfare: when you employ a small number they must be solid. When you employ a large mass they must be well ordered. With a small force it is advantageous to harass the enemy; with a large mass it is advantageous to use orthodox tactics. When employing a large mass, advance and stop; when employing a small number, advance and withdraw. If your large mass encounters a small enemy force, surround them at a distance, but leave one side open. Conversely, if you divide your forces and attack in turn, a small force can withstand a large mass. If their masses are beset by uncertainty you should take advantage of it. If you are contending for a strategic position, abandon your flags as if in flight, and when the enemy attacks turn around to mount a counterattack. If the enemy is vast, then concentrate your troops and let them surround you. If the enemy is fewer and fearful, avoid them and leave a path open.

Ssu-ma Fa, 5

In general, the strategy for employing the military is this: If your strength is ten times theirs, surround them; if five, then attack them; if double, then divide your forces. If you are equal in strength to the enemy, you can engage him. If fewer, you can circumvent him. If outmatched, you can avoid him. Thus a small enemy that acts inflexibly will become the captives of a large enemy.

The Art of War, 3

As for military methods: the first is termed measurement; the second, estimation of forces; the third, calculation of numbers of men; the fourth, weighing relative strength; and the fifth, victory.

Terrain gives birth to measurement; measurement produces the estimation of forces. Estimation of forces gives rise to calculating the numbers of men. Calculating the numbers of men gives rise to weighing strength. Weighing strength gives birth to victory.

The Art of War, 4

The army does not esteem the number of troops being more numerous for it only means one cannot aggressively advance. It is sufficient for you to muster your own strength, analyze the enemy, and take them. Only someone who lacks strategic planning and slights an enemy will inevitably be captured by others.

The Art of War, 9

King Wei said: "Suppose we go forth and the enemy comes forth. We still do not know whether they are many or few. How should we employ the army?"

Sun Pin said: "The method is called 'Dangerous Completion.' If the enemy is well ordered, deploy into three formations. One should confront the enemy, two can provide mutual assistance. When they can halt, they should halt; when they can move, they should move. Do not seek a quick victory."

Military Methods, 3

King Wei asked: "How do we attack someone of equal strength?"

Sun Pin said: "Confuse them so that they disperse their forces, then unite our troops and strike them, do not let the enemy know about it. But if they don't disperse then secure your position and halt. Do not attack in any situation that appears suspicious."

Military Methods, 3

SUPERIOR NUMBERS

If you are double the enemy, halt and do not move, be full and await them.

Military Methods, 3

King Wei said: "If we are strong while the enemy is weak, if we are numerous while the enemy is few, how should we employ them?"

Sun Pin bowed twice and said: "This is the question of an enlightened King! To be numerous and moreover strong yet still inquire about employing them is the Tao to make the state secure. The method is called 'Inducing the Army.' Disrupt your companies and disorder your ranks, in order to accord with the enemy's desires. Then the enemy will certainly engage you in battle."

Military Methods, 3

When your strategic power exceeds the enemy's when deploying to approach them employ a flanking attack on the wings.

Military Methods, 14

OUTNUMBERED OR INFERIOR IN
COMPONENT STRENGTH

Valleys with streams and treacherous ravines are the means by which to stop chariots and defend against cavalry. Narrow passes and mountain forests are the means by which a few can attack a large force.

Six Secret Teachings, 27

King Wu asked the T'ai Kung: "Suppose we have led the army deep into the territory of the feudal lords until we are opposed by the enemy's assault forces. The enemy is numerous, while we are few. The enemy is strong, while we are weak. The enemy approaches at night, some attacking the left, others the right. The Three Armies are quaking. We want to be victorious if we choose to fight, and solid if we choose to maintain a defensive posture. How should we act?"

The T'ai Kung said: "In this case we refer to them as 'Shaking Invaders.' It is more advantageous to go out and fight; you cannot be defensive. Select skilled soldiers and strong crossbowmen, together with chariots and cavalry, to comprise the right and left flanks. Then urgently strike their forward forces, quickly attacking the rear as well. Some should strike the exterior, others the interior. Their troops will certainly be confused, their generals afraid."

King Wu asked: "Suppose the enemy has blocked off our forward units some distance away, and is pressing a fervent attack on our rear. They have broken up our elite troops, and cut off our skilled soldiers. Our interior and exterior forces cannot communicate with each other. The Three Armies are in chaos, all running off in defeat. The officers and troops have no will to fight, the generals and commanders no desire to defend themselves. What should we do?"

The T'ai Kung said: "Illustrious is your question, my King! You should make your commands clear and be careful about your orders. You should have our courageous, crack troops who are willing to confront danger sally forth, each man carrying a torch, two men to a drum. You must know the enemy's location, then strike both the interior and exterior. When our secret signals have all been communicated, order them to extinguish the torches, and stop beating all the drums. Then the interior and exterior should respond to each other, each according to the appropriate time. When our Three Armies urgently attack, the enemy will certainly be defeated and vanquished."

Six Secret Teachings, 45

King Wu asked the T'ai Kung: "Suppose we have led the army deep into the territory of the feudal lords where we suddenly encounter a martial, numerically superior enemy. If his martial chariots and valiant cavalry attack our left and right flanks, and our Three Armies become so shaken that their flight is unstoppable, what should I do?"

The T'ai Kung said: "In this situation you have what is termed a defeated army. Those who are skillful in employing their forces will manage a victory. Those who are not will perish."

King Wu asked: "What does one do?"

The T'ai Kung replied: "Have our most skilled soldiers and strong crossbowmen, together with our martial chariots and valiant cavalry, conceal themselves on both sides of the retreat route, about three miles ahead and behind the main force. When the enemy pursues us, launch a simultaneous chariot and cavalry assault from both sides. In such circumstances the enemy will be thrown into confusion, and our fleeing soldiers will stop by themselves."

Six Secret Teachings, 46

King Wu asked: "Suppose the enemy's chariots and cavalry are squarely opposite ours, but the enemy is numerous while we are few, the enemy strong while we are weak. Their approach is disciplined and spirited, and our formations are unable to withstand them. What should we do?"

The T'ai Kung replied: "Select our skilled soldiers and strong crossbowmen, and have them lie in ambush on both sides, while the chariots and cavalry deploy into a solid formation and assume position. When the enemy passes our concealed forces, the crossbowmen should fire en masse into their flanks. The chariots, cavalry, and skilled soldiers should then urgently attack their army, some striking the front, others striking the rear. Even if the enemy is numerous they will certainly flee."

Six Secret Teachings, 46

King Wu asked the T'ai Kung: "If I want to attack a large number with only a few, or attack the strong with the weak, what should I do?"

The T'ai Kung said: "If you want to attack a large number with only a few, you must do it at sunset, setting an ambush in tall grass, pressing them on a narrow road. To attack the strong with the weak you must obtain the support of a great state, and the assistance of neighboring states."

King Wu asked: "We do not have any terrain with tall grass, and moreover there are no narrow roads. The enemy has already arrived; we cannot wait until sunset. I do not have the support of any great state, nor, furthermore, the assistance of neighboring states. What then?"

The T'ai Kung said: "You should set out specious arrays and false enticements to dazzle and confuse their general, to redirect his path so that he will be forced to pass tall grass. Make his route long so you can arrange your engagement for sunset. When his advance units have not yet finished crossing the water, or his rear units have not yet reached the encampment, spring our concealed troops, vehemently striking his right and left flanks, while your chariots and cavalry stir chaos among his forward and rear units. Even if the enemy is numerous, they will certainly flee.

"To serve the ruler of a great state, to gain the submission of the officers of neighboring states, make their gifts generous, and speak extremely deferentially. In this fashion you will obtain the support of a great state, and the assistance of neighboring states."

Six Secret Teachings, 49

Marquis Wu asked: "If the enemy is numerous while we are few, what can I do?"

Wu Ch'i replied: "Avoid them on easy terrain, attack them in narrow quarters. Thus it is said for one to attack ten, nothing is better than a narrow defile. For ten to attack a hundred, nothing is better than a deep ravine. For a thousand to attack ten thousand, nothing is better than a dangerous pass. Now if you have a small number of troops, should they suddenly arise, striking the gongs and beating the drums, to attack the enemy on a confined road, then even though his numbers are very great they will all be startled and move about. Thus it is said, when employing larger numbers concentrate upon easy terrain; when using small numbers concentrate upon naturally confined terrain."

Wu-tzu, 5

Marquis Wu asked: "Their forces are extremely numerous, martial, and courageous. Behind them are ravines and dangerous passes; on their right are mountains; on the left a river. They have deep moats and high ramparts, and are defending their position with strong crossbowmen. Their withdrawal is like a mountain moving; their advance like a tempest. As their food stocks are also plentiful, it will be difficult to defend against them very long. What should be done?"

Wu Ch'i replied: "A great question indeed! This is not a problem of the strength of chariots and cavalry, but of having the plans of a Sage. If you can prepare a thousand chariots and ten thousand cavalry, and support them with foot soldiers, you can divide them into five armies, each one traversing a different route. Now if the five armies simultaneously move along five different routes the enemy will certainly be confused, and won't know where to concentrate his efforts. If the enemy fortifies his defenses in order to solidify his troops, quickly dispatch spies in order to observe their plans. If they listen to our persuasions they will abandon their positions and depart. If they don't listen to our persuasions they will kill our emissaries and burn the treaties. Then divide your forces and engage them in five battles. However if you win any of the battles do not pursue the retreating enemy. If you don't win then withdraw in extreme haste, thereby feigning a retreat. After reforming, swiftly attack them, with one force tying them up in the front, another cutting off the rear, while two of your armies move silently to the left and right flanks to suddenly attack them. If the five armies strike simultaneously they will certainly gain the advantage. This is the Tao for attacking the strong."

Wu-tzu, 5

King Wei asked: "If the enemy is numerous while we are few, if the enemy is strong while we are weak, how should we employ them?"

Sun Pin said: "The strategy is termed 'Yielding to Awesomeness.' You must conceal the army's tail to ensure that the army will be able to withdraw. Long weapons should be in front, short ones to the rear. Establish roving crossbow units in order to provide support in exigencies. Your main force should not move in order to wait for the enemy to manifest his capabilities."

Military Methods, 3

King Wei said: "Is there a Tao for one to attack ten?"

Sun Pin said: "There is. Attack where they are unprepared, go forth where they will not expect it."

Military Methods, 3

T'ien Chi said: "If the enemy is numerous and martial but we must fight, is there a Tao?"

Sun Pin said: "There is. Augment your fortifications and expand your soldiers' determination. Strictly order and unify the masses. Avoid the enemy and make him arrogant. Inveigle and tire him. 'Attack where he is not prepared, go forth where he will not expect it.' You must be prepared to continue such actions for a long time."

Military Methods, 3

T'ien Chi asked Sun Pin: "If our troops being few unexpectedly come into mutual contact with the enemy, how should we manage it?"

Sun Pin said: "Transmit orders to have our crossbows race and to spread out our bowmen."

Military Methods, 4

When under duress, shifting the army is the means by which to prepare for a strong enemy.

Military Methods, 14

"Suppose our army encounters the enemy and both establish encampments. Our men and weapons are numerous but our chariots and cavalry are few. If the enemy's men are ten times ours, how should we attack them?"

"To attack them, you should conceal yourselves in the ravines and take the defiles as your base, being careful to avoid broad, easy terrain. This is because easy terrain is advantageous for chariots while ravines are advantageous to infantry. This is the Tao for striking chariots in such circumstances."

Military Methods, 17

"Suppose our army encounters the enemy and both establish encampments. Our chariots and cavalry are numerous, but our men and weapons are few. If the enemy's men are ten times ours, how should we attack them?"

"To attack them, carefully avoid ravines and narrows; break open a route and lead them, coercing them toward easy terrain. Even though the enemy is ten times more numerous, easy terrain will be conducive to our chariots and cavalry, and our Three Armies can attack. This is the Tao for striking infantry."

Military Methods, 17

"Suppose our army encounters the enemy and both establish encampments. Our provisions and food supplies have been disrupted. Our infantry and weapons are inadequate to be relied upon. If we abandon our base and attack, the enemy's men are ten times ours. How should we strike them?"

"To strike them when the enemy's men have already deployed into and are defending the narrows, we should . . . turn about and inflict damage upon their vacuities. This is the Tao for striking an enemy on contentious terrain."

Military Methods, 17

"Suppose our army encounters the enemy and both establish encampments. The enemy's generals are courageous and difficult to frighten. Their weapons are strong, their men numerous and self-reliant. All the warriors of their Three Armies are courageous and untroubled. Their generals are awesome; their soldiers are martial; their officers strong; and their provisions well supplied. None of the feudal lords dares contend with them. How should we strike them?"

"To strike them, announce that you do not dare fight. Show them that you are incapable; sit about submissively and await them in order to make their thoughts arrogant and apparently accord with their ambitions. Do not let them recognize your ploy. Thereupon strike where unexpected; attack where they do not defend; apply pressure where they are indolent; and attack their doubts. Being both haughty and martial, when their Three Armies break camp the front and rear will not look at each other. Therefore strike their middle just as if you had the infantry strength to do it. This is the Tao for striking a strong, numerous foe."

Military Methods, 17

35

Deployments, Formations, and Their Employment

GENERAL PRINCIPLES FOR DEPLOYMENTS

King Wu asked the T'ai Kung: "In employing the army there are the Heavenly Deployment, the Earthly Deployment, and the Human Deployment. What are these?"

The T'ai Kung replied: "When you accord with the sun and moon, the stars, planets, and the handle of the Big Dipper, one on the left, one on the right, one in front, and one to the rear, this is referred to as the Heavenly Deployment.

"When the hills and mounds, rivers and streams are similarly to your advantage to the front, rear, left, and right, this is referred to as the Earthly Deployment.

"When you employ chariots and horses, when you use both the civil and martial, this is referred to as the Human Deployment."

Six Secret Teachings, 32

The pinnacle of military deployment approaches the formless. If it is formless, then even the deepest spy cannot discern it or the wise make plans against it. In accord with the enemy's disposition we impose measures on the masses that produce victory, but the masses are unable to fathom them. Men all know the disposition by which we attain victory, but no one knows the configuration through which we control the victory. Thus a victorious battle strategy is not repeated, the configurations of response to the enemy are inexhaustible.

The Art of War, 6

Now the army likes heights and abhors low areas, esteems the sunny (yang) and disdains the shady (yin). It nourishes life and occupies the substantial. An army that avoids the hundred illnesses is said to be certain of victory.

The Art of War, 9

King Wei said: "If the ground is level and the troops well ordered, but after engaging in battle they retreat, what does it mean?" Sun Pin said: "It means that the deployment lacked a front."

Military Methods, 3

Sun Pin said: "If you want to understand the nature of the army, the crossbow and arrows are the model. Arrows are the troops, the crossbow is the general. The one who releases them is the ruler. As for arrows, the metal is at the front, the feathers are at the rear. Thus they are powerful and excel in flight, for the front is heavy and the rear is light. Today in ordering the troops the rear is heavy and the front light, so when deployed in formation they are well ordered, but when pressed toward the enemy they do not obey. This is because in controlling the troops men do not model on the arrow."

Military Methods, 10

NATURE AND CHARACTERISTICS OF VARIOUS FORMATIONS

As for military formations; when advancing, the most important thing for the ranks is to be dispersed; when engaged in battle, to be dense, and for the weapons to be of mixed types. Instructions to the people should be thorough;

quietness is the basis of order; awesomeness becomes advantageous when it is made manifest. When people preserve each other according to righteousness, then they will be stimulated to action. When many well-conceived plans prove successful, the people submit to them. If they sincerely submit at the appropriate time, then subsequent affairs will be well ordered. When things are manifest, then the eye discerns them clearly. When plans have been decided the mind is strong. When advancing and withdrawing are without doubt, one can give the appearance of being without plans. When judging infractions and punishing the guilty, do not wantonly change their designations, nor change their flags.

Ssu-ma Fa, 3

In general, the chariots realize security through close formations; the infantry becomes solid through kneeling; armor becomes solid through weight; victory is attained through the lightness of the weapons.

Ssu-ma Fa, 4

The Awl Formation is the means by which to penetrate solid formations and destroy elite units. The Wild Geese Formation is the means by which to abruptly assault the enemy's flanks and respond to changes. Selecting the troops and strong officers is the means by which to break through enemy formations and capture their generals. Strong crossbowmen running along and firing are the means by which to take pleasure in battle and sustain it. The Fierce Wind Formation is the means by which to return. Masses of troops are used to divide the effort and achieve victory.

Military Methods, 3

As for employing the eight formations in battle: in accord with the advantages of the terrain use appropriate formations from among the eight. Employ a deployment that segments the troops into three, each formation having an elite front, and each elite front having a rear guard. They should all await their orders before moving. Fight with one of them, reserve the other two. Employ one to attack the enemy, use the other two to consolidate the gains. If the enemy is weak and confused, use your picked troops first to exploit it. If the enemy is strong and well disciplined, use your weak troops first in order to entice them.

Military Methods, 7

Breaking apart and intermixing like clouds are the means by which to create a tactical imbalance of power and explosive movement.

Military Methods, 14

To hunt down the enemy's army use an elongated formation; labor and exhaust them by constraining and contravening them. To deploy the regiments use an endangering . . . formation. Engage in arrow warfare with the Cloud Formation. Defend against and surround the enemy with an entangled, flowing formation. Seize the enemy's fierce beak with a closing envelopment. Attack the already defeated by wrapping and seizing them. When racing to rescue an army employ a close formation. In fierce combat use alternated rows. Employ heavy troops in order to attack light troops. Employ light troops in order to attack the dispersed. When attacking mountain cliffs employ the "Arrayed Walls." On . . . terrain employ a square formation. When you confront heights and deploy your forces, employ a piercing formation. For ravines . . . employ a circular formation.

Turbulent winds and shaking formations are the means by which to exploit doubts. To facilitate exhausting the enemy use the Awl Formation. To realize a sharp-edged deployment use the Awl Formation. The Floating Marsh Formation and flank attacks are the means by which to fight an enemy on a confined road. Solid formations and massed battalions are the means to attack an enemy's fiery strength. The Whirlwind Formation and swift chariots are the means by which to pursue a fleeing enemy.

Military Methods, 14

In general, there are ten deployments: square, circular, diffuse, concentrated, Awl, Wild Geese, hooked, Dark Rising, incendiary, and aquatic. Each of them has its advantages: The square deployment is for cutting. The circular deployment is for unifying. The diffuse deployment is for rapid, flexible response. The concentrated deployment is to prevent being cut off and taken. Deployment into the Awl Formation is for decisively severing the enemy. Deployment into the Wild Geese Formation is for exchanging archery fire. Deployment into the hooked formation is the means by which to change targets and alter plans. The Dark Rising deployment is for causing doubts in the enemy's masses and difficulty for his plans. The incendiary deployment is the means to seize enemy encampments. The aquatic deployment is the means to inundate the solid.

Military Methods, 16

The tactics for square deployment: you must thin out the troops in the middle and make those on the sides thicker. The reserve ready response formations are at the rear. By thinning out the middle the general can effect a rapid response. By expanding and making the sides heavy, the general can cut the enemy. Retaining the ready response reserves in the rear is the means by which to. . . .

In the tactics for the diffuse deployment armor is scarce and men are few. For this reason make it firm. Martial prowess lies in the flags and pennants; showing large numbers of men lies in your weapons. Thus the soldiers must disperse and maintain their internal separation. Make the flags, banners, and feathered pennants numerous; sharpen your blades to act as your flanks. For them not to be compressed by the enemy when diffuse or surrounded when concentrated lies in exercising great care. The chariots do not race, the infantry does not run. The tactics for diffuse deployment lie in creating numerous small operational units. Some advance, others retreat. Some attack, others hold and defend. Some launch frontal assaults, others press their developing weaknesses. Thus the diffuse deployment is able to seize the enemy's elite forces.

The tactics for concentrated deployment: Do not augment the spacing between the men. When they are compressed, gather your blades at the head of the formation and then extend it forward while the front and rear mutually preserve each other. Amidst the changes of battle do not alter it. If the mailed soldiers are afraid, have them sit. Use sound to direct them to sit and arise. Do not dispatch any forces after enemy troops that go off; do not stop those who come forth. Some of our troops should attack their circuitous routes of approach, others should "insult" their elite troops. Make them as dense as feather down without any gaps; when they turn about and retreat they should be like a mountain. Then the concentrated deployment cannot be taken.

Deployment into the Awl Formation should be like a sword. If the top is not sharp it will not penetrate; if the blade is not thin it will not cut; if the foundation is not thick you cannot deploy the formation. For this reason the tip must be sharp, the blade must be thin, and the foundation must be substantial. Only then can a deployment into the Awl Formation decisively sever the enemy.

Deployment into the Wild Geese Formation . . . middle. This refers to the function of the Wild Geese deployment. The front ranks should be like a baboon, the rear ranks should be like a wildcat. Attack from three sides, not letting the enemy escape your net to preserve themselves. This is referred to as the function of the Wild Geese deployment.

When deployed into the hooked formation the front ranks must be square, while those conjoined on the left and right must be hooked. When the three sounds of the drums, gongs, and pipes are already complete, flags in the five colors must be prepared. When the sounds of our commands are clearly discriminated and the troops all know the five flags, and there is no front or rear, no. . . .

In the Dark Rising deployment you must make the flags, pennants, and feathered banners numerous; the drums should be integrated and resounding. If the mailed troops are confused have them sit; if the chariots are disordered array them in rows. When they have been ordered . . . with a great pounding and tumult, as if descending from Heaven, as if coming out from Earth, the infantry should come forth and be unwavering. Throughout the day they will not be taken. This is referred to as the Dark Rising deployment.

Military Methods, 16

The standard deployment for formations is always facing toward the enemy. There are also internally oriented formations, externally oriented formations, standing formations, and sitting formations. Internally oriented formations provide the means to preserve the center; externally oriented formations provide the means to prepare against external threats. Standing formations are the means to move, sitting formations the means to stop. Mixed formations, with some soldiers standing, others sitting, respond to each other in accord with the need to move or stop, with the general being in the middle. The weapons of the seated soldiers are the sword and axe; the weapons of the standing soldiers are the spear-tipped halberd and crossbow; the general also occupies the middle.

Wei Liao-tzu, 23

METHODS FOR ATTACKING SPECIFIC FORMATIONS

Dividing your troops into four and splitting them into five are the means by which to attack their circular formations and destroy their square ones.

Six Secret Teachings, 27

"Suppose our army encounters the enemy and both 'guest' and 'host' have deployed. The disposition of the enemy's men is like a woven, flat basket. If I estimate the enemy's intentions, he seems to want us to penetrate his lines and be overwhelmed. How should we strike them?"

"To strike them the thirsty should not drink, the hungry should not eat. Segment into three operational groups and employ two to assemble and strike their critical point. When the enemy has already initiated a response toward the middle our talented officers and selected soldiers should then strike their two flanks. . . . their Three Armies will be severely defeated. This is the Tao for striking basket-like deployments."

Military Methods, 17

"Suppose our army encounters the enemy and both establish encampments. The provisions and foodstuffs for both sides are equal and ample; our men and arms balanced with the enemy's; while both 'guest' [or invader] and 'host' [or defender] are afraid. If the enemy has deployed in a circular formation in order to await us and relies upon it for his solidity, how should we strike them?"

"To strike them the masses of our Three Armies should be divided to comprise four or five operational groups. Some of them should assault them and then feign retreat, displaying fear to them. When they see we are afraid they will divide up their forces and pursue us with abandon, thereby confusing and destroying their solidity. The four drums should rise up in unison, our five operational forces should all attack together. When all five arrive simultaneously the Three Armies will be united in their sharpness. This is the Tao for striking a circular formation."

Military Methods, 17

"**S**uppose our army encounters the enemy and both establish encampments. The enemy is rich while we are poor; the enemy is numerous while we are few; the enemy is strong while we are weak. If they approach in a square formation, how should we strike them?"

"To strike them deploy in the diffuse formation and fragment them; if they are properly assembled, separate them; engage them in battle and then feign retreat; and kill the general for their rear guard without letting them become aware of it. This is the Tao for striking a square formation."

Military Methods, 17

"**S**uppose our army encounters the enemy and both establish encampments. The enemy is already numerous and strong, and have assumed an extended horizontal deployment. We have deployed and await them, but our men are few and incapable of withstanding them. How should we strike them?"

"To strike them you must segment our soldiers into three operational groups and select the 'death warriors.' Two groups should be deployed in an extended array with long flanks; one should consist of talented officers and selected troops. They should assemble to strike at the enemy's critical point. This is the Tao for killing their general and striking horizontal deployments."

Military Methods, 17

"Suppose our army encounters the enemy and both establish encampments. If the enemy's troops are already numerous and strong; muscular, agile, and resolute; and have deployed into a sharp formation in order to await us, how should we strike them?"

"To strike them you must segment into three operational groups to separate them. One should be stretched out horizontally, two should go off to strike their flanks. Their upper ranks will be afraid and their lower ranks confused. When the lower and upper ranks are already in chaos, their Three Armies will then be severely defeated. This is the Tao for striking a sharp deployment."

Military Methods, 17

The dense conquer the diffuse; the full conquer the vacuous; byways conquer roads; the urgent conquer the slow; the numerous conquer the few; the rested conquer the weary.

If they are dense, make them denser; if they are diffuse, disperse them; if they are full, make them fuller; if they are vacuous, make them more vacuous; if they are taking shortcuts, make them shorter; if they are on the road, make the road longer; if they are urgent, make them more urgent; if they are slow, make them slower; if they are numerous, make them more numerous; if they are few, make them fewer; if they are rested, make them more rested; if they are tired, make them more tired.

The dense and diffuse mutually change into each other; the full and vacuous mutually change into each other; the urgent and slow mutually change into each other; the numerous and few mutually change into each other; the rested and tired mutually change into each other.

Do not oppose the dense with the dense; do not oppose the dispersed with the dispersed; do not oppose the full with the full; do not oppose the vacuous with the vacuous; do not oppose the urgent with the urgent; do not oppose the slow with the slow; do not oppose the numerous with the numerous; do not oppose the few with the few; do not oppose the rested with the rested; do not oppose the weary with the weary.

The dense and diffuse mutually oppose each other; the full and vacuous mutually oppose each other; shortcuts and roads mutually oppose each other; the urgent and slow mutually oppose each other; the numerous and few mutually oppose each other; the rested and weary mutually oppose each other.

A dense enemy can be dispersed; the full can be made vacuous; one taking shortcuts can be forced onto main roads; the urgent can be slowed; the numerous can be made few; the rested can be made fatigued.

Military Methods, 29

36

Basic Principles of Terrain

In general, the strategy for employing the military is this: After the general has received his commands from the ruler, united the armies, and assembled the masses: Do not encamp on entrapping terrain. Unite with your allies on focal terrain. Do not remain on isolated terrain. Make strategic plans for encircled terrain. On fatal terrain you must do battle. There are roads that are not followed. There are armies that are not attacked. There are fortified cities that are not assaulted. There is terrain for which one does not contend. There are commands from the ruler that are not accepted.

Thus the general who has a penetrating understanding of the advantages of the nine changes knows how to employ the army. If a general does not have a penetrating understanding of the advantages of the nine changes, even though he is familiar with the topography, he will not be able to realize the advantages of terrain. One who commands an army but does not know the techniques for the nine changes, even though he is familiar with the five advantages, will not be able to control men.

The Art of War, 8

Configuration of terrain is an aid to the army. Analyzing the enemy, taking control of victory, estimating ravines and defiles, the distant and near, is the Tao of the superior general. One who knows these and employs them in combat will certainly be victorious. One who does not know these or employ them in combat will certainly be defeated.

The Art of War, 10

One who does not know the plans of the feudal lords cannot forge preparatory alliances. One who does not know the topography of mountains and forests, ravines and defiles, wetlands and marshes cannot maneuver the army. One who does not employ local guides will not secure advantages of terrain. One who does not know one of these four or five cannot command the army of a hegemon or a true king.

The Art of War, 11

The chariots and cavalry that participate in a battle should be divided into three forces, one for the right, one for the left, and one for the rear. If the terrain is easy make the chariots numerous; if difficult, make the cavalry numerous. If constricted then increase the crossbows. On both difficult and easy terrain you must know the "tenable" and "fatal" ground. Occupy tenable ground, attack on fatal ground.

Military Methods, 7

As for the Tao of terrain, yang constitutes the exterior, yin constitutes the interior. The direct constitutes the warp, techniques constitute the woof. When the woof and the warp have been realized deployments will not be confused. The direct traverses land where vegetation thrives, techniques take advantage of where the foliage is half dead.

Military Methods, 8

37

Specific Configurations of Terrain

CONTENTIOUS TERRAIN

If when we occupy it, it will be advantageous to us, while if they occupy it, it will be advantageous to them, it is "contentious terrain." On contentious terrain do not attack. On contentious terrain I race our rear elements forward.

The Art of War, 11

CONSTRICTED AND DEADLY TERRAIN

Holding defiles and narrows is the means by which to be solidly entrenched. For narrow roads and small bypaths set out iron caltrops eight inches wide, having hooks four inches high and shafts of more than six feet, numbering twelve hundred. They are for defeating retreating cavalry. On narrow roads, small bypaths, and constricted terrain set out iron chains, one hundred twenty of them, to defeat infantry and cavalry, to urgently press the attack against the invaders, and to intercept their flight.

Six Secret Teachings, 27, 31

You must quickly get away from deadly configurations of terrain such as precipitous gorges with mountain torrents, Heaven's Well, Heaven's Jail, Heaven's Net, Heaven's Pit, and Heaven's Fissure. Do not approach them. When we keep them at a distance, the enemy is forced to approach them. When we face them, the enemy is compelled to have them at their rear.

The Art of War, 9

When on the flanks the army encounters ravines and defiles, wetlands with reeds and tall grass, mountain forests or areas with heavy, entangled undergrowth, you must thoroughly search them because they are places where an ambush or spies would be concealed.

The Art of War, 9

As for constricted configurations, if we occupy them first we must fully deploy throughout them in order to await the enemy. If the enemy occupies them first and fully deploys in them, do not follow them in. If they do not fully deploy in them, then follow them in.

The Art of War, 10

Where the entrance is constricted, the return is circuitous, and with a small number they can strike our masses, it is "encircled terrain." On encircled terrain use strategy.

The Art of War, 11

Where there are mountains and forests, ravines and defiles, wetlands and marshes, wherever the road is difficult to negotiate, it is "entrapping terrain." On entrapping terrain move through quickly. On entrapping terrain I speedily advance along the roads.

The Art of War, 11

Where if one fights with intensity he will survive but if he does not fight with intensity he will perish, it is "fatal terrain." On fatal terrain engage in battle.

The Art of War, 11

Marquis Wu asked: "Is there a Tao for advancing and halting the Three Armies?"

Wu Ch'i replied: "Do not confront 'Heaven's furnace' or 'Dragon's head.' Heaven's furnace is the mouth of a deep valley. Dragon's head is the base of a high mountain. You should keep the Green Dragon banner on the left, White Tiger on the right, Vermilion Bird in the front, Mysterious Military to the rear, with Twinkler above, from where military affairs will be controlled. When about to engage in combat determine the wind's direction. If favorable yell and follow it; if contrary, assume a solid formation and await the enemy."

Wu-tzu, 3

The five killing grounds are Heaven's Well, Heaven's Jail, Heaven's Net, Heaven's Fissure, and Heaven's Pit. These five graves are killing grounds. Do not occupy them, do not remain on them.

Military Methods, 8

When the enemy is bottled up in a ravine, release the mouth in order to entice them farther away.

Military Methods, 14

DISPERSIVE TERRAIN

When the feudal lords fight in their own territory, it is "dispersive terrain." On dispersive terrain do not engage the enemy.

The Art of War, 11

FOCAL TERRAIN

Land of the feudal lords surrounded on three sides such that whoever arrives first will gain the masses of All under Heaven is "focal terrain." On focal terrain unite and form alliances with nearby feudal lords.

The Art of War, 11

HEAVY TERRAIN

When one penetrates deeply into enemy territory, by-passing numerous cities, it is "heavy terrain." On heavy terrain plunder for provisions.

The Art of War, 11

LIGHT TERRAIN

When they enter someone else's territory, but not deeply, it is "light terrain." On light terrain do not stop.

The Art of War, 11

MARSHES, WETLANDS, RIVERS, AND LAKES

Marshy depressions and secluded dark areas are the means by which to conceal your appearance.

Six Secret Teachings, 27

Unorthodox technical skills are the means by which to cross deep waters and ford rivers. Strong crossbows and long weapons are the means by which to fight across water.

Six Secret Teachings, 27

King Wu said: "In front of us lies a large body of water, or broad moat, or deep water hole that we want to cross. However, we do not have equipment such as boats and oars. The enemy has fortifications and ramparts that limit our army's advance, and block off our retreat. Patrols are constantly watchful; passes are fully defended. Their chariots and cavalry press us in front, their courageous fighters attack us to the rear. What should we do?"

The T'ai Kung said: "Large bodies of water, broad moats, and deep water holes are usually not defended by the enemy. If they are able to defend them, their troops will certainly be few. In such situations you should use the Flying River with winches, and also the Heavenly Huang, to cross the army over. Our courageous, strong, skilled soldiers should move where we indicate, rushing into the enemy, breaking up his formations, all fighting to the death.

"First of all burn the supply wagons and provisions, and clearly inform the men that those who fight courageously will live, while cowards will die. After they have broken out and crossed the bridges, order the rear elements to set a great conflagration visible from far off. The troops sallying forth must take advantage of the cover afforded by grass, trees, hillocks, and ravines. The enemy's chariots and cavalry will certainly not dare pursue them too far. Using the flames as a marker, the first to go out should be ordered to proceed as far as the flames and then stop, reforming a four-sided attack formation. In this fashion the Three Armies will be fervent and sharp, and fight courageously, and no one will be able to withstand us."

Six Secret Teachings, 34

King Wu asked the T'ai Kung: "Suppose we have led the army deep into the territory of the feudal lords where we are confronting the enemy across a river. The enemy is well equipped and numerous; we are impoverished and few. If we cross the water to attack we will not be able to advance, while if we want to outlast them our supplies are too few. We are encamped on salty ground. There are no towns in any direction, and moreover no grass or trees. There is nothing the Three Armies can plunder, while the oxen and horses have neither fodder nor place to graze. What should we do?"

The T'ai Kung said: "The Three Armies are unprepared; the oxen and horses have nothing to eat; the officers and troops have no supplies. In this situation seek some opportunity to trick the enemy and quickly get away, setting up ambushes to your rear."

King Wu said: "The enemy cannot be deceived. My officers and troops are confused. The enemy has occupied positions cutting across both our front and rear. Our Three Armies are defeated and in flight. What then?"

The T'ai Kung said: "When you are searching for an escape route, gold and jade are essential. You must obtain intelligence from the enemy's emissaries. In this case cleverness and secrecy are your treasures."

King Wu said: "Suppose the enemy knows I have laid ambushes, so their main army is unwilling to cross the river. The general of their second army then breaks off some units and dispatches them to ford the river. My Three Armies are sorely afraid. What should I do?"

The T'ai Kung said: "In this situation divide your troops into assault formations, and have them improve their positions. Wait until all the enemy's troops have emerged, then spring your concealed troops, rapidly striking their rear. Have your strong crossbowmen on both sides shoot into their left and right flanks. Divide your chariots and cavalry into the Crow and Cloud Formation, arraying them against their front and rear. Then your Three Armies should vehemently press the attack. When the enemy sees us engaged in battle, their main force will certainly ford the river and come up. Then spring the ambushing forces, urgently striking their rear. The chariots and cavalry should assault the left and right. Even though the enemy is numerous they can be driven off.

"In general, the most important thing in employing your troops is that when the enemy approaches to engage in battle you must deploy your assault formations, and have them improve their positions. Thereafter divide your chariots and cavalry into the Crow and Cloud Formation. This is the unorthodox in employing your troops. What is referred to as the Crow and Cloud Formation is like the crows dispersing and the clouds forming together. Their changes and transformations are endless."

Six Secret Teachings, 48

In general, in warfare keep the wind to your back, the mountains behind you, heights on the right, and defiles on the left. Pass through wetlands, cross over damaged roads. Complete double the normal march before encamping, and select ground for encamping configured like a turtle's back.

Ssu-ma Fa, 5

When you cross salt marshes and wetlands, concentrate on quickly getting away from them; do not remain. If you engage in battle in marshes or wetlands, you must stay in areas with marsh grass and keep groves of trees at your back. This is the way to deploy the army in marshes and wetlands.

The Art of War, 9

When it rains upstream, foam appears. If you want to cross over the river, wait until it settles. After crossing rivers you must distance yourself from them. If the enemy is fording a river to advance, do not confront them in the water. When half their forces have crossed, it will be advantageous to strike them. If you want to engage the enemy in battle, do not array your forces near the river to confront the invader but look for tenable ground and occupy the heights. Do not confront the current's flow. This is the way to deploy the army where there are rivers.

The Art of War, 9

Marquis Wu asked: "When it has been continuously raining for a long time, so the horses sink into the mire and the chariots are stuck, while we are under enemy attack on all four sides and the Three Armies are terrified, what should I do?"

Wu Ch'i replied: "In general desist from employing chariots when the weather is rainy and the land wet, but mobilize them when it is hot and dry. Value high terrain, disdain low ground. When racing your strong chariots, whether advancing or halting, you must adhere to the road. If the enemy arises be sure to follow their tracks."

Wu-tzu, 5

Marquis Wu asked: "If we encounter the enemy in a vast, watery marsh where the chariot wheels sink down to the point that the shafts are under water; both our chariots and cavalry are floundering; and we haven't prepared any boats or oars, so can't advance or retreat—what should we do?"

Wu Ch'i replied: "This is referred to as water warfare. Do not employ chariots or cavalry, but have them remain on the side. Mount some nearby height and look all about. You must ascertain the water's condition, know its expanse, and fathom its depth. Then you can conceive an unorthodox stratagem for victory. If the enemy begins crossing the water, press them when half have crossed."

Wu-tzu, 5

What causes trouble for the army is the terrain. What causes difficulty for the enemy is ravines. Thus it is said that three miles of wetlands will cause trouble for the army; crossing through such wetlands will result in leaving the main force behind.

Military Methods, 3

Five types of terrain are conducive to defeat: gorges with streams; valleys; river areas; marshes; and salt flats. Crossing rivers; confronting hills; going contrary to the current's flow, occupying killing ground; and confronting masses of trees— all these that I have just mentioned, in all five, one will also not be victorious.

Military Methods, 8

Unusual movements and perverse actions are the means by which to crush the enemy at fords.

Military Methods, 14

The tactics for defensive aquatic warfare: You must make the infantry numerous and the chariots few. Command them to fully prepare all the necessary equipment, such as hooks, repelling poles, cypress wood, pestles, light boats, oars, baskets, and sails. When advancing, you must follow close on; when withdrawing do not press together. When mounting a flank attack follow the current's flow, taking their men as the target.

The tactics for aggressive aquatic warfare: nimble boats should be used as flags, swift boats should be used as messengers. When the enemy goes off pursue him; when the enemy comes forth press him. Resist or yield . . . in accord with the situation, organize against them. When they shift their forces, make them change their plans; when they are deploying, strike them; when they are properly assembled, separate them. Accordingly, the weapons include spades and the chariots have defensive infantry. You must investigate their numerical strength as many or few, strike their boats, seize the fords, and show the people that the infantry is coming. These are the tactics for aquatic warfare.

Military Methods, 16

MOUNTAINS AND PRECIPITOUS TERRAIN

Occupying high ground is the means by which to be alert and assume a defensive posture.

Six Secret Teachings, 27

King Wu asked the T'ai Kung: "Suppose we have led the army deep into the territory of the feudal lords where we encounter high mountains with large flat rock outcroppings, on top of which are numerous peaks, all devoid of grass and trees. We are surrounded on all four sides by the enemy. Our Three Armies are afraid, the officers and troops confused. I want to be solid if we choose to defend our position, and victorious if we fight. What should we do?"

The T'ai Kung said: "Whenever the Three Armies occupy the heights of a mountain they are trapped on high by the enemy. When they hold the land below the mountain they are imprisoned by the forces above them. If you have already occupied the top of the mountain, you must prepare the Crow and Cloud Formation in which the troops act like the crows dispersing and the clouds forming together. The Crow and Cloud Formation should be prepared on both the yin and yang sides of the mountain. Some will encamp on the yin side, others will encamp on the yang side. Those that occupy the yang side must prepare against attacks from the yin side. Those occupying the yin side must prepare against attacks from the yang side. Those occupying the left side of the mountain must prepare against the right side. Those on the right, against the left. Wherever the enemy can ascend the mountain, your troops should establish external lines. If there are roads passing through the valley, sever them with your war chariots. Set your flags and pennants up high. Be cautious in commanding the Three Armies; do not allow the enemy to know your true situation. This is referred to as a 'mountain wall.'

"After your lines have been set, your officers and troops deployed, rules and orders already issued, and tactics, both orthodox and unorthodox, already planned, deploy your assault formation at the outer perimeter of the mountain, and have them improve the positions they occupy. Thereafter divide your chariots and cavalry into the Crow and Cloud Formation. When your Three Armies urgently attack the enemy, even though the latter are numerous, their general can be captured."

Six Secret Teachings, 47

To cross mountains follow the valleys, search out tenable ground, and occupy the heights. If the enemy holds the heights, do not climb up to engage them in battle. This is the way to deploy an army in the mountains.

Where there are hills and embankments you must occupy the yang side, keeping them to the right rear. This is to the army's advantage and exploits the natural assistance of the terrain.

The Art of War, 9

As for precipitous configurations, if we occupy them we must hold the heights and yang sides to await the enemy. If the enemy occupies them first, withdraw our forces and depart. Do not follow them.

The Art of War, 10

A mountain on which one deploys on the south side is a tenable mountain; a mountain on which one deploys on the eastern side is a fatal mountain.

Military Methods, 8

In the spring do not descend; in the fall do not ascend. Neither the army nor any formation should attack to the front right. Establish your perimeter to the right; do not establish your perimeter to the left.

Military Methods, 8

To create awesomeness, deploy with mountains as the right wing.

Military Methods, 14

When circumventing mountains and forests use segmented units in succession.

Military Methods, 14

Descending dragons' hidden power and deployed ambushes are the means by which to fight in the mountains.

Military Methods, 14

"Suppose our army encounters the enemy and both establish encampments. The enemy's men have concealed themselves in the mountains and taken the passes as their base. Our distant forces cannot engage them in battle, but nearby we have no foothold. How should we strike them?"

"To strike them you must force them to move from some of the passes they have taken . . . and then they will be endangered. Attack positions that they must rescue. Force them to leave their strongholds in order to analyze their tactical thinking and then set up ambushes and establish support forces. Strike their masses when they are in movement. This is the Tao for striking those concealed in strongholds."

Military Methods, 17

PLAINS AND LEVEL TERRAIN

Deploying on clear, open ground without any concealment is the means by which to fight with strength and courage.

Six Secret Teachings, 27

On level plains deploy on easy terrain with the right flank positioned with high ground to the rear, fatal terrain to the fore, and tenable terrain to the rear. This is the way to deploy on the plains.

The Art of War, 9

If we can go forth and the enemy can also advance, it is termed "accessible." In an accessible configuration, first occupy the heights and yang side, and improve the routes for transporting provisions. Then when we engage in battle, it will be advantageous.

The Art of War, 10

As for expansive terrain, if our strategic power is equal, it will be difficult to provoke them to combat. Engaging in combat will not be advantageous.

The Art of War, 10

When engaged in combat on easy terrain, to effect a martial retreat employ your soldiers in a rear guard action.

Military Methods, 14

STALEMATED TERRAIN *Do unexpected to break*

If it is not advantageous for us to go forth nor advantageous for the enemy to come forward, it is termed "stalemated." In a stalemated configuration, even though the enemy tries to entice us with profit, we do not go forth. Withdraw our forces and depart. If we strike them when half the enemy has come forth, it will be advantageous.

The Art of War, 10

SUSPENDED TERRAIN

If we can go forth but it will be difficult to return, it is termed "suspended." In a suspended configuration, if they are unprepared go forth and conquer them. If the enemy is prepared and we sally forth without being victorious, it will be difficult to turn back and is not advantageous.

The Art of War, 10

TRAVERSABLE TERRAIN

When we can go and they can also come, it is "traversable terrain." On traversable terrain do not allow your forces to become isolated. On traversable terrain I focus on defense.

The Art of War, 11

VALLEYS

King Wu asked the T'ai Kung: "Suppose we have led the army deep into the territory of the feudal lords where we encounter the enemy in the midst of a steep valley. I have mountains on our left, water on our right. The enemy has mountains on the right, water on the left. They divide the valley with us in a standoff. If we choose to defend our position I want to be solid, and victorious if we want to fight. How should we proceed?"

The T'ai Kung said: "If you occupy the left side of a mountain you must urgently prepare against an attack from the right side. If you occupy the right side of a mountain, then you should urgently prepare against an attack from the left. If the valley has a large river but you don't have boats and oars, you should use the Heavenly Huang pontoon bridge to cross the Three Armies over. Those that have crossed should widen the road considerably in order to improve your fighting position. Use the Martial Assault chariots at the front and rear; deploy your strong crossbowmen into ranks; and solidify all your lines and formations. Employ the Martial Assault chariots to block off all the intersecting roads and entrances to the valley. Set your flags out on high ground. This posture is referred to as an Army Citadel.

"In general, the method for valley warfare is for the Martial Assault chariots to be in the forefront, and the Large Covered chariots to act as a protective force. Your skilled soldiers and strong crossbowmen should cover the left and right flanks. Three thousand men will comprise one detachment, which must be deployed in the assault formation. Improve the positions the soldiers occupy. Then the Army of the Left should advance to the left, the Army of the Right to the right, and the Army of the Center to the front, all attacking and advancing together. Those that have already fought should return to their detachment's original positions, the units fighting and resting in succession until you have won."

Six Secret Teachings, 50

Marquis Wu asked: "If I encounter the enemy in a deep valley, where gorges and defiles abound to the sides, while his troops are numerous and ours few, what should I do?"

Wu Ch'i replied: "Traverse hilly regions, forests, valleys, deep mountains and vast wetlands quickly, departing from them posthaste. Do not be dilatory. If in high mountains or a deep valley the armies should suddenly encounter each other you should first beat the drums and set up a clamor, taking advantage of it to advance your archers and crossbowmen, both shooting the enemy and taking prisoners. Carefully investigate their degree of control: if they are confused then attack without doubt."

Wu-tzu, 5

Marquis Wu asked: "On the left and right are high mountains, while the land is extremely narrow and confined. If when we meet the enemy we dare not attack them, yet cannot escape, what shall we do?"

Wu Ch'i replied: "This is referred to as valley warfare. Even if your troops are numerous they are useless. Summon your talented officers to confront the enemy, the nimble-footed and sharpest weapons to be at the forefront. Divide your chariots and array your cavalry, concealing them on all four sides several miles apart, so that they will not show their weapons. The enemy will certainly assume a solid defensive formation, not daring to either advance or retreat. Thereupon display your flags and array your banners, withdraw outside the mountains, and encamp. The enemy will invariably be frightened and your chariots and cavalry should then harass them, not permitting them any rest. This is the Tao for valley warfare."

Wu-tzu, 5

WOODS, FORESTS, AND DENSE VEGETATION

Mountain forests and dense growth are the means by which to come and go silently. Deep grass and dense growth are the means by which to effect a concealed escape.

Six Secret Teachings, 27

For fighting in wild expanses and in the middle of tall grass there is the square-shank, arrow-shaped spear, twelve hundred of them. The method for deploying these spears is to have them stick out of the ground one foot five inches. They are used to defeat infantry and cavalry, to urgently press the attack against invaders, and intercept their flight.

Six Secret Teachings, 31

King Wu asked the T'ai Kung: "Suppose we have led our troops deep into the territory of the feudal lords where we encounter a large forest which we share with the enemy in a standoff. If we assume a defensive posture I want it to be solid, or if we fight, to be victorious. How should we proceed?"

The T'ai Kung said: "Have our Three Armies divide into the assault formation. Improve the positions the troops will occupy, and station the archers and crossbowmen outside, with those carrying spear-tipped halberds and shields inside. Cut down and clear away the grass and trees, and extensively broaden the passages in order to facilitate our deployment onto the battle site. Set our pennants and flags out on high, and carefully encourage the Three Armies without letting the enemy know our true situation. This is referred to as Forest Warfare.

"The method of forest warfare is to form the spear bearers and halberdiers into squads of five. If the woods are not dense, cavalry can be used in support. Battle chariots will occupy the front. When opportune they will fight; when not opportune, they will desist. Where there are numerous ravines and defiles in the forest, you must deploy in the Assault Formation in order to be prepared both front and rear. If the Three Armies urgently attack, even though the enemy is numerous, they can be driven off. The men should fight and rest in turn, each with their section. This is the main outline of forest warfare."

Six Secret Teachings, 43

Amidst grasses and heavy vegetation use yang visible pennants. When the road is thorny and heavily overgrown, use a zig-zag advance.

Military Methods, 14

38

Tactical Principles
for Specific
Situations

Thus the strategy for employing the military: Do not approach high mountains; do not confront those who have hills behind them. Do not pursue feigned retreats. Do not attack animated troops. Do not swallow an army acting as bait. Do not obstruct an army retreating homeward. If you besiege an army you must leave an outlet. Do not press an exhausted invader. These are the strategies for employing the military.

The Art of War, 7

BESIEGED OR SURROUNDED

King Wu asked the T'ai Kung: "If the enemy surrounds us, severing both our advance and retreat, breaking off our supply lines, what should we do?"

The T'ai Kung said: "These are the most distressed troops in the world! If you employ them explosively you will be victorious; if you are slow to employ them, you will be defeated. In this situation if you deploy your troops into martial assault formations on the four sides, use your military chariots and valiant cavalry to startle and confuse their army, and urgently attack them, you can thrust across them."

King Wu asked, "After we have broken out of the encirclement, if we want to take advantage of it to gain victory, what should we do?"

The T'ai Kung said: "The Army of the Left should urgently strike out to the left, and the Army of the Right should urgently strike out to the right. But do not get entangled in protracted fighting with the enemy over any one road. The Central Army should alternately move to the front and then the rear. Even though the enemy is more numerous, their general can be driven off."

Six Secret Teachings, 33

King Wu asked the T'ai Kung: "Suppose we have led our troops deep into the territory of the feudal lords where the enemy unites from all quarters and surrounds us, cutting off our road back home, and severing our supply lines. The enemy is numerous and extremely well provisioned, while the ravines and gorges are also solidly held. We must get out— how can we?"

The T'ai Kung said: "In the matter of effecting a certain escape your equipment is your treasure, while courageous fighting is foremost. If you investigate and learn where the enemy's terrain is empty and vacuous, the places where there are no men, you can effect a certain escape.

"Order your generals and officers to carry the Mysterious Dark Pennants and take up the implements of war. Require the soldiers to put wooden gags into their mouths. Then move out at night. Men of courage, strength, and swiftness, who will risk danger, should occupy the front, to level fortifications and open a passage for the army. Skilled soldiers and strong crossbowmen should compose an ambushing force that will remain in the rear. Your weak soldiers, chariots, and cavalry should occupy the middle. When the deployment is complete slowly advance, being very cautious not to startle or frighten the enemy. Have the Martial Attack Fu-hsü Chariots defend the front and rear, and the Martial Flanking Great Covered Chariots protect the left and right flanks.

"If the enemy should be startled, have your courageous, strong risk takers fervently attack and advance. The weaker troops, chariots, and cavalry should bring up the rear. Your skilled soldiers and strong crossbowmen should conceal themselves in ambush. If you determine that the enemy is in pursuit, the men lying in ambush should swiftly attack their rear. Make your fires and drums numerous, and attack as if coming out of the very ground, or dropping from Heaven above. If the Three Armies fight courageously no one will be able to withstand us!"

Six Secret Teachings, 34

Marquis Wu asked: "The enemy is nearby, pressing us. Even if I want to retreat there is no road. My soldiers are terrified. What can I do?"

Wu Ch'i replied: "The technique for dealing with this is as follows: If your troops are numerous and theirs few, divide them and attack. If, on the contrary, their troops are numerous and yours few, then use improvised measures to harry them, never giving them any rest. Then, even though they are numerous, they can be forced to submit."

Wu-tzu, 5

Reckless withdrawals and round-about entries are the means by which to release the army from difficulty.

Military Methods, 14

DEFENDING AGAINST INVADERS AND COUNTER-ATTACKING

Marquis Wu asked: "If a savage raiding force suddenly appears, plundering our lands and fields, seizing our cattle and horses, what should I do?"

Wu Ch'i replied: "When a savage raiding force appears you must carefully consider its strength and well maintain your defensive position. Do not respond to their attacks by going out to engage them. When they are about to withdraw at the end of the day their packs will certainly be heavy and their hearts will invariably be afraid. In withdrawing they will concentrate upon speed, and inevitably there will be stragglers.

You should then pursue and attack them, and their troops can be overcome."

Wu-tzu, 5

King Wei asked: "How do we attack exhausted invaders?"
Sun Pin said: ". . . You can make plans while waiting for them to find a route to life."

Military Methods, 3

To counter raiding forces that forcefully penetrate the interior use "Death Warriors." The resolute are the means to defend against invasion.

Military Methods, 14

INITIAL STANDOFFS AND STALEMATES

King Wu asked the T'ai Kung: "Both the enemy and our army have reached the border where we are in a standoff. They can approach, and we can also advance. Both deployments are solid and stable; neither side dares to move first. We want to go forth and attack them, but they can also come forward. What should we do?"

The T'ai Kung said: "Divide the army into three sections. Have our advance troops deepen the moats and increase the height of the ramparts, but none of the soldiers should go forth. Array the flags and pennants, beat the leather war drums, and complete all the defensive measures. Order our rear army to stockpile supplies and foodstuffs, without causing the enemy to know our intentions. Then send forth our elite troops to secretly launch a sudden attack against their center, striking where they do not expect it, attacking where they are not prepared. Since the enemy does not know our real situation, they will stop and not advance."

Six Secret Teachings, 36

King Wu asked: "Suppose the enemy knows our real situation and has fathomed our plans. If we move, they will be able to learn everything about us. Their elite troops are concealed in the deep grass. They press us on the narrow roads, and are attacking where convenient for them. What should we do?"

The T'ai Kung said: "Every day have the vanguard go forth and instigate skirmishes with them in order to psychologically wear them out. Have our older and weaker soldiers drag brushwood to stir up the dust, beat the drums and shout, and move back and forth—some going to the left, some to the right, never getting closer than a hundred paces from the enemy. Their general will certainly become fatigued, and their troops will become fearful. In this situation the enemy will not dare come forward. Then our advancing troops will unexpectedly not stop, some continuing forward to attack their interior, others the exterior. With our Three Armies all fervently engaging in the battle, the enemy will certainly be defeated."

Six Secret Teachings, 36

King Wu asked the T'ai Kung: "Suppose we have led our troops deep into the territory of the feudal lords and are confronting the enemy. The two deployments, looking across at each other, are equal in numbers and strength, and neither dares to move first. I want to cause the enemy's general to become terrified; their officers and men to become dispirited; their battle array to become unstable; their reserve army to want to run off; and those deployed forward to constantly look about at each other. I want to beat the drums, set up a clamor, and take advantage of it so that the enemy will then run off. How can we do it?"

The T'ai Kung said: "In this case send our troops out about ten miles from the enemy and have them conceal themselves on both flanks. Send your chariots and cavalry out about one hundred miles and have them return unobserved to assume positions cutting across both their front and rear. Multiply the number of flags and pennants, and increase the number of gongs and drums. When the battle is joined, beat the drums, set up a clamor, and have your men all rise up together. The enemy's general will surely be afraid, and his army will be terrified. Large and small numbers will not come to each other's rescue; upper and lower ranks will not wait for each other; and the enemy will definitely be defeated."

Six Secret Teachings, 37

King Wu asked: "Suppose because of the enemy's strategic configuration of power we cannot conceal troops on the flanks, and moreover our chariots and cavalry have no way to cross behind them and assume positions both to the front and rear. The enemy anticipates my thoughts and makes preemptive preparations. Our officers and soldiers are dejected, our generals are afraid. If we engage in battle we will not be victorious. What then?"

The T'ai Kung said: "Truly a serious question. In this case five days before engaging in battle, dispatch distant patrols to observe their activities and analyze their forward movement in order to prepare an ambush and await them. We must meet the enemy on deadly ground. Spread our flags and pennants out over a great distance, disperse our arrays and formations. We must race forward to meet the enemy. After the battle has been joined, suddenly retreat, beating the gongs incessantly. Withdraw about three miles, beyond our prepared ambush, then turn about and attack. Your concealed troops should simultaneously arise. Some should penetrate the flanks, others attack their vanguard and rear-guard positions. If the Three Armies fervently engage in battle, the enemy will certainly run off."

Six Secret Teachings, 37

King Wei of Ch'i, inquiring about employing the military, said to Sun Pin: "If two armies confront each other, their two generals looking across at each other, with both of them being solid and secure so that neither side dares to move first, what should be done?"

Sun Pin replied: "Employ some light troops to test them, commanded by some lowly but courageous officer. Focus on fleeing, do not strive for victory. Deploy your forces in concealment in order to abruptly assault their flanks. This is termed the 'Great Attainment.' "

Military Methods, 3

PURSUIT

King Wu asked: "The enemy, knowing we are following him, conceals elite troops in ambush while pretending to continue to retreat. When we reach the ambush their troops turn back, some attacking our front, others our rear, while some press our fortifications. Our Three Armies are terrified, and in confusion fall out of formation and leave their assigned positions. What should we do?"

The T'ai Kung said: "Divide into three forces, then follow and pursue them, but do not cross beyond their ambush. When all three forces have arrived, some should attack the front and rear, others should penetrate the two flanks. Make your commands clear, choose your orders carefully. Fervently attack, advancing forward, and the enemy will certainly be defeated."

Six Secret Teachings, 38

In antiquity they did not pursue a fleeing enemy too far, nor follow a retreating army too closely. By not pursuing them too far it was difficult to draw them into a trap; by not pursuing so closely as to catch up it was hard to ambush them. They regarded the forms of propriety as their basic strength and benevolence as the foundation of their victory. After they were victorious their teachings could again be employed. For this reason the true gentleman values them.

Ssu-ma Fa, 2

In general, when pursuing a fleeing enemy do not rest. If some of the enemy stop on the road, then be wary!

Ssu-ma Fa, 5

39

Invasion
Measures

Do not set fire to what the people have accumulated, do not destroy their palaces or houses, nor cut down the trees at gravesites or altars. Do not kill those who surrender, nor slay your captives. Instead show them benevolence and righteousness, extend your generous Virtue to them. Cause their people to say "the guilt lies with one man." In this way the entire realm will then submit.

Six Secret Teachings, 40

In general, in warfare: if you advance somewhat into the enemy's territory with a light force it is dangerous. If you advance with a heavy force deeply into the enemy's territory you will accomplish nothing. If you advance with a light force deeply into enemy territory you will be defeated. If you advance with a heavy force somewhat into the enemy's territory you can fight successfully. Thus in warfare the light and heavy are mutually related.

Ssu-ma Fa, 4

In general, the Tao of an invader is that when one has penetrated deeply into enemy territory, the army will be unified, and the defenders will not be able to conquer you.

The Art of War, 11

In general, when employing the military do not attack cities that have not committed transgressions, nor slay men who have not committed offenses. Whoever kills people's fathers and elder brothers; whoever profits himself with the riches and goods of other men; whoever makes slaves of the sons and daughters of other men, is in all cases a brigand. For this reason the military provides the means to execute the brutal and chaotic, and to stop the unrighteous. Wherever the army is applied the farmers do not leave their occupations in the fields, the merchants do not depart from their shops, and the officials do not leave their offices, due to the martial plans all proceeding from one man. Thus even without the forces bloodying their blades, All under Heaven give their allegiance.

Wei Liao-tzu, 8

If the territory is vast but the cities small, you must first occupy their land. If the cities are large but the land narrow, you must first attack their cities. If the country is vast and the populace few, then isolate their strategic points. If the land is confined but the people numerous, then construct high mounds in order to overlook them. Do not destroy their material profits nor seize the people's agricultural seasons. Be magnanimous toward their government officials, stabilize the people's occupations, and provide relief for their impoverished, for then your Virtue will be sufficient to overspread All under Heaven.

Wei Liao-tzu, 22

If you gain a strategic position, defend it. If you get a dangerous defile, block it. If you take difficult terrain then establish encampments to hold it. If you secure a city then cut it off to enfeoff the generals. If you seize territory then divide it up as a reward for the officers. If you obtain riches then distribute them among your troops.

Huang Shih-kung, 1

The T'ai-tsung said: "The army values being the 'host'; it does not value being a 'guest.' It values speed, not duration. Why?"

Li Ching said: "The army is employed only when there is no alternative, so what advantage is there in being a 'guest' or fighting long? Sun-tzu says, 'When provisions are transported far off, the common people are impoverished.' This is the exhaustion of a guest. He also said, 'The people should not be conscripted twice, provisions should not be transported thrice.' This comes from the experience of not being able to long endure. When I compare and weigh the strategic power of host and guest, then there are tactics for changing the guest to host, changing the host to guest.

"By foraging and capturing provisions from the enemy you change a guest into a host. As Sun-tzu said, 'If you can cause the sated to be famished, and the rested to be tired,' it will change a host into a guest. Thus the army is not confined to being host or guest, slow or fast, but only focuses on its movements invariably attaining the constraints, and thereby being appropriate.

"In antiquity, Yüeh attacked Wu with two armies, one to the left, the other to the right. When they blew the horns and beat the drums to advance, Wu divided its troops to oppose them. Then Yüeh had its central army secretly ford the river. Without sounding their drums, they suddenly attacked and defeated Wu's army. This is a case of changing a guest into a host. The ancients had many cases like this."

Questions and Replies, 2

40

[handwritten: Manpower intensive]

[handwritten: Logistically Draining]

Urban Warfare, Sieges, and Assaults

[handwritten: He who has the high ground has advantage]

MOUNTING ASSAULTS AGAINST FORTIFICATIONS

Distant observation posts and far-off scouts, explosive haste and feigned retreats are the means by which to force the surrender of walled fortifications and compel the submission of towns.

Six Secret Teachings, 27

King Wu asked the T'ai Kung: "Suppose, being victorious in battle, we have deeply penetrated the enemy's territory and occupy his land. However, large walled cities remain that cannot be subjugated, while their second army holds the defiles and ravines, standing off against us. We want to attack the cities and besiege the towns, but I'm afraid that their second army will suddenly appear and strike us. If their forces inside and outside unite in this fashion, they will oppose us from both within and without. Our Three Armies will be in chaos; the upper and lower ranks will be terrified. What should be done?"

The T'ai Kung said: "In general, when attacking cities and besieging towns, the chariots and cavalry must be kept at a distance. The encamped and defensive units must be on constant alert in order to obstruct the enemy both within and without. When the inhabitants have their food cut off, those outside being unable to transport anything in to them, those within the city walls will be afraid, and their general will certainly surrender."

Six Secret Teachings, 40

King Wu said: "Suppose that when the supplies inside the city are cut off, external forces being unable to transport anything in, they clandestinely make a covenant and take an oath, concoct secret plans, and then sally forth at night, throwing all their forces into a death struggle. Some of their chariots, cavalry, and elite troops assault us from within, others attack from without. The officers and troops are confused, the Three Armies defeated and in chaos. What should be done?"

The T'ai Kung said: "In this case you should divide your forces into three armies. Be careful to evaluate the terrain's configuration and then strategically emplace them. You must know in detail the location of the enemy's second army, as well as his large cities and secondary fortifications. Leave them a passage in order to entice them to flee. Pay attention to all the preparations, not neglecting anything. The enemy will be afraid, and if they do not enter the mountains or the forests, they will return to the large towns, or run off to join the second army. When their chariots and cavalry are far off, attack the front, do not allow them to escape. Since those remaining in the city will think that the first to go out have a direct escape route, their well-trained troops and skilled officers will certainly issue forth, with the old and weak alone remaining. When our chariots and cavalry have deeply penetrated their territory, racing far off, none of the enemy's army will dare approach. Be careful not to engage them in battle; just sever their supply routes, surround and guard them, and you will certainly outlast them."

Six Secret Teachings, 40

Now as to the Tao for attacking the enemy and besieging his cities: after his cities and towns have already been shattered, enter each of the palaces, take control of their bureaucrats, and collect their implements of administration. However, wherever your army goes do not cut down the trees, destroy houses, take the grain, slaughter the animals, or burn their supplies. Thus you will show the populace that you do not harbor vicious intentions. Accept those who seek to surrender and settle them.

Wu-tzu, 5

Attacking state capitals and towns with water will prove effective.

Military Methods, 14

In general, when assembling an army a thousand miles away ten days are required, and when a hundred miles one day, while the assembly point should be the enemy's border. When the troops have assembled and the general has arrived, the army should penetrate deeply into their territory, sever their roads, and occupy their large cities and large towns. Have the troops ascend the walls, and press the enemy into endangered positions. Have the several units of men and women each press the enemy in accord with the configuration of the terrain, and attack any strategic barriers. If you occupy the terrain around a city or town and sever the various roads about it, follow up by attacking the city itself. If the enemy's generals and armies are unable to believe in each other, the officers and troops unable to be in harmony, and there are those unaffected by punishments, we will defeat them. Before the rescue party has arrived, a city will have already surrendered.

If fords and bridges have not yet been constructed, strategic barriers not yet repaired, dangerous points in the city walls not yet fortified, and the iron caltrops not yet set out, then even though they have a fortified city they do not have any defense!

If the troops from distant forts have not yet entered the city, the border guards and forces in other states not yet returned, then even though they have men, they do not have any men! If the six domesticated animals have not yet been herded in, the five grains not yet harvested, the wealth and materials for use not yet collected, then even though they have resources they do not have any resources!

Now when a city is empty and void, and its resources are exhausted, we should take advantage of this vacuity to attack them. *The Art of War* says: "They go out alone, they come in alone. Even before the enemy's men can cross blades with them, they have attained victory." This is what is meant.

Wei Liao-tzu, 5

When the general is light, the fortifications low, and the people's minds unstable, they can be attacked. If the general is weighty and the fortifications are high, but the masses are afraid, they can be encircled. In general, whenever you encircle someone you must provide them with a prospect for some minor advantage, causing them to become weaker day by day. Then the defenders will be forced to reduce their rations until they have nothing to eat. When their masses fight with each other at night they are terrified. If the masses avoid their work they have become disaffected. If they just wait for others to come and rescue them, and when the time for battle arrives they are tense, they have all lost their will and are dispirited. Dispirit defeats an army; distorted plans defeat a state.

Wei Liao-tzu, 22

TACTICAL RESPONSES FOR SIEGE SITUATIONS

King Wu asked the T'ai Kung: "Suppose the enemy's advance forces have penetrated deep into our territory and are ranging widely, occupying our land, and driving off our cattle and horses. Then their Three Armies arrive *en masse* and press us outside our city walls. Our officers and troops are sorely afraid, our people are in bonds, having been captured by the enemy. If we assume a defensive posture I want it to be solid, or if we fight, to be victorious. What should we do?"

The T'ai Kung said: "An invading enemy in situations such as this is referred to as an 'Explosive Force.' Their oxen and horses will certainly not have been fed, their officers and troops will have broken their supply routes, having explosively attacked and advanced. Order our distant towns and other armies to select their elite soldiers and urgently strike their rear. Carefully consult the calendar, for we must unite on a moonless night. The Three Armies should fight intensely, for then even though the enemy is numerous, their general can be captured."

Six Secret Teachings, 44

King Wu said: "Suppose the enemy divides his forces into three or four detachments, some fighting with us and occupying our territory, others stopping to round up our oxen and horses. Their main army has not yet completely arrived, but they have had their swift invaders press us below the city walls. Therefore our Three Armies are sorely afraid. What should we do?"

The T'ai Kung said: "Carefully observe the enemy. Before they have all arrived, make preparations and await them. Go out about four miles from the walls and establish fortifications, setting out in good order our gongs and drums, flags and pennants. Our other troops will comprise an ambushing force. Order large numbers of strong crossbowmen to the top of the fortifications. Every hundred paces set up an 'explosive gate,' outside of which we should place the *chevaux-de-frise*. Our chariots and cavalry should be held outside, while our courageous, strong, fierce fighters should be secreted in this outer area. If the enemy should reach us, have our light-armored foot soldiers engage them in battle, then feign a retreat. Have the forces on top of the city wall set out the flags and pennants and strike the war drums, completing all preparations to defend the city. The enemy will assume we are going to defend the wall, and will certainly press an attack below it. Then release the forces lying in ambush, some to assault their interior, others to strike the exterior. Then the Three Armies should urgently press the attack, some striking the front lines, others the rear. Even their courageous soldiers will not be able to fight, while the swiftest will not have time to flee. This is termed 'explosive warfare.' Although the enemy is numerically superior, they will certainly run off."

Six Secret Teachings, 44

In general, when nearing an enemy's capital, you must have a road by which to advance; when about to withdraw, you must ponder the return route.

Ssu-ma Fa, 5

In general, when the defenders go forth, if they do not occupy the outer walls of the cities nor the borderlands, and when they retreat do not establish watchtowers and barricades for the purpose of defensive warfare, they do not excel at defense. The valiant heroes and brave stalwarts, sturdy armor and sharp weapons, powerful crossbows and strong arrows should all be within the outer walls, and then all the grain stored outside in the earthen cellars and granaries collected, and the buildings outside the outer walls broken down and brought into the fortifications. This will force the attackers to expend ten or a hundred times the energy, while the defenders will not expend half theirs. The enemy aggressors will be harmed greatly, yet generals through the ages have not known this.

Now the defenders should not neglect their strategic points. The rule for defending a city wall is that for every ten feet you should employ ten men to defend it, artisans and cooks not being included. Those who go out to fight do not defend the city; those that defend the city do not go out to fight. One man on defense can oppose ten men besieging him; ten men can oppose a hundred men; a hundred men can oppose a thousand men; a thousand men can oppose ten thousand men. Thus constructing a city's interior and exterior walls by accumulating loose soil and tamping it down does not wantonly expend the strength of the people, for it truly is for defense.

If a wall is ten thousand feet long, then ten thousand men should defend it. The moats should be deep and wide, the walls solid and thick, the soldiers and people prepared, firewood and foodstuffs provided, the crossbows stout and arrows strong, the spears and halberds well suited. This is the method for making defense solid.

If the attackers are not less than a mass of at least a hundred thousand, while the defenders have an army outside that will certainly come to the rescue, it is a city that must be defended. If there is no external army to inevitably rescue them, then it isn't a city that must be defended.

Now if the walls are solid and rescue certain, then even stupid men and ignorant women will all, without exception, protect the walls, exhausting their resources and blood for them. For a city to withstand a siege for a year, the strength of the defenders should exceed that of the attackers, and the strength of the rescue force exceed that of the defenders.

Now if the walls are solid but rescue uncertain, then the stupid men and ignorant women, all without exception, will defend the parapets but they will weep. This is normal human emotion. Even if you thereupon open the grain reserves in order to relieve and pacify them, you can not stop it. You must incite the valiant heroes and brave stalwarts with their sturdy armor, sharp weapons, strong crossbows, and stout arrows to exert their strength together in the front, and the young, weak, crippled, and ill to exert their strength together in the rear.

If an army of a hundred thousand is encamped beneath the city walls, the rescue force must break open the siege, and the city's defenders must go out to attack. When they sally forth they must secure the critical positions along the way. But the rescue forces to the rear of the besiegers should not sever their supply lines, and the forces within and without should respond to each other.

In this sort of rescue, display a halfhearted commitment. If you display a halfhearted commitment, it will overturn the enemy and we can await them. They will put their stalwarts in the rear, and place the old in the forefront. Then the enemy won't be able to advance, nor be able to stop the defenders from breaking out. This is what is meant by the tactical balance of power in defense.

Wei Liao-tzu, 6

41

Incendiary
Warfare

DEFENSE AGAINST INCENDIARY ATTACK

King Wu asked the T'ai Kung: "Suppose we have led our troops deep into the territory of the feudal lords where we encounter deep grass and heavy growth which surround our army on all sides. The Three Armies have traveled several hundred miles; men and horses are exhausted and have halted to rest. Taking advantage of the extremely dry weather and a strong wind, the enemy ignites fires upwind from us. Their chariots, cavalry, and elite forces are firmly concealed in ambush to our rear. The Three Armies become terrified, scatter in confusion, and run off. What can be done?"

The T'ai Kung said: "Under such circumstances use the cloud ladders and flying towers to look far out to the left and right, to carefully investigate front and rear. When you see the fires arise, then set fires in front of our own forces, spreading them out over the area. Also set fires to the rear. If the enemy comes, withdraw the army and take up entrenched positions on the blackened earth to await their assault. In the same way, if you see flames arise to the rear, you must move far away. If we occupy the blackened ground with our strong crossbowmen and skilled soldiers protecting the left and right flanks, we can also set fires to the front and rear. In this way the enemy will not be able to harm us."

King Wu asked: "Suppose the enemy has set fires to the left and right, and also to the front and rear. Smoke covers our army, while his main force appears from over the blackened ground. What should we do?"

The T'ai Kung said: "In this case—assuming you have prepared a burnt section of ground—disperse the Martial Attack chariots to form a fighting barrier on all four sides, and have strong crossbowmen cover the flanks. This method will not bring victory, but will also not end in defeat."

Six Secret Teachings, 41

The tactics for incendiary warfare: when your ditches and ramparts have already been completed, construct another outer ring of ditches and moats. Every five paces pile up firewood, being certain to equalize the quantities in each pile. A designated number of attendants should be assigned to them. Order men to make linked *chevaux-de-frise*; they must be light and sharp. If it is windy, avoid . . . and if the vapors from the fire overspread you, while if you engage in battle you will not conquer them, stand down and retreat.

Military Methods, 16

MOUNTING INCENDIARY ATTACKS

There are five types of incendiary attack: The first is to incinerate men, the second to incinerate provisions, the third to incinerate supply trains, the fourth to incinerate armories, and the fifth to incinerate formations.

Implementing an incendiary attack depends on the proper conditions. Equipment for incendiary attack should be fully prepared before required. Launching an incendiary attack has its appropriate seasons, igniting the fire the proper days. As for the seasons, it is the time of the dry spell; as for the day, when the moon is in *chi*, *pi*, *i*, or *chen*. When it is in these four lunar lodges, these are days the wind will arise.

The Art of War, 12

In general, in incendiary warfare you must respond to the five changes of fire: If fires are started within their camp, then you should immediately respond with an attack from outside. If fires are ignited but their army remains quiet, then wait; do not attack. When they flare into a conflagration, if you can follow up, then do so; if you cannot, then desist. If the attack can be launched from outside without relying on inside assistance, initiate it at an appropriate time. If fires are ignited upwind, do not attack downwind.

The Art of War, 12

Use chariots to mount incendiary attacks on supplies under transport.

Military Methods, 14

The tactics for incendiary warfare: if the enemy is downwind in an area abundant with dry grass where the soldiers of their Three Armies would not have anywhere to escape, then you can mount an incendiary attack. When there is a frigid fierce wind, abundant vegetation and undergrowth, and firewood and grass for fuel already piled up while their earthworks have not yet been prepared, in such circumstances you can mount an incendiary attack. Use the flames to confuse them, loose arrows like rain. Beat the drums and set up a clamor to motivate your soldiers. Assist the attack with strategic power. These are the tactics for incendiary warfare.

Military Methods, 16

Index

Government, weakness in, 84,
86, 87, 96, 98, 131, 136,
165–168
Guest and host, 204, 263, 264,
293, 294

Heaven, 75, 81, 96, 105, 106,
110, 118, 175, 202, 207,
213, 218, 226

Instruction and training, 93, 138,
148, 172, 175, 188, 189,
258
Intelligence
military, 90, 92, 108,
120–123, 159, 194, 207,
211, 221, 226, 227, 230,
237, 250, 268
political, 120–123, 131
Invasion, 97, 177, 179,
249–251, 270, 272, 283,
285–289, 292, 293, 295

Material Resources, 93, 104,
105, 113
Military Organization, 137, 162,
163
Motivation, 87, 104, 110, 114,
141, 142, 145, 146, 153,
168, 170–179, 201, 250,
273

Negligence, 76

People's welfare, primacy of, 78,
83, 85–89, 94, 95, 97, 103,
105, 106, 110, 130, 144
Planning, 75, 90–92, 95, 211
Power, strategic, 77–79, 103,
105, 114, 123, 134, 148,
179, 202–205, 208, 219,
280, 289, 290
Preparation, 93–95, 103–105,
113, 114, 245, 246

Provisions, 121, 125, 194, 217,
227, 230, 238, 294
Pursuit, 193, 291

Retreat, 209, 210, 222, 285
Rewards and punishments, 86,
113, 134, 135, 138, 139,
141, 146, 163, 164,
171–174, 176, 181–188,
208, 223, 226, 228
Righteousness, 87, 93, 98, 104,
160, 171, 172, 209
Rulership, 75, 79–86, 94–96, 99,
129–135, 169

Seasons, 81, 86, 94, 95, 104,
106, 110, 111
Secrecy, 103, 104, 109, 114,
126, 136, 215, 233
Soft, the, 81, 145
Spies, 104, 110, 122, 123, 253,
257
Subversive measures, 150–152,
202, 209, 217, 219,
231–234

Tactical principles, 111, 221,
237, 248, 285–291
ambushes, 212, 213, 221,
224, 251, 270, 273, 274,
279, 299
attacking, 222, 237, 238–241,
243, 247, 248, 276, 279
balk plans, 107, 109, 111,
112, 223, 224, 234
defending, 93, 108, 201,
237, 238, 240, 241,
243–246, 276, 287, 288,
298, 299
disrupt the enemy, 109,
111–113, 216, 222, 234
escapes, 250, 273, 274,
285–287, 290, 298, 302,
303

Suggested Further Reading

Further discussion of the topics raised by Sun-tzu's *Art of War* and many other focal subjects in Chinese military and intelligence history may be found in the following Westview Press books, translated and authored by Ralph D. Sawyer.

Fire and Water:
The Art of Incendiary and Aquatic Warfare in China
0-8133-4065-9, $28.00 / $42.50CAN, cloth
Fire and Water traces the evolution and development of warfare, both use and techniques, from antiquity through the introduction of true gunpowder weapons, including cannon and muskets, and similarly unfolds the evolution of aquatic methodology, emphasizing the strong interconnection between the two with the inception of riverine combat. Based upon an examination of the Chinese military writings, the author examines and recounts comparatively significant battles in which these tactics were employed over the centuries. Although this is not a naval history, the extensive employment of incendiary attacks in naval conflict will be a focal subject, and the means for overcoming riverine obstacles, such as floating bridges, explored.

The Tao of War:
The Martial Tao Te Ching
0-8133-4081-0, $15.95 / $25.00CAN, paper
Wang Chen, a ninth-century military commander, was sickened by the carnage that had plagued the glorious T'ang dynasty for decades. "All within the seas were poisoned," he wrote, "and pain and disaster was rife throughout the land." Wang Chen wondered, how can we end conflicts before they begin? How can we explain and understand

the dynamics of conflict? For the answer he turned to a remarkable source—the *Tao Te Ching*. Here is Wang Chen's own rendering of and commentary on the ancient text, insightfully expanded and amplified by translator Ralph D. Sawyer, a leading scholar of Chinese military history. Although the *Tao* long influenced Chinese military doctrine, Wang Chen's interpretations produced the first reading of it as a martial text—a "tao of war." Like Sun-tzu's *Art of War*, certainly the most famous study of strategy ever written, the *Tao* provides lessons for the struggles of contemporary life. In the way that the ancient *Art of War* provides inspiration and advice on how to succeed in competitive situations of all kinds, even in today's world, Wang Chen's *The Tao of War* uncovers action plans for managing conflict and promoting peace.

A book to put on the shelf next to *Art of War*, Wang Chen's *The Tao of War* is a reference of equally compelling and practical advice.

Sun Tzu:
Art of War
0-8133-1951-X $15.95 / $25.00CAN, paper

"The *Art of War* has become so accepted as a 'must read' book . . . that it needs no further justification. . . . The most accurate, concise, and usable English-language translation available."

—*Military Review*

The *Art of War* is almost certainly the most famous study of strategy ever written and has had an extraordinary influence on the history of warfare. The principles Sun-tzu expounded were utilized brilliantly by such great Asian war leaders as Mao Tse-tung, Giap, and Yamamoto. First translated two hundred years ago by a French missionary, Sun Tzu's *Art of War* has been credited with influencing Napoleon, the German General Staff, and even the planning for Desert Storm. Many Japanese companies make this book required reading for their key executives. And increasingly, Western businesspeople and others are turning to the *Art of War* for inspiration and advice on how to succeed in competitive situations of all kinds.

Ralph Sawyer places this classic work of strategy in its proper historical context. Sawyer supplies a portrait of Sun-tzu's era and outlines several battles of the period that may have either influenced Sun-tzu or been conducted by him. While appreciative of the philosophical richness of the *Art of War*, his edition addresses Sun-tzu's practical origins and presents a translation that is both accurate and accessible.

The Complete Art of War
Sun-tzu, Sun Pin
ISBN 0-8133-3085-8, $35.00/$52.95CAN, cloth

"The combination of a . . . clear translation with an informative commentary make this an essential element in the study of Chinese martial philosophy. . . . An excellent [book]."
—*Military & Naval History Journal*

The only single-volume edition available of the classic essays on strategy by the great Sun-tzu and his descendant, Sun Pin. With Sawyer's thoughtful chapter-by-chapter commentaries, *The Complete Art of War* is designed to guide the reader to new insights into the nature of human conflict and a greater understanding of every field of human activity—from playing the game of politics to building a successful marriage, from closing a deal to managing a large organization, and even from making war to making peace.

The Seven Military Classics of Ancient China
ISBN 0-8133-1228-0, $37.50/$56.50CAN, cloth
The *Seven Military Classics* is one of the most profound studies of warfare ever written. Here translated in their entirety for the first time, the seven separate essays in this volume (written between 500 BC and AD 700) include Sun-tzu's famous *Art of War*. This is the definitive English-language edition of a unique contribution to the military literature.

Sun Pin: Military Methods
ISBN 0-8133-8888-0, $32.00/$47.95CAN, paper

"Sawyer's translation . . . further adds in an important way to our knowledge of the place of warfare in classical Chinese civilization."
—**John Keegan**

In addition to translating this "eighth military classic," Sawyer has prepared insightful chapter-by-chapter commentaries and a vivid general introduction that describes Sun Pin's life and times, analyzes in detail Sun Pin's tactics in important battles, and compares Sun-tzu's strategic thinking with Sun Pin's.

One Hundred Unorthodox Strategies:
Battle and Tactics of Chinese Warfare
ISBN 0–8133–2861–6, $22.00/$32.95CAN, paper

"Not only insightful, but impeccable."
—*War in History*

"Sawyer's commentary, written in language understandable to both soldiers and businessmen, is useful beyond its application to the study of military theory. . . . Enjoyable and enlightening."
—*Military Review*

Beginning with Sun-tzu's *Art of War*, the anonymous author of this Sung dynasty military manual abstracted the one hundred generally paired tactical principles—such as fast/slow, unorthodox/orthodox—he felt to be essential to battlefield analysis and martial conceptualization before appending a similar number of historical examples.

The Tao of Spycraft:
Intelligence Theory and Practice in Traditional China
ISBN 0–8133–4240–6, $19.95/$26.95CAN, paper

"Ralph Sawyer has once again written a text which combines the virtues of scholarly integrity, shrewd analysis, and plain fun. This book is not only for those interested in the history and theory of intelligence, but for those simply intent on a good read."
—**Robert L. O'Connell,**
author of *Ride of the Second Horseman*

In *The Tao of Spycraft*, for the first time anywhere Ralph Sawyer unfolds the long and venerable tradition of spycraft and intelligence work in traditional China, revealing a vast array of theoretical materials and astounding historical developments.